HOW
BERNIE
WON

HOW BERNIE WON

INSIDE THE REVOLUTION
THAT'S TAKING BACK OUR COUNTRY—
AND WHERE WE GO FROM HERE

JEFF WEAVER

THOMAS DUNNE BOOKS ✦ ST. MARTIN'S PRESS

THOMAS DUNNE BOOKS.
An imprint of St. Martin's Press.

www.thomasdunnebooks.com
www.stmartins.com

Designed by Steven Seighman

The Library of Congress Cataloging-in-Publication Data is available upon request.

ISBN 978-1-250-14475-1 (hardcover)
ISBN 978-1-250-14476-8 (ebook)

Our books may be purchased in bulk for promotional, educational, or business use. Please contact your local bookseller or the Macmillan Corporate and Premium Sales Department at 1-800-221-7945, extension 5442, or by email at MacmillanSpecialMarkets@macmillan.com.

First Edition: May 2018

10 9 8 7 6 5 4 3 2 1

This book is dedicated to the staff and volunteers of the campaign. They were the heart and soul of the Revolution and I was honored to work for them.

CONTENTS

ACKNOWLEDGMENTS

THERE ARE MANY PEOPLE who deserve thanks for their support during my time as the campaign manager of Bernie 2016. First and foremost is my family. A campaign affects not only those working on it but those around them. In many ways, more so. Barbara, Sydney, Paul, and Will, your love and unwavering support through this journey made it possible. Thanks also to the many friends who pitched in to help my family during the campaign, especially the Tomans.

I also want to express my appreciation to the staff (Greg, Gareth, Sam, and the rest of the crew) and the customers of Victory Comics. You made sure that Virginia's Comic and Gaming Superstore kept going strong during my absence. My friend Al Stoltz and his family as always had my back, as well.

To all the Bernie 2016 staffers who fought against incredible odds to move our country forward, you have my undying gratitude. Although we came up a little short of the nomination, your work has changed politics. In that very real sense, we did win in 2016. I know each of you will take the skills you learned into future progressive campaigns. A special thanks to the headquarters staff I worked with most closely—and to each of our state directors and their staff, who deserve much of the credit for our success, as do the advance staffers who made sure we pulled off

Bernie's packed event schedule. I also have to mention our constituency outreach teams. Despite the false narratives, your work ensured that the political revolution became the multiracial coalition our country desperately needs.

Thanks to our consultants and vendors, especially Devine, Mulvey, Longabaugh; Tulchin Research; HaystaqDNA; Revolution Messaging; our researcher Edward Chapman; Solidarity Strategies and our trio of mail vendors. Each of you brought invaluable expertise and gave Bernie 2016 the modern campaigning tools that most progressive campaigns never have access to.

The individuals and organizations who endorsed Bernie's run faced incredible pressure to stay out of the race or to support Secretary Clinton. Thank you for your courageous stand.

Bernie 2016 was ultimately successful due to the hard work of hundreds of thousands of volunteers and the generosity of millions of small donors. All those phone calls, door knocks, and $27 contributions made the impossible possible. Your commitment to Bernie 2016 was inspiring then and continues to be. I want to give a nod to those who supported me personally with words of encouragement, defense on social media, and even by wearing blue superhero capes at the convention.

Millions of people across the country voted for Bernie (and many more wanted to vote but were disenfranchised by closed primaries, improper voting roll purges, and outright voter suppression). Despite the establishment and media narrative about the futility of our fight for progressive change, you expressed your support in the most American way possible—at the ballot box. The impact your votes have had on the politics of our country is a testament to why it is so important to protect the right of every American to vote.

This book would not have been possible without the support of my agent Ron Goldfarb and the dedication and incredible patience of Tom Dunne and all the folks at St. Martin's Press/Thomas Dunne Books. I appreciate your recognition of the lasting significance of Bernie 2016 and your willingness to give readers a glimpse behind the scenes of our campaign.

Finally, I want to thank Bernie and Jane Sanders. Together they have dedicated their lives to creating a more just and equitable world. They have never lost sight of what is important—improving the lives of everyday people in every community. For allowing me to do my small part in this continuing fight, I am forever grateful.

INTRODUCTION

THIS BOOK IS A CHRONICLE of Bernie Sanders' 2016 campaign for president of the United States. It is an attempt to give the reader a behind-the-scenes look at the inner workings of this historic endeavor.

I have tried to be true to events as they occurred, but this account is admittedly written from my own perspective. I have worked for most of my adult life with Bernie Sanders in his effort to create a more just and equitable society. He inspired me as a young man of twenty, and he continues to do so to this day. I hope the reader comes away with an appreciation for why I consider him one of the great modern American political figures and why I am honored to have been his lieutenant in this most recent fight.

The number of people who are responsible for the success of the political revolution Bernie gave voice to is huge. At the peak of the campaign we had some 1,200 staff and canvassers. Hundreds of thousands of people knocked on countless doors, made phone calls, or otherwise volunteered. Even a book this size cannot capture every important detail of how we took on the entire establishment, almost won the Democratic nomination, and changed modern American politics for the foreseeable future. I apologize in advance for those whose important contributions do not get the recognition here that they deserve.

As with any campaign this size, we had our share of personality conflicts and personal disagreements. Except to the extent they are important to the story line, I have omitted them. I am pleased to have served with each and every person on the campaign, and I have no ax to grind with any of them, here or elsewhere. I wish every one of them well and hope they all continue to push the political revolution forward in their own way, even if we choose not to exchange holiday greeting cards. That being said, I have included accounts of some internal policy disagreements because it is important to understand what was going on at critical moments.

In addition, I have spent a lot of time in a very intense environment with many people. I hold many confidences from people on our own team, from folks in the media, and even from Clinton-world. I have no interest in gratuitously embarrassing anyone; I have no interest in airing anyone's personal matters; and I have taken my responsibility as a keeper of trust in the writing of this book seriously. I have at times, because a fact is important to the story, attributed comments to an unnamed source, the way reporters use information "on background." If you don't blush when you read them, no one will know you were the source. I have tried, however, to limit the use of unattributed material. A book based almost entirely on such sources does a great disservice to its readers and its subject. Without the source, it is not possible to weigh the credibility of what is recounted; nor is it possible to make judgments about whether a recollection is just a self-serving narrative meant to advance the source's or the writer's personal or political agenda.

With every good story, there are heroes and there are villains. Such is the case here. Most of our opponents competed in an honorable way—most of the time. But that is not universally true. I have tried to be fair to everyone who opposed us—even those whom I believe acted in a scurrilous manner or worse. But many will no doubt find the portrayal of at least some of their actions unflattering. It would be wrong to sugarcoat, for instance, the extent to which the Democratic National Committee worked to advance the Clinton campaign and, as has been widely documented, worked to harm Bernie's. Of course, I was not privy to what was going on in the other camp, and the lens through which they would view events would shade them differently. I will leave that to their book.

Campaigns are hard-fought efforts. There is an overwhelming personal and organizational drive to win. That was as true in our campaign as in any other. Bernie Sanders himself is a fierce competitor. It is a quality that has allowed him to continue fighting for his beliefs against tremendous odds for decades. It was true of our opponents also. Many of our opponents' actions laid out in the book that were harmful to our campaign were entirely within the bounds of acceptable political conduct. Just because they are detailed here does not mean that I consider them to have been out of bounds or that I think the actors should be condemned.

On the other hand, there were times when our opponents inside the Clinton campaign and outside it, or elements clearly sympathetic to them, went beyond decency—engaging in slander, deceit, and behavior destructive not only to our campaign but to the democratic process. I have called those out as well. I leave it to the reader to make her or his own determination in the end about what is acceptable in the heat of a vigorously contested presidential campaign.

During the general election, following Bernie's lead, I and many other Bernie supporters made common cause with the Clinton organization to stop Donald Trump. I know this was not a universally hailed decision. During that time, Bernie, I, and others campaigned with the Clinton folks, got to know many of them, and got a look at how their operation worked. The reader may see the portrayal of some of our opponents in the primary process become more positive as we worked to defeat the rise of Donald Trump. Our assessment of many of them on a personal level did improve when we were in a more cooperative posture.

The Clinton campaign's relationship to Bernie and the larger movement changed, for tactical reasons, in that moment, and the narrative reflects that. This is not to say that we will or will not be in common cause with everyone going forward. The point is not to Monday-morning-quarterback the Clinton campaign's strategy. I am open to as much hindsight criticism for my role in Bernie's campaign as is anyone on any other campaign.

I am confident that all the people who worked for Hillary Clinton engage in the same self-criticism I do, and mentally play out what-if scenarios. Given Donald Trump's victory, it weighs on me greatly that we did not win the primary. There has been a lot of finger-pointing in the wake of Clinton's defeat. To the extent our campaign bears any responsibility for Trump's victory it is that we did not defeat Hillary Clinton.

Speaking only for myself, I had doubts throughout the spring that the Clinton campaign was the best opponent against Trump. In many media appearances, I expressed that concern. Understandably, given that we were in the midst of a campaign, those comments were dismissed as self-serving. Like everyone else I believed that Hillary Clinton would ultimately win the general election, but I also believed that Trump could win.

If we are to defeat the forces of reaction and corporatism, it is critical to understand what lessons should be drawn from the 2016 race. The personal difficulty of reflection and self-reflection should not stand in the way of remedying the very serious problems that need to be addressed to create a winning progressive majority.

Organizing and executing a presidential primary campaign—particularly the type of insurgent campaign Bernie was mounting—is a formidable challenge, as I have learned both from my own experience and from my many discussions with people who have been involved in other efforts. I have worked in many types of organizations, big and small, public and private. I drew on my experiences from all of them, but primarily from military models of organization. A presidential campaign requires a large organization to move quickly and decisively, at times on a minute-by-minute basis, to parry, and to advance its goals. A political campaign requires effectively deploying large numbers of people in an ever-changing environment and, in the case of a presidential primary campaign, an ever-changing geographic environment, as we moved from state to state. In our case, it required a plan for how a much smaller force, with fewer resources and less infrastructure, would be able to defeat a much larger one.

I know a number of people will reject the comparison of a political campaign to a military one for a host of reasons, including its inherent authoritarian nature. But as people with military experience will tell you, this type of structure only really functions well when there is an ongoing and real back-and-forth between the various levels of the organization. In that regard, I believed then, and I believe now, that devolution of appropriate authority to "local commanders," if you will—such as state directors "on the ground"—was a critically important organizational feature of our campaign.

Having an organizational concept and implementing it in the real world is not necessarily the same thing. The speed with which we created and grew Bernie 2016 necessarily meant that many middle-management structures that one would expect to find in a 1,200-person organization were never implemented. We had a very small national staff, vastly outnumbered by our state-based organizing efforts, with very little structure in the middle. It certainly allowed us to be nimbler, but it put a lot of strain on the campaign and on individuals who worked in it. State directors and constituency department managers picked up much of that responsibility, but it was admittedly imperfect. As with all management issues, whether I was personally involved or not, I take full ownership of the shortcomings.

We also found, particularly in 2015, that there was a reluctance on the part of many experienced people to join our campaign: They felt that it would quickly burn out, or that there would be professional retribution from establishment elements of the Democratic Party, or both. Those fears were not unfounded, but they did make it challenging to build out a staff with extensive experience, particularly at the beginning. That was a benefit to many staffers, who were able to take on responsibilities far above what they would have had on any other presidential campaign. Most rose to the occasion in an impressive way.

Finally, a word about how we talk about politics. All too often we talk about this or that group as if everyone in it is identical to everyone else—millennial voters, black voters, women voters, working-class voters, and so forth. There are some contexts in which it is appropriate to generalize. It is empirically true that people who belong to a certain constituency will have, in many cases, similar outlooks. (The commercial advertising sector would not exist if this were not true.) This is understandable and expected due to shared personal and cultural experiences and values. Talking about groups of voters can be an effective shorthand in political discussions.

However, viewing groups of similar voters as monolithic also creates social pressure on individual members of those constituencies to act in a certain way, or it can be used to drive a false political narrative. It is entirely correct to note that Bernie Sanders was overwhelmingly supported by millennial voters. In fact, age was the primary determinant of whom a voter would support in the 2016 Democratic primary. At the same time, it is also true that there were large numbers of millennials who strongly supported Hillary Clinton.

On the flip side, Hillary Clinton received broad support in the African American community, although that support waned as the campaign went along. At the same time, Bernie Sanders was supported by millions of African Americans and, in particular, as was the case with voters of all races, by younger African Americans. I know from our experience that there was considerable frustration among Bernie supporters who were members of political constituencies that were viewed as monolithically supporting Hillary Clinton. And I'm sure it was true of Clinton supporters in similar circumstances.

Part of this problem is the result of the fact that to do in-depth polling of smaller segments of the voting population requires a commitment of financial resources to reach out to statistically valid sample sizes. Much of the media does not want to put out that extra expense to truly understand, for instance, how different parts of a minority community view candidates. It is also true that it can be politically expedient for some to pretend that every member of a group either does or should support one or another candidate.

Finally, most people belong to more than one constituency: For example, a college-educated millennial Latina is young, a woman, educated, and of Latino heritage. She might also be straight or LGBTQ, she might be single or married, she might be religious or not religious, she may have kids or not, be employed or not, she may be native-born or an immigrant.

How voters synthesize all facets of themselves as political actors and interact with others in the political sphere could fill more than one book.

In this book, readers will find references to different groups of voters. I intend it as a shorthand to indicate what the research and voting results showed was the dominant view within categories of people. At the same time, I do not want anyone to take from that that I believe any such group was monolithic, or that the support any individual gave to one candidate or another was in some way inappropriate because she or he deviated from how most members of the group voted. In fact, I spent a lot of time arguing during the campaign that the media was missing much of what was really happening because they became locked into static notions of how some supposedly monolithic group of voters was going to behave either in a particular contest or in the campaign as a whole.

So enough with caveats, qualifications, and preemptive mea culpas . . .

It was late afternoon on February 1, 2016. The Iowa caucus was about to begin. I was driving with Tad Devine, the head of our campaign's media firm and one of our key strategists, down the Des Moines winter streets to our campaign headquarters to monitor the returns. The offices were in a shopping center. Bernie and Jane would watch the returns from a hotel suite. A winter storm was threatening from the west. We all knew that weather could seriously affect election turnout—and we needed a Yuge turnout to win.

Our success relied heavily on voters who did not regularly participate in the Iowa caucus. Would those people come out if the weather was bad? On the other hand, the Clinton campaign's supporters were statistically older. Would they be more likely to stay home in bad weather even if they were more likely to be consistent caucusgoers?

To eat up the time on the ride, Tad and I discussed the weather and turnout. "Do you think this storm is going to keep our people away?" I asked him. "Well, that depends," he began. Tad has a certain tone of voice when he's about to opine on the political. "Her voters are more consistent voters, but ours are much more enthusiastic." It was all speculation and in the end a meaningless conversation, because we could neither control the weather nor at this late hour do anything more to ensure our voters turned out.

Regardless, I felt the storm was a bad omen. But was it a bad omen for the Clinton campaign or ours?

Tad called a contact in the media and got the early entrance poll results. The major media outlets all participated in entrance and exit surveying of voters in key contests so they could have a sense of what was happening before they had to report on it.

"Well," he said, "we're down twelve right now in the early entrance polls."

My astute political observation was limited to, "That's not good."

"Don't worry," Tad reassured me. "The early arrivals are all party regulars who will be overwhelmingly for Clinton. Our people will show up later."

I felt crushed. Only days before, the *Des Moines Register* poll—considered the gold standard of Iowa caucus polling—had us down only three. No one had really expected us to win the Iowa caucus when the campaign began. The polls had had us down 50 points. But we had come a long way since then, and the expectations of the media had been raised substantially. Beating the benchmark set by the *Des Moines Register* is the measure of success in the Iowa caucus. Beat it and the media will declare you are a winner even if you come up a little short of an outright victory. Underperform and they declare you a loser. No one would care how far we had come since the spring of 2015. Tad's assessment that Clinton voters were more likely to show up early did help quell my anxiety, but only a bit.

It seemed so long ago that Bernie and I had met in the Thunder Grill at Union Station in Washington, DC, to discuss my coming on to manage the campaign. As Tad and I pulled into the shopping center parking lot, I was filled with dread. Despite all our apparent progress since the meeting at the Thunder Grill, those storm clouds on the horizon could be a sign that Bernie Sanders' insurgent campaign was going to be snuffed out in the very first contest.

I like to think of our country as one home in which the interests of each member are bound up with the happiness of all. We ought to know, by now, that the welfare of your family or mine cannot be bought at the sacrifice of our neighbor's family. —FDR

PART ONE

BERNIE AT THE BEGINNING

1

TRAVELING THE GREEN MOUNTAIN BYWAYS

MILLIONS OF AMERICANS WERE FIRST introduced to Bernie
Sanders and his political revolution in 2015. My introduction came thirty
years earlier. In the spring of 1986, I had been suspended from Boston
University for being arrested at an anti-apartheid protest on campus. It
had been a tumultuous year. Before my suspension from BU, the administration had tried to throw me and three other students out of our dorms
for putting political signs in our windows. The courts in Massachusetts had
vindicated our First Amendment rights and stopped the evictions. That
didn't change the fact that I was returning home to St. Albans, Vermont,
without a college degree, without a job, and with an arrest record.

When I got back home, I decided to reach out to the independent
gubernatorial campaign of Burlington mayor Bernie Sanders. Bernie was
running against Madeleine Kunin, the Democratic incumbent, and Peter
Smith, the Republican challenger and Vermont's lieutenant governor.
Both Kunin and Smith had previously served in the state senate, and
Kunin had also served as lieutenant governor. Both candidates were well
known across the state and had won statewide office.

Within a few days, Phil Fiermonte, who was working on the campaign,
visited me at my home, thirty miles north of Burlington. Phil had also been
involved in the anti-apartheid movement. We would become coworkers

and great friends—and remain so to this day. Before he left the house, I was the Franklin County coordinator of Sanders for Governor.

Knowing what I do now about campaigns and politics, it should have been a warning sign that a twenty-year-old with no campaign experience whatsoever was suddenly the county coordinator for a gubernatorial campaign. But at the time I was overjoyed. My newfound college activism was going to be put to work right at home in Vermont.

I got word a short time later that I was going to staff Bernie at the Enosburg, Vermont, Dairy Festival. Of course, I had no idea what that really meant, but it was my first opportunity to meet Mayor Sanders. My job was to hold the Bernie sign on a stick as we walked around. (For some reason, the campaign color was purple.) And I held the bag of Bernie buttons. Bernie would hand them out as he shook hands with the voters. He'd fill his jacket pockets with buttons to have them at the ready for the next handshake. The ritual was always the same. "Hi, I'm Mayor Bernie Sanders, running for governor." Back then, there were a lot of people who did not know him or recognize him. If they seemed reasonably friendly, he'd move to the second part of the pitch: "Would you like a button?" He would always hold the button with the metal pin pinched between his fingers so the voter could see the face of it. Vermonters are polite. They usually took it. When he ran out, I'd scoop buttons out of the bag so he could refill his pockets.

I didn't truly understand that the expression "death by a thousand cuts" could be more than a figure of speech until I spent a day repeatedly reaching into a bag of buttons, trying not to wince as I was pricked by every open metal pin. I had to reconcile the positive feeling of yet another Vermonter warmly accepting a button from Bernie with the knowledge that each one he handed out brought me closer to the moment I'd have to drive my hands back in that bag to get more.

Bernie always got great energy from positive interactions with voters, just as he would on a larger scale in 2015 and 2016 speaking to tens of thousands of rally attendees.

He must have been happy with my sign-wielding and button refills, because he called me the next week. "Jeff, this is Mayor Sanders. What would you think about coming down and working in Burlington a couple of days a week?" I said yes, and it was 24/7 until election day—and for much of the rest of my adult life.

It turned out that I was part of the second set of staffers brought on (there were two of us). I learned that he had once had a larger staff. But they had spent the small amount of money he had been able to raise and then suggested he withdraw from the race. Not Bernie's style, then or now. His unwillingness to quit even when faced with insurmountable odds has been one of his great strengths in his lifelong fight for progressive change.

Bernie was, and remains, a tireless campaigner. I quickly became his full-time driver, sign holder, button refiller, parade companion, and all-around duties-as-assigned guy. Most days it was just the two of us traveling around Vermont by car from town to town, from public meeting to public meeting, from local newspaper to local newspaper. The campaign was supported by a kitchen cabinet of advisers, most of whom were part of Bernie's mayoral administration. Jane Sanders was a key adviser even then and has remained so to this day.

Bernie's crowds were nothing like those so many Americans have become accustomed to recently. We'd show up in a small town and there might be seven people. Twenty-five was considered excellent. Bernie would appear anywhere he could communicate with Vermonters. My father at the time owned a teen pageant in Vermont, and Bernie appeared as the guest speaker. Not a standard campaign stop, by any measure, but it was a good-sized crowd for a Bernie speech in those days.

I was introduced to Bernie's complicated relationship with much of the media. He was and is very impatient with the media's attraction to light news, conventional political thinking, and sensationalism. To him, the most important issues facing working people did not and do not get the consistent coverage that they warrant. The stories are too complex, the solutions too difficult to convey in a short newspaper story—and certainly too difficult for the time limitation of television news. It was impossible to convey bold new ideas when the media just wanted sound bites.

Back then there was no internet or social media, just television, radio, and newspapers. Bernie's frustration was often evident. In his tenure as mayor, he took on almost every establishment institution in Burlington, which had earned him no friends at the *Burlington Free Press* or with much of the rest of the media. The exceptions were small-town papers and locally owned radio stations. While the editors or hosts may not have shared Bernie's views, they were generally willing to give him the space or the time to present his positions in some detail.

Interestingly, he used to commiserate with Republican Richard Snelling, a former governor who was running against Senator Patrick Leahy in 1986, about their feelings about the media. Vermont is a small place, and during campaign season all the candidates for political office will typically attend any parades or community events. We often ran into the other candidates. When we invariably ran into Snelling after a parade, he and Bernie would compare notes. In the partisan era in which we live, unhappiness with media coverage may be the last area of bipartisan agreement among political figures.

Bernie's message discipline became quickly evident. Just as in 2015–16, he had a 1986 stump speech, written on yellow legal paper, that he gave in town after town, meeting after meeting. Its centerpiece was income inequality and tax fairness—the "unfair and regressive property tax." By the end of the campaign, I'd tease him by reciting the speech by heart as we drove down the road to the next stop. But that message discipline and consistent use of the stump speech, while unexciting to the media, was a great strength for him then, as it would prove to be in the recent presidential race. It allowed him to carry out an intensely crammed schedule of events. On very little sleep, he could reliably deliver the stump speech three or four times a day or more. When I asked about it one time, his response was that while the media may have heard it countless times, the people had not, because it was different from what they heard from every other political figure and in news reporting. It was true then and it's still true.

The summer of 1986 turned into fall. Vermont's hills and valleys turned from deep green to the multicolored spectacle that draws visitors from all over. As Bernie and I trekked across the state, we could feel the excitement for him growing. I felt he just might win. Of course, I had no frame of reference and was completely committed to the vision Bernie was conveying to people across the state.

Election day came, and that night we learned that Bernie had gotten 14 percent of the vote. How could this have happened? Looking back, I empathize with all the young people who gave their all for Bernie Sanders during the 2016 presidential campaign only to have us come up short of the nomination. I understand their disappointment so deeply.

The 1986 governor's race laid the groundwork for his close run for Congress in 1988, which he lost, and eventually for his winning race for Congress in 1990. He had successfully presented his progressive message to Vermonters, and he (and the rest of us) gained a much greater appreciation for what it took to run a statewide campaign. He also had the chance to personally interact with thousands of Vermonters at town halls, parades, and county fairs. Vermonters expect their political leaders to engage in retail politics. Bernie has never lost a race in Vermont since his election to Congress in 1990. Without the losing race in 1986, he would not have become a viable candidate for president in 2016. Who can foresee what the ultimate outcome of the groundwork that Bernie and millions of Americans laid out in 2016 will be?

As a side note, the top vote-getter of the 1986 race was incumbent Democratic governor Madeleine Kunin, but she did not get 50 percent of the vote. That meant under Vermont law that the legislature got to pick the winner. The legislature picked Kunin, as they should have, given that she had the plurality. In 2016, she would be one of the few leaders of the anti-Bernie forces in Vermont.

In 1988, Bernie asked me to come back to work on his bid for Congress. It was an open seat, as the incumbent House member, Jim Jeffords, was running for the U.S. Senate. The Republican was again former Lt. Governor Peter Smith. The Democrat was Paul Poirier, the Vermont House majority leader. Having run in 1986, Bernie was much better known across the state, so he started much further ahead in terms of name recognition and experience.

I was brought on to play an enhanced version of the role I held in 1986. I traveled with him around the state, but I was much more a sounding board and a junior adviser than I had been just a couple of years before. Obviously, we personally were much more familiar with each another, having spent so much time together in 1986.

This was the year that the CBS newsmagazine *60 Minutes* decided to do a feature on Bernie that would only run if Bernie won the election. A *60 Minutes* crew followed us for a few days, and then Harry Reasoner came to Vermont to film his portion of the segment. The *60 Minutes* crew followed us everywhere. As Bernie and I blew down the interstate in my red Yugo (okay, maybe "blowing down the interstate" is hyperbole), I remember the crew passing us on the right in their minivan. The sliding side door was open, and a cameraman was sitting in the doorway with his feet dangling out of the vehicle.

It was then that Bernie decided to highlight his dissatisfaction with the coverage or lack of coverage he was getting from the Vermont media, in this case the Associated Press. The AP had refused to cover one of his press conferences. My memory is that it was a press conference on the plight of Vermont's family dairy farmers (an issue Bernie has dealt with throughout his legislative career, and on which I spent a large amount of my time on Capitol Hill). Bernie had the crew follow us to the AP office, which was upstairs in a building in Montpelier, Vermont's capital. Maintaining a sense of fairness even when he was upset with someone, Bernie asked the *60 Minutes* crew to wait five minutes before coming up. He and I trudged up the stairs to the AP office. Bernie asked if bureau chief Chris Graff was there. Chris came out and Bernie said to him that there was a *60 Minutes* crew three minutes behind him.

What can only be described as controlled panic ensued. There was little doubt that everyone in that room wanted to slip under their desks or be teleported away to some safe place. As the *60 Minutes* cameras rolled, Bernie confronted the AP about its failure to cover the press conference. It was fascinating to see people who always have the luxury of being on the asking end of a question-and-answer session having their actions scrutinized. Chris Graff handled himself well under the admittedly stressful and frankly impossible situation. But Bernie had effectively made the point that his fight for working Vermonters was going to necessarily include taking on establishment media who did not view the trials of ordinary people as important enough to cover.

The polls at the end of the race were not clear, because their results were within the margin of error. Bernie ran into his Republican opponent before the polls closed on election day. Smith embraced him and they wished each other good luck. It could have gone either way.

We watched the returns coming in. In the presidential contest, Bernie had supported the Reverend Jesse Jackson in the primary and endorsed Governor Dukakis in the general election. All night long, Governor Dukakis was ahead, and so was Bernie. Then, as some of the late returns came in, Vice President George H. W. Bush moved ahead in Vermont. The coverage turned to the congressional race. Bernie was now down and never regained the lead.

Bernie ended up losing the 1988 race by 3 percentage points to Republican Peter Smith.

The Democrat came in a distant third at 19 percent. In many ways, this night was even more disappointing than 1986. The issue of guns had played a pivotal role in that very tight race. Bernie had been the only candidate to come out in favor of an assault weapons ban. This put him at odds with his Democratic and Republican opponents, both of whom had come out against it. Theirs was the politically advantageous position in Vermont at the time. While a majority of Vermonters, like a majority of Americans, supported such a ban, all the intensity was on the side of the opposition to the ban. But that kind of calculation was not what was important to Bernie. He told people where he stood regardless of the consequences. It easily cost him 3 points in that race.

Bernie's politically courageous position on gun safety legislation was one for which he would get almost no credit in his presidential bid as the Clinton campaign distorted his record and glossed over Hillary Clinton's long history of being on every side of the issue. That included 2008, when she said she did not think one-size-fits-all federal gun laws made sense, and her campaign sent out mailers attacking then senator Obama's stronger gun control positions. Her attacks were so over-the-top that Obama dubbed her Annie Oakley.

As late as the fall of 2015, in preparation for a Brady Center to Prevent Gun Violence event in which Hillary Clinton was to receive an award, her staff was carefully modulating her position on gun safety legislation. She was deciding to not embrace the expansive legislation passed by New York State called the SAFE Act in the wake of the Sandy Hook tragedy. Clinton policy adviser Corey Ciorciari wrote, in a subsequently leaked email to other senior staff, "Don't see a need to fully embrace the SAFE Act. There are some controversial items in there. We can highlight pieces that fit within our agenda." Clinton research director Tony Carrk replied, "I agree. SAFE is not a safe bet."

Even though Bernie lost in 1988, he set down an important political marker. He had shown that in Vermont he was the viable alternative to the Republicans, and that the third-place finishing Democrat had in fact been the spoiler. Throughout 1986 and 1988, Bernie had had to contend with a constant media narrative that he was going to be responsible for electing the Republican by taking away Democratic votes. Of course, no candidate or party owns anyone's votes, but that was an issue he was forced to deal with repeatedly. That changed in 1988. Bernie was now more popular than the Democratic establishment in Vermont. And any Democrat running against him statewide was likely to come in third and tip the race for the Republicans.

One of the aspects of Bernie that too few people get to see is that he has a sense of humor. In most of his public appearances, he is so focused on the fight at hand that few are aware it's there. After hundreds of hours on the road, I can tell you it is.

One day it was raining and we were unprepared. "Let's stop and get raincoats," Bernie suggested, pointing to a discount department store in a South Burlington shopping center. He frequently despaired over how difficult it is to find American-made and union-made clothing. On this occasion, he ended up buying us each a raincoat made in China. Over the next couple of weeks, they completely fell apart. First the seams started coming undone. Then the pockets were falling off. In the end, they were in tatters. Whenever one of us developed a new tear or unraveling seam, we broke out laughing.

During the 1988 race, Bernie and I developed a game that is still to this day a great source of amusement between the two of us—Honk-A-Mania. On breaks in the schedule, we would go to the nearest, most active intersection, because Bernie wanted to get in as much campaigning as possible. (That's a trait that continued into the 2016 race. Reporters traveling with him early on found out the hard way that he doesn't even have a scheduled lunch break.)

While we stood at the intersection, I would hold the Bernie sign, and Bernie would wave to cars passing by. Of course, we'd get some negative reactions. The finger. Mooning. Whenever that happened, I'd invariably suggest that we should put them down as "undecided." It never failed to elicit a chuckle from Bernie.

To break up the tedium of waving at cars repeatedly, we started counting positive responses in a timed period and trying to beat our old "record." As Bernie's campaign caught fire in 1988 and then again in 1990, the number of positive responses increased exponentially. We started only counting "honks" in our tallies, as opposed to other signs of encouragement, like thumbs-ups or waves. It got to the point where we would get sustained flurries of honks that would go on for minutes at a time at busy intersections—like the five corners in Essex Junction. As the honking reached a crescendo, Bernie would wave more and more furiously to keep it coming and then would shout out in a dramatically extended fashion, "HONK-A-MANIA!"

The 1990 congressional race was a rematch of 1988, except that the Democrats did not put up a viable candidate. In fact, the Democrats didn't push anyone at all to run, but a University of Vermont professor, Dolores Sandoval, decided to jump in. Vermont was becoming increasingly blue, which weighed in Bernie's favor. But we were concerned that the nominal

Democratic candidate would tip the reelection of then representative Peter Smith. The spoiler issue had come full circle. The Democratic candidate was now the "third party."

Peter Smith was an old-style New England Republican. They really don't exist anymore, even if Maine senator Susan Collins pretends to be one. Smith was pro-choice and pro-education. But he made two critical mistakes in his first term.

Shortly after his election, he double-crossed those opposed to an assault weapons ban by switching his position in a Washington, DC, press conference. That incensed people who had supported him in 1988, and some of them chose to support Bernie in 1990, even though Bernie held the same position on the assault weapons ban. But Bernie had been consistent and honest about his views. The sense on the street was that Smith had not. Homemade signs sprang up in many areas of rural Vermont: "Peter Pinocchio Smith." Many people for whom this was a top issue believed that they could teach Smith a lesson by defeating him and then get rid of Bernie two years later. Underestimating Bernie is never a smart strategy.

The second error Smith made was supporting the first Bush administration's budget bills, which slashed future increases in Medicare payments and made other cuts. Bernie went after him relentlessly on this front. For Bernie, this was the central issue of the campaign. Smith claimed to be a traditional New England Republican, but in Washington, on critical issues for working people, he was voting with the increasingly right-wing Republican establishment.

Bernie, the ever-tireless campaigner, traveled from one end of the state to the other, talking about Smith's record of supporting the Bush administration's cuts to social spending. As always, it was tough to get the media to focus on the complexities of this issue, but Bernie didn't let up.

The race remained super-tight until Smith made his fatal mistake. He ran an ad attacking Bernie on his values. The offensive ad said that Bernie did not have Vermont values, and it showed pictures of Bernie and Fidel Castro moving together from opposite ends of the screen until they were side by side. Vermonters hate that kind of negative advertising. Smith's campaign collapsed. Bernie won by 16 points.

The backlash against Smith's negativity left a big impression on Bernie, and even more so on Jane. Jane in 2016 would be the most consistent voice on the campaign against negative paid advertising.

In the 2016 presidential race, the Clinton campaign claimed that Bernie's victory in 1990 was due to the support of the gun rights community. The facts show that's not true. There is no doubt that the anti-assault-weapons-ban voters were very upset with Smith. But the truth is that the entire change in Bernie's vote from 1988 to 1990 (from 3 points down in 1988 to 16 points up in 1990) equalled the 19 percent total that Democratic Vermont representative Paul Poirier had received in 1988. Bernie won in 1990 because the Democratic vote moved entirely in his direction. Although on the ballot as an independent, Bernie was the candidate of the rank and file of the Democratic Party in Vermont.

The Democratic candidate Dolores Sandoval got 3 percent of the vote, so it may be fair to say that Bernie got 16 points from Democratic voters and 3 percent from people upset with Smith. But with a 16-point margin, that 3 percent was a fraction of the margin of victory. This type of empirical analysis fell flat with reporters in the 2016 campaign. Much spicier to buy into the false Clinton campaign narrative that Bernie was somehow an adherent of the NRA.

2

MR. SANDERS GOES TO WASHINGTON

BERNIE WAS NOW OFF TO CONGRESS, and I was off to Washington with him. We had to deal with all the issues familiar to freshman congresspeople—first, securing a staff and an office. But Bernie had other challenges to face. And so did the Democratic Party leadership in the House.

The House of Representatives was and is organized along strictly partisan lines. The party in charge controls the speakership and all the committee chairs. It also controls the agenda on the floor. No bill gets to the floor without the consent of the majority party, which in most cases also decides whether individual members will even be able to offer amendments to those bills. The ratio of Democrats and Republicans on committees roughly corresponds to the ratio in the overall House, and each party picks which of its members serve on each committee.

When Bernie was running for Congress as an independent, he pledged to caucus with the Democrats. But that was no guarantee they would want to caucus with him. No "non-aligned" member had been elected to the U.S. House in recent memory. If they chose not to admit him to the caucus, there was a possibility that he would have no committee assignments at all.

Before he even arrived in Washington, there was an effort to bar him from the caucus. This effort was led by what were called Blue Dogs, conservative southern Democrats. (The Blue Dogs of that time are all but extinct in the U.S. House today, having been replaced by Republicans. The Democratic right is now dominated by corporatists rather than old-style southern and rural members. But in 1990 the Blue Dogs still held sway.)

The House Democratic leadership—Speaker Tom Foley, Majority Leader Dick Gephardt, and especially Minority Whip Dave Bonior—treated Bernie with respect and fairness. It was while having these discussions about Bernie's status that he and I met for the first time a young staffer who was Dick Gephardt's floor manager—George Stephanopoulos. We also met a Congressional Research Service analyst who would serve as a resource on seniority/party status issues for many years thereafter, Judy Schneider. We relied on her research and analysis when Bernie arrived in the House and during his transition to the U.S. Senate.

Ultimately, a compromise was reached. Bernie would count as a Democrat for purposes of House organization. He would be counted in the Democratic total in calculating committee ratios. He received Democratic committee appointments, and he would accrue seniority on the Democratic side of the aisle. He would start, however, as the least senior member of his entering class. Crisis averted.

Many of the staff were already in place when we arrived in Washington. Doug Boucher was tapped to be chief of staff, and John Franco came from Vermont to be the legislative director. Our team would also include Steffie Woolhandler, of Physicians for a National Health Program; and Carolyn Kazdan, who had helped on the campaign. Jane and I were tasked with rounding out the staff. After wading through three large brown paper grocery bags of résumés, we hired Katie Clark as our front desk person and Ruthan Wirman as scheduler/executive assistant. Ruthan had worked for now senator Bill Nelson when he was in the House. She knew how to navigate the ins and outs of the House bureaucracy and became a mentor to many of the young staffers who would join our office over the following years.

Being a freshman member meant there were few choices left when it was Bernie's turn to pick office space. His office ended up being on the fifth floor of the Cannon Building, in a cramped suite that included space that had once housed Richard Nixon's congressional office. Some of our interns worked out of the storage cage across the hall.

From his earliest days in Congress, Bernie liked to hold staff brainstorming sessions. These were and are very free-flowing discussions. He likes to hear different approaches to issues and likes staff covering different fields to offer views that those immersed in a topic may not have considered. It allows him to synthesize what initiatives or legislation he wants to advance. It is also a chance from a management perspective for him to make sure that certain staffers are not drowning in work when the issues they cover are under active consideration in the House (and later the Senate). And he gets to interact directly with junior staffers.

On the downside, these meetings always did seem to happen as the day was otherwise ending. Not for Bernie, though. He was often in the office until 11:00 p.m. or later, long past the time everyone else had left. No staffer, perhaps other than Michael Briggs on the presidential campaign, regularly worked longer hours than Bernie did.

One of Bernie's concerns has been how he stays connected with the people who sent him to Washington—how to avoid becoming a creature of the Beltway. With very, very few exceptions, he went home to Vermont every weekend. He would hold meetings with Vermonters and spend time with his family, who remained in the Green Mountain State.

When he was first elected to the House, one of the other ways he wanted to stay in touch with the folks back home was to personally answer every letter that came in. I don't think any of us anticipated the volume of mail he would receive. As he struggled to keep up with it in the evenings, the piles of mail on and around his desk grew and grew. This was not a satisfactory process. As it turns out, many people will write about the same topic. So we moved to a system where he would draft or approve a single letter that could be sent to all the senders on a particular topic. It has evolved further as his national profile has grown. But he still personally sees many letters that are sent from Vermonters.

Bernie's agenda in his first term was as extensive and ambitious as it is now. And, as always, he was driven to move as much of it as quickly as possible. His list of agenda items included creating a single-payer health program that could be implemented on a state-by-state basis, reforming labor laws, ensuring middle- and working-class taxpayers didn't foot the bill for the savings and loan crisis, saving family farms, and protecting veterans. In hindsight, of course, the House is not set up to allow freshman members to jam through anything, let alone the bold program that Bernie was advocating.

What little opportunity there was at the beginning of his first term to tackle domestic priorities evaporated when President George H. W. Bush decided to attack Iraq on January 17, 1991. Bernie strongly opposed the war. The vast majority of the rest of the Democratic caucus did as well: 68 percent of House Democrats and 82 percent of Senate Democrats (including then senator Joe Biden) voted no.

Bernie takes war seriously and personally. He has a deep emotional connection with people, especially the middle- and working-class people who are asked to fight and die in our military and the civilians whose lives are devastated by war going on around them. Having won a seat in the United States Congress against all the odds, Bernie was now coming to grips with the very real limitations of a single legislator's power over issues of war and peace.

The war was over relatively quickly, with reportedly around six hundred Americans killed or wounded. When the Democratic House leadership cravenly put a resolution on the floor complimenting President George H. W. Bush on his "unerring judgment," Bernie voted no. That resolution also had kind words for the troops—language Bernie did support—but there was no opportunity to vote separately on those provisions. It was an anguishing vote for him. Bernie got some negative reactions to that vote from people back in Vermont, and it hurt him deeply. But President Bush's judgment had not been unerring. Every alternative to war had not been tried, and as result American service members and Iraqi civilians paid the price.

And the truth of the war Bernie opposed turned out to be much darker than the administration let on. Bernie first started hearing about the true level of casualties in the Gulf War at one of his many town hall meetings in Vermont. At those meetings, he started hearing from veterans about the multisymptom illness they were experiencing since their service in the Gulf. These reports started coming in through several sources, including the veterans' community. The Defense Department and the Department of Veterans Affairs were not anxious to acknowledge that there was some unrecognized illness or injury that affected far more people than the official casualty numbers. Spending defense dollars on the cost of the last war is not a popular position in the Pentagon.

Bernie threw himself into exposing the truth about what is now called Gulf War Syndrome and getting veterans the health care and benefits they deserved. His primary partner in this fight was Republican congressman Chris Shays. This was just one of the many bipartisan efforts Bernie would undertake in his congressional career. Other left/right efforts included protecting Americans' reading habits from government surveillance, opposing the bailout of the Mexican peso (in reality the bailout of big financial investors whose money was at risk), and opposing taxpayer bailouts of the banking industry. For someone who is unfairly caricatured as an ideologue, Bernie worked with Republicans whenever common ground could be found.

On the issue of Gulf War Syndrome, Bernie spent countless hours in hearings, in meetings with Defense and Veterans Department bureaucrats, and in consultation with veterans' groups and researchers around the country who were trying to understand and treat the increasingly large number of veterans that the federal government was abandoning.

A subsequent Department of Veterans Affairs report put the number of veterans of the Gulf War experiencing symptoms of Gulf War Syndrome at 250,000. If 250,000 out of some 600,000 Americans serving in the Gulf War were injured, it would represent the highest casualty rate in any American war and an enormous cost to the federal government to treat and compensate these veterans. That was a far cry from the administration's claims of minimal casualties, and it was not information that they wanted the public to know.

In the face of all the stonewalling, Bernie would not take no for an answer. As he often described it, the federal government owed a "debt" to the women and men who came home injured. To him, that debt had to be repaid. No bureaucrat was going to dissuade him from believing what he was seeing with his own eyes. Beyond Congress, he worked with anyone who was willing to join the fight, including former presidential candidate Ross Perot. Bernie still displays on his office wall a replica of the Arthurian sword Excalibur sent to him by Ross Perot in recognition of Bernie's fight for Gulf War veterans.

That fight for veterans ultimately paid off. Gulf War Syndrome is now recognized as a service-connected illness, and those suffering with it are entitled to the benefits they earned. This kind of year-in, year-out fight for ordinary people is tough to translate in the sound-bite world of a presidential campaign. There's no bill number attached to it—no key vote that can be pointed to. This is just one example of the falsity of the narrative peddled during the presidential campaign that Bernie was not an effective member of Congress. For those of us who were there with him on Capitol Hill, it was galling.

Bernie also showed during his first term that he was willing to take on tough fights for vulnerable people far from Vermont. The first Bush administration put forward an onerous anticrime bill. Its central features were mass incarceration and increased use of the death penalty. Bernie was and is a staunch opponent of the death penalty and of mandatory minimums. The country was in a different place in 1991 in terms of its views on these issues—they were far more popular. Bernie voted at every opportunity to take out or weaken provisions in both these areas. In the end, he took to the floor of the House to denounce the bill. He called for investment in poor communities rather than locking people up. He called the bill "a punishment bill, a vengeance bill." And he explicitly called out the disproportionate impact of the death penalty on African Americans. "Let's not keep putting poor people into jail and disproportionately punishing blacks."

Of course, Republican presidents are not the only ones who used bad crime bills to get votes, as we were to learn a few years later.

Bernie's first term in office ended with a legislative victory. With the help of then congresswoman Mary Rose Oakar, he passed a cancer registry bill that would allow the collection of information about the prevalence of different cancers across the country. This information was important because it would alert public health officials to geographic clusters of cancers so that potential causes, like environmental factors, could be identified.

Bernie faced far-right Republican Tim Philbin in his first reelection campaign, in 1992. In the primary, Philbin had beaten a more moderate Republican who was mayor of Vermont's second-largest city. Philbin was the type of Gingrich Republican who, two years later, would win across the country and sweep the Democrats out of power in the House. But in 1992 in Vermont that type of politics was rejected by voters. A key part of Philbin's attack was Bernie's support of gun safety legislation. Bernie's margin of victory was almost 28 points.

In that same election, Bill Clinton was elected president with 43 percent of the national vote in a three-way race. Bill Clinton's election represented a major turn in the Democratic Party. After twelve years out of the White House following Reagan's 1980 victory, a new corporate-friendly wing of the Democratic Party had come into power. Its agenda was pro–free trade and a coziness with big-money interests that was to characterize Bill Clinton's presidency and the career of Hillary Clinton. The "centrist" Democratic Leadership Council (DLC, referred to by some as Democrats for the Leisure Class) hailed Clinton's victory in the fight to have the party abandon the economic populism that had been central to the identity of the Democratic Party and its coalition of supporters throughout its modern existence. They called themselves New Democrats. In fact, for the working-class elements of the core Democratic base, they didn't seem like Democrats at all.

Bill Clinton and the New Democrats relied on the votes of the traditional Democratic base. But because the economic policies of Clintonism were ultimately at odds with the interests of middle- and working-class families, it used a policy of triangulation against the most vulnerable members of that base, with thinly veiled attacks meant to play on race and homophobia. With his so-called welfare reform bill and the Defense of Marriage Act (DOMA), Bill Clinton took dog-whistle politics to a new level in the Democratic Party. This should not have come as a surprise to anyone. It was foreshadowed in the 1992 Democratic presidential primary, when Clinton left New Hampshire so that he could personally oversee the execution of Ricky Ray Rector, a black man whose attempted suicide left him so mentally impaired that, as widely reported, he saved his dessert from his last meal so he could eat it later. A veteran reporter on the trail in 2016 would characterize to me Bill Clinton's political use of Rector's execution as "the most disgusting political act I had ever seen."

Some readers may be wondering why I'm dredging up the 1990s Clinton administration. The reason is that its impact on American politics in general, and on the corporatist takeover of the Democratic Party, in particular, underlies much of the differences within the party that continue to this day and that spilled out into the 2016 Democratic primary.

Bill Clinton's administration represented an aberration in the historical trajectory of the Democratic Party toward more inclusion, more economic equality, and broader and broader opportunity. Although they were sold as examples of economic moderation, Clintonism's free-trade deals—the North American Free Trade Agreement (NAFTA) and most-favored-nation status with China—accelerated the deindustrialization of the nation and the resulting long-term impoverishment of working people of all races. Hillary Clinton herself played an active role in promoting the passage of NAFTA, as reported by ABC News and other media sources.

Bill Clinton apologists will point to the short-term economic numbers of the 1990s to justify their policy choices, while ignoring the tech bubble that helped create the appearance of wealth creation, and the longer-term damage done to wages and jobs as factories continued to leave the country throughout the 2000s. As recent studies have shown, the percentage of the economic pie going to the bottom 50 percent of income earners continued to decline during Bill Clinton's presidency as the percentage going to the top 1 percent rose. Looking at this historical data, there is no difference in the movement of income to the top earners from Reagan to Bush to Clinton to Bush.

President Obama inherited an economy in crisis when he came into office. The disastrous policies of his predecessor George W. Bush bear most of the blame for that debacle. But some of the seeds of the economic collapse were sown by the financial deregulation of the Clinton administration in the 1990s. This deregulation provided the fuel for the economic calamity of 2007 and 2008. Lit by the match of lax Bush administration oversight of the financial industry and, as Bernie calls it, "the greed and recklessness of Wall Street," that fuel exploded in the faces of middle-income and working families.

Clintonism also tore at the fabric of the Democratic Party. Working-class voters ultimately understood the damage that had been done to them by the Clinton economic policies. People of color, particularly young people of color, became rightfully cynical about the Democratic Party's sincerity as a vehicle for creating a more fair and inclusive society. All these chickens would come home to roost in 2016 for Hillary Clinton.

Bernie's role in the House in the Clinton years was to fight the most onerous parts of the administration's economic and triangulation agenda and look for opportunities to improve the more positive aspects of their proposals. He fought hard against Clinton trade pacts such as NAFTA, the welfare reform bill, and DOMA. At the same time, he actively supported the health care reform efforts that were spearheaded by Hillary Clinton. Bernie's hope was that, in the event something passed, it might include his legislation allowing states to pursue a single-payer plan if they chose. Unfortunately, health care reform efforts were thwarted by the Republicans and their corporate health care allies.

Nineteen ninety-four would prove a pivotal political year during Bernie's tenure that would have ramifications for the presidential campaign. The Clinton administration, in its effort to show how tough on crime (black people) it was, pushed a massive anticrime bill. The bill passed through various incarnations but included the Violence Against Women Act (VAWA) and ultimately a ban on several semiautomatic weapons. This vote was an extremely difficult one for Bernie. We had many discussions about how to deal with it, because it included a host of provisions he opposed, like mandatory minimums and the death penalty. I remember Bernie's disgust that the Clinton administration was using the same politics as the previous Republican administration had.

But the inclusion of VAWA and the assault weapons ban put Bernie in a difficult position. He had been clear in both 1988 and 1990 that he supported a ban on assault weapons—a position Vermont politicians like Howard Dean wouldn't touch with a ten-foot pole.

To have voted against the final version of the 1994 Crime Bill would have been seen as an abandonment of his position against assault weapons. He had paid a high price politically in Vermont for support of the ban and likely lost the 1988 congressional race because of it. Now, with the opportunity to enact the ban, he felt he could not back away. He was also committed to the VAWA provisions.

He spoke on the floor about the need to support VAWA to help end the scourge of violence against women. "All six of the women slain in Vermont during 1993 died at the hands of an intimate partner or a family member," he pointed out. "Nationally, three out of every ten women who are victims of homicide were murdered by a spouse or an intimate partner, and every fifteen seconds a woman is battered by her husband or a boyfriend."

But he wanted the record to be clear that he opposed the bill's increased use of incarceration and the death penalty. So he went to the floor. "All the jails in the world and all the executions in the world are not going to make that situation right [end crime]. We can either educate or electrocute. We can create meaningful jobs rebuilding our society or we can build more jails."

Bernie voted for the Crime Bill despite its seriously flawed provisions, not because of them—unlike Bill Clinton.

Nineteen ninety-four also demonstrated the degree to which Clinton administration policies were shattering the Democratic brand. Republicans picked up a net gain of fifty-four seats in the House, giving Republicans under the leadership of Congressman Newt Gingrich control for the first time since the election of 1952. Republicans picked up eight U.S.

Senate seats. Bernie was reelected by only 3 points in the face of the Republican wave in a race where he openly attacked the NRA. It was the closest he would ever come to being unseated in his congressional career. Two years later, Bernie would hire Tad Devine as his media consultant on the recommendation of his good friend, fellow Congressman Pete DeFazio.

The results of the 1994 elections might have made some presidents rethink their approach. In this case, perhaps triangulation did not compensate for economic centrist policies like NAFTA. Instead the Clinton administration doubled down. In the run-up to the 1996 presidential campaign, the Clinton administration pushed its welfare reform bill. Bernie strongly opposed this punitive legislation, triangulated against the poorest in this country and disproportionately impacting communities of color. But he was not alone. When it passed, Peter Edelman resigned his Clinton administration post in protest. Edelman was the husband of the Children's Defense Fund's Marian Wright Edelman. (Hillary Clinton in the 2016 campaign often tried to establish her progressive bona fides by pointing to her early work at the CDF under Marian Wright Edelman. The irony was lost on the media.)

In that same year, the Clinton administration supported passage of DOMA. This legislation barred federal recognition of same-sex couples (since declared unconstitutional) and permitted states to deny recognition of same-sex unions created in other states (arguably on its face a violation of the Constitution's "full faith and credit" clause). After it passed, Bill Clinton's reelection campaign ran ads touting DOMA on Christian radio throughout the South. DOMA and the circumstances around its passage would become a big issue in the 2016 campaign and a big problem for Hillary Clinton.

In the fall of 2015 on the *Rachel Maddow Show*, Hillary Clinton defended the Clinton administration's support of DOMA on the grounds that it was meant to prevent something even worse—a constitutional amendment. Voting for a bad piece of legislation can in some circumstances be justified to prevent an even worse law from being enacted. But voting for is different from publicly trumpeting the bad law. And in the case of DOMA, Hillary Clinton's defense wasn't even true. There was no constitutional amendment looming in 1996. The *Washington Post* gave her claim four Pinocchios. Even her friend and supporter Hilary Rosen spoke out against Hillary Clinton's claim: "@BernieSanders is right. Note to my friends Bill and #Hillary: Pls stop saying DOMA was to prevent something worse. It wasn't, I was there."

Staff emails from the time show the extent to which the Clinton campaign scrambled to limit the damage that Hillary Clinton's claim had caused.

I left Bernie's office in 1995 to finish law school and then to work at Crowell & Moring, a DC law firm, doing mostly government contracts–related work. Bernie wasn't surprised that I was leaving, given that I was going to law school. Not knowing the future, it was personally difficult to leave having been through so much with Bernie.

The lawyers I practiced with at C&M were top-notch and great mentors. At Crowell I had my first introduction to the corporate world, as their client base included some of the country's largest defense and health care contractors. Too many people on the left have no idea how that world works, and I'm certainly not an expert. But my understanding about how big companies think and operate increased greatly and has been invaluable to me since. A break from the day-to-day weeds of politics also gives you perspective about how most people take in information about it. When you are in it you know every detail, every nuance. But for the vast majority of people, Congress and politics are just one small part of life, and news about it competes with a million other professional, family, and personal priorities.

In 1998, I got a call from Jane Sanders. I was traveling for work at the time. She said that Bernie needed a new chief of staff and wanted to know if I would be interested in talking about it if Bernie were. She asked me to think about it. It's never been clear to me if my possible return to the office was something that Bernie and Jane had already discussed, or if Jane knew Bernie needed a new chief of staff and wanted to talk with me before she suggested me to him. She and I had a couple more short conversations about it. The prospect of coming back in this new capacity started to grow on me. Ruthan Wirman called from the office to set up a meeting between Bernie and me.

Bernie and I sat on a park bench outside the Capitol. Even though we had a long history together, he wanted to be sure I was up to the new responsibilities. I call it his revetting process. He wants to be sure a choice is the right one for the moment and not one based on what's easy or familiar. During my three-plus-year absence I had in fact had many professional experiences that made me a much better choice than I would have been when I left. He wanted someone who would be an assertive advocate for him. Legal practice is the perfect training ground for that skill. A few days later he offered me the job. Just as in 2015, I had a hard time saying no to Bernie. My wife and I discussed the move, including the pay cut. She was fully behind it and I put in my notice with the firm.

By this time, Bernie was more senior and had established professional relationships with his colleagues on both sides of the aisle. He had also become a master of using the looser floor rules around appropriations bills to push amendments to votes and in securing Republican votes for those amendments. In fact, from 1995 to 2007, Bernie successfully passed, by recorded vote, more amendments on the floor of the Republican-controlled U.S. House than any other member. None of these amendments would have passed in a chamber with a majority of Republicans without at least some Republican votes.

Even an amendment that doesn't pass can have a big impact. During consideration of the farm bill, a coalition Bernie put together with Democratic congressman David Obey and Republican congressman David Vitter came within a few votes on the floor of passing a major overhaul of federal dairy policy. (For those not familiar with the "dairy wars," dairy politics are as byzantine as the policies are themselves. They are characterized by bitter regional, ideological, and industry feuding.) To get a bipartisan, multiregion coalition to agree on a single dairy reform plan, let alone such a sweeping one, was a miracle unto itself.

The plan was opposed by the top Republican and the top Democrat on the House Agriculture Committee and the Republican leadership. Upper Midwest Republicans abandoned the coalition (and their farmers) in the end, even as Democrats from that region and members of both parties from the South and the mid-Atlantic/New England regions hung together. The leaders on the House Agriculture Committee were shocked by the strength of the vote, which they had expected to crush. Top Ag Committee staffers stood on the floor in obvious shocked disbelief as the votes came in.

As they publicly acknowledged, the strong showing substantially bolstered the hand of senators, including Vermont's senators, who were pushing for dairy reform on their side of the Capitol. Before the vote, hard-pressed family dairy farmers were going to get almost nothing in the bill. Now their plight couldn't be ignored. It wasn't going to be the far-reaching plan Bernie and his coalition advocated, but it would be real and substantial help.

That victory, like so much Bernie accomplished in Congress, was made possible by pushing the envelope policy-wise and broadening the scope of the debate, even in coalition with Republicans, so that change gets made even if it's not the "whole loaf." That view was reflected in his agenda as a presidential candidate. He articulated an ambitious agenda of progressive change. His opponents and many in the media ridiculed it as pie-in-the-sky. But pragmatic Bernie understands that you achieve the maximum result not by putting forth tepid proposals that you've pre-negotiated with yourself but by moving the goalposts in a bold, progressive way.

3

BERNIE GOES TO THE BIG HOUSE

BERNIE'S OPPORTUNITY TO RUN for the U.S. Senate came to us as a bit of a surprise. I was heading into the House office when my phone rang. It was Luke Albee, Senator Leahy's then chief of staff. "Jim Jeffords is going to announce that he's not running for reelection," he reported. In Vermont politics, this news was a bombshell. I immediately hung up and called Bernie. "I think you have to run," I told him. I was not sure it would be his view. He didn't need my encouragement. He was in.

Bernie running for the Senate was very much in keeping with the tradition in Vermont. Vermont has only one congressional district, and it had been customary in Vermont politics for the House member to ascend to the Senate once there was a vacancy. Jim Jeffords had been the House member when Bob Stafford retired and had successfully run for the seat. Congressman Richard Mallory was widely expected to win the open Senate seat in 1974 but was upset in the post-Watergate era by Chittenden County prosecutor Pat Leahy.

As I was living in the DC area and the campaign was going to be run out of Vermont, I was charged with finding a campaign manager for the effort. Every day for a week Bernie and I would go over a list of names of potential candidates. After a week Bernie asked me to run it myself. I'd end up commuting weekly to Vermont for the last six months of the campaign.

He and I both realized, though, that this campaign was going to be entirely different from the many House races he had run. The stakes nationally were much higher, and the resources that could be brought to bear were considerable. Two years before, Vermont's Democratic senator Patrick Leahy had spent $2 million on his reelection campaign. That number seems quaint by the standards of other states, but it was a huge number at the time in Vermont.

We saw it as a particular problem for our campaign, given that Bernie had not and would not in his Senate race take corporate PAC money. Given how relatively inexpensive campaigns in Vermont were at that time, we were very concerned that if the Republican candidate gained any traction, the national Republicans and their corporate allies would pour money into the state in the hopes of getting a cheap pickup. There were also several national Republicans who were bitter because Jim Jeffords had been elected as a Republican but left the party to sit as an independent as he became increasingly uncomfortable with its far-right move.

But on that first day and on the days that followed, our bigger concern was clearing the field on the Democratic side so that Bernie became the sole viable candidate to face the Republicans. This was complicated by the fact that Bernie would run as an independent, as he had in all his House races.

Over the course of his House career, he had become the de facto Democrat in his congressional races. That only made sense. He caucused with the House Democrats, he had seniority on that side of the aisle, and he voted for the Democratic House leadership. And, importantly, he had the overwhelming support of rank-and-file Democrats in Vermont. For those reasons, the national Democrats would never have helped a candidate seeking to unseat Bernie. Plus, as a practical matter, no serious Democratic politician in Vermont would have risked his or her political career by going after Bernie in a House race.

But this was different. Bernie did not have a relationship with the

Senate Democratic leadership. He had no way of knowing if they would support a more establishment candidate, of which there were many. Bernie certainly did not fit the profile of the candidate the national Democrats all too often back—wealthy, self-funding, centrist. And even if they didn't, it would be very easy for anyone to get on the ballot on the Democratic line, split the vote, and elect a Republican.

Senator Leahy helped with both of these problems. He intervened for Bernie with the Senate Democratic leadership to keep them from supporting a different candidate. Keeping the Democratic Senatorial Campaign Committee (DSCC) from backing someone else would make it very difficult, if not impossible, for anyone else to raise the money needed to take on Bernie in a primary. The DSCC pretty quickly came in behind Bernie.

The second issue—keeping someone from getting on the Democratic line on the Vermont ballot—took more time. The goal was to have Bernie win the Democratic primary, decline the nomination, and then have the Democratic State Committee endorse him and not replace him on the Democratic line. In the meantime, we would gather the signatures for him to appear on the ballot as an independent. (Under Vermont law, you cannot appear on the ballot as both an independent and with any other affiliation.) In that way, Bernie would be an independent candidate for the Senate with the endorsement of the Vermont State Democratic Party and the DSCC. In other words, he would be the candidate of the Democrats, even if not the Democratic candidate.

The problem was that the state Democratic Party rules didn't allow the state party to support candidates not running on the Democratic line. The rules had to be changed. Senator Leahy's people got the ball rolling. Bernie called every member of the Vermont state committee.

In my time with him, this was the first time he had made this kind of effort to reach out in a systematic way to the Democratic Party infrastructure. It's the understatement of the century to say that Bernie prefers meeting with everyday people a hundred times more than making these types of political calls. But he understood the importance of the fight he was taking on in his quest to be Vermont's next U.S. senator. In the end, the rules were changed, and the likelihood that anyone would appear on the Democratic line evaporated.

Bernie's Republican opponent in the 2006 race was Rich Tarrant, a self-made businessman who had recently sold his company for some $1.2 billion. That was a big problem. Tarrant would have, for all practical purposes, unlimited funds to try to win the U.S. Senate seat. And he was running to win. He brought in out-of-state Republican operatives to run his campaign. We feared this would not be the type of civilized race focused on issues that our small state was used to.

Bernie's Senate campaign focused on his record of fighting for average Vermonters in the U.S. House and his ability to bring those fights to a larger platform in the U.S. Senate. He also ran hard against the Bush administration's policies on war and peace and the economy. Bernie had served almost sixteen years in the House, so he had a long record for his opponent to distort. For the first time in his career, we did self-opposition research on Bernie's voting record. This is common practice in politics— you want to know the potential lines of attack by your opponents and be ready for them. But we had never done it before. We brought on Paul Hortenstine to do research (both self and opposition) and to be the campaign press secretary. He was a thorough, aggressive, and effective campaign staffer. Just what the doctor ordered for what we would face in 2006.

Still, the issue of Rich Tarrant's resources loomed large. We understood that our fund-raising would have to be kicked into high gear if we were going to compete. Bernie had the advantage of "incumbency." As Vermont's lone congressperson, he had been elected statewide every two years since 1990. Even so, his opponent had hundreds of millions at his disposal in a state where the most ever spent in a Senate race had been $2 million.

The foundation of Bernie's fund-raising in 2006 was going to be small-dollar individual contributions, as it had always been. But we needed more of them. Even a decade ago, the internet was not the huge source of political contributions it is today. In those long-ago days, Bernie's small-dollar fund-raising was through direct mail. Yes, the kind that comes through the post office. And just as he would be successful online in 2016, in 2006 he had great success with direct mail.

Bernie personally drafted all the direct-mail appeals. They usually took the form of a four-page, single-spaced letter heavy on policy prescriptions. They reflected who he was—as his policy-laden 2016 stump speech would—and how he liked to treat his small donors with respect, not gimmicks. He handpicked the target universe from commercially available lists. It was amazingly successful. Those who do direct-mail fund-raising expect to lose money on the front end, as they prospect from commercial lists to build a donor list that can then profitably be resolicited. Bernie's appeals made money even in the prospecting phase.

In addition to direct mail, we would look to potential allies who could help fund the race. Labor, of course, strongly backed Bernie's senatorial bid. The labor movement recognized his long and unequivocal support of working people during his House tenure. They were almost unanimously on board. But in these pre–*Citizens United* days, the amount of support each union could provide was limited.

We reached out successfully to the trial lawyers for help as well. Bernie had long opposed so-called tort reform, which is just another front in corporate America's fight to escape any kind of accountability for their actions. Corporate interests flood the presidential and congressional electoral process to gain influence over politicians and the laws and regulations they produce. As a result, the one place average people can still get at least a fighting chance against corporate power and excess is in the courtroom. Needless to say, corporate interests are always doing whatever they can to shut down that venue as well.

Realizing the severity of our resource imbalance against Tarrant, Bernie did a few fund-raisers on the West Coast, in New York City, and a few other places. He has never been comfortable asking people for money, and he felt strongly that fund-raising robbed him of valuable time he could be using to talk to voters.

Rich Tarrant put his money to work early. In an unprecedented move, in May 2006 he began an ad campaign that was a weekly serial of his life story. Each week would present the next episode in the life of Rich Tarrant. The ads were very well done and were running often.

Our challenge was to turn Tarrant's main advantage—his money—against him. We had to make every one of his innumerable ads a reminder to our fellow Vermonters that Tarrant was the candidate of big money and Bernie was the candidate of the average person. In many ways that was a perfect position to be in for an authentically progressive candidate like Bernie. Leahy's chief Luke Albee's view was that the race was summed up by the contrast between Bernie's populism and Tarrant's wealth. "C'mon," he said to me, "his name is Rich." Foreshadowing Trump's talking points from 2016, Tarrant told NPR, "I will never apologize for success. But also, I'm not beholden to special interests."

We went on the offensive right out of the gate. Soon satellite pictures of Tarrant's Florida residence with its boat slip were in the news. As was the homestead exemption he took on the Florida house. And it was a good thing, too, because our fears about his campaign going negative turned out to be all too true. When you have unlimited money like Tarrant, you can afford to run the slick, warm 'n' fuzzy weekly biography ad series as well as negative ads. And he did.

Tarrant went after Bernie's opposition to mandatory minimum sentencing. The ads accused Bernie of coddling child molesters. NPR's Peter Overby reported that Tarrant's ads "accuse Sanders of quietly voting to protect child molesters" and portrayed him as being "against single working mothers." In that same story, University of Vermont professor Gary Nelson described Tarrant's ads as "the nastiest set of commercials Vermont has ever seen."

One ad charged that Bernie was soft on terrorists because he opposed intelligence spending bills that he believed were bloated. Harkening back to 9/11, it used visuals of airliners. Senator Harry Reid told Bernie that Tarrant's ads against him were the most vicious of the cycle. The gloves were off.

Tarrant's company had applied for state tax breaks only available to companies that would certify they'd otherwise move jobs out of Vermont.

Not a good fact for someone seeking to represent Vermonters in Washington. But in the paid media Bernie never went negative, as would be the case all the way through his presidential campaign. Instead he responded to Tarrant's paid media assaults with a direct-to-camera ad that effectively made the case that all of Tarrant's negative ads were a distortion of Bernie's long record of service to his fellow Vermonters: "For months my opponent, Rich Tarrant, has been spending millions telling us about himself. Well, it's his money and he can spend it if he wants. But he has no right to distort my record or what I stand for." That ad was paired with another, featuring several Vermonters, including Republicans, who testified to the fact that Bernie is an honest public figure who fights for everyday people. These ads were done by Tad Devine.

One of the highlights of the campaign was a visit from Senator Barack Obama in March to endorse Bernie and Peter Welch. Peter Welch was running for the House seat Bernie was vacating to run for the U.S. Senate. Senator Obama was one of a number of elected officials who came that year to endorse Bernie. But you could see that there was something very different, very remarkable about this young senator. He had an ease about him, a comfort in himself and in his interactions with other people that is uncommon in politics.

Often when political figures come to campaign, their staff provides a list of things the person will and won't do, what the schedule must look like, what food must be available, and so forth. It varies from person to person and is usually handled at the staff level. In an extreme case, one person who came to campaign for us limited the time that a town hall meeting could last and required any questions to be submitted ahead of time. Senator Obama had provided none of that, but we had had the usual conversations with his staff about what the format of the event would be so that he would know what to expect.

The event was held at a freestanding chapel at the University of Vermont. Picture a minichurch. As was the case all over the country, Senator Obama drew a huge crowd. Over 1,000 people were crowded inside and hundreds more were outside. People were literally hanging off the windows so they could see him. It was a giant turnout, and there was a fair amount of chaos. Per the schedule, the event inside would take place and then Senator Obama, Bernie, and Peter Welch would go outside to briefly greet the overflow crowd at the end.

As the overflow crowd continued to grow, Bernie decided that he and Peter Welch would go outside to begin addressing the people. When Senator Barack Obama arrived, I was to explain the situation and escort him to join them. That way, people who could not get in would not have to wait outside until the end of the event before being addressed. It was an unseasonably warm day in Vermont, but Bernie is always concerned about the physical comfort of his audience.

Bernie and Peter Welch headed out to the front steps of the chapel, while I stayed behind to inform Senator Obama that the run-of-show had changed. He arrived not long after, coming into the backstage area. "I'm sorry, Senator, but there's been a change in the schedule," I said apologetically. "Congressman Sanders is addressing the overflow crowd first and would like you to join him out there."

He looked at me. I was expecting at least some consternation on his part. Most senators don't like surprises, even little ones. Instead, he gave me one of those big, warm Barack Obama smiles. Maybe he could tell that I was nervous about the situation. "No problem," he said. "This is your event and you just tell me where to go." I led him through the chapel, which sent the crowd waiting in the pews into a frenzy, and out to the front steps. He rocked the speech to the overflow crowd and to the folks inside that he addressed afterward. It was no surprise to any of us when his presidential campaign caught fire in 2008. Both in his personal dealings and in his ability to inspire a crowd, we had already seen in 2006 that he was head and shoulders above.

Throughout his Senate run, Bernie was crisscrossing the state, holding meetings and rallies in town after town. We launched a mail program targeted to constituencies that are not reliably Democratic. I personally designed pieces that we sent to seniors, veterans, and rural voters. Bernie had championed these voters in the U.S. House, but it was important to remind folks. And we had a field program, spearheaded by Phil Fiermonte, whose members were knocking on doors, making phone calls, and tabling at events across the state. That combination of positive advertising, Bernie's packed calendar, a vigorous field program, and "pointed" free media engagement created a wall that the Tarrant campaign, for all its money, couldn't breach.

In August, Bernie asked for an updated finance report on the campaign. He hated doing traditional fund-raising in small gatherings. He looked at the direct-mail fund-raising totals and the cash on hand and said, "We're going to be fine with the direct mail. I'm not doing any more traditional fund-raisers." I can't say that I was happy to hear Bernie say it, given the monetary resources we were up against. But it wasn't a suggestion on his part.

The personal relationship between the candidates continued to degenerate and culminated in some extremely heated debates that can still be found on YouTube. Let's just say there was no love lost between Bernie and Tarrant after Tarrant spent his campaign alleging Bernie loved child molesters and terrorists. (In fairness, I suppose Tarrant didn't appreciate the narrative that he was a narcissistic carpetbagger who was using money and lies to buy a U.S. Senate seat.) Polling continued moving in Bernie's direction. A couple of weeks before election day, Tarrant's spending dried up. He knew he was whipped and he wasn't going to pour more of his own money in.

Bernie beat Tarrant by over 20 points. Tarrant had spent over $8 million. Bernie had—surprisingly—spent over $6.5 million. In many ways, this was a foreshadowing of 2016. People would respond with overwhelming generosity, giving small sums to sustain Bernie's fight for the common person against big-money interests. Two thousand six was also important because it gave us our first preview of what it is like to go up against the type of well-funded modern campaign we would face in 2016. All the same, the 2006 race was fought on much more favorable terrain in terms of Bernie's name recognition and initial levels of support.

He certainly did not start the 2006 campaign at 36 percent in the polls as he did in 2016.

Bernie's transition to the Senate was much less unusual than his arrival in the House in 1990. There was no effort to exclude him from the Democratic caucus, no question that he would be treated as anything other than a full-fledged member of the Democratic Senate majority. That being said, the Senate and the House have extremely different cultures.

The primary difference is that every single senator has the power to say no, but no one senator has the power to say yes. By that I mean that any senator can hold up legislation by threatening a filibuster. But no senator or group of senators fewer than sixty can force debate to end on a measure and require a vote. By contrast, in the House, the leadership of the majority party has almost unlimited control of the floor.

The impact of everyone being able to say no in the Senate is a culture of interpersonal hypercourtesy. There's a lot of walking on eggshells—making sure one doesn't inadvertently give personal offense to another senator. Personal notes are sent back and forth between senators. As an example, very early on I remember walking with Bernie through one of the many subterranean tunnels beneath the Senate office buildings. We ran into Pete Domenici, a Republican, with whom Bernie exchanged hellos. Everything seemed fine. Bernie was in his usual hurry and not one to really chit-chat anyway.

Shortly thereafter, Bernie received a note from Senator Domenici, who profusely apologized for not having stopped to talk to Bernie at greater length. Neither Bernie nor I had noticed anything wrong with the exchange in the tunnel. But Bernie appreciated it as a sincere and courteous gesture. There was a lot to learn about the U.S. Senate.

What Bernie did realize was the opportunities that the Senate provided to make the lives of ordinary people better. In his first year, he turned his attention to a group of people who were suffering incredibly: the migrant tomato workers of Immokalee, Florida. He had learned of an organizing campaign to get the buyers of the tomatoes these workers picked—mainly fast-food restaurants—to pay a penny a pound more so wages could go up. YUM! Brands (which includes Taco Bell, Pizza Hut, and KFC) had already agreed. But others, like Burger King, were holding out. In addition, the growers were opposed to the campaign and doing everything they could to prevent it from being successful.

Bernie traveled to Immokalee. On the day he arrived, authorities made arrests for human slavery there. Workers lived in terrible housing. Early in the predawn hours, they would gather to be chosen to go to the fields to pick tomatoes at extremely low wages. Clearly, many were being victimized by uncertain immigration status. At a community meeting, Bernie pledged to the workers that he would take their case to Washington.

When he got back to DC, he met with Senator Ted Kennedy, who was then head of the Senate Committee on Health, Education, Labor and Pensions (HELP). Senator Kennedy agreed to hold a hearing—to be chaired by Bernie—to expose the plight of the migrant workers. Bernie had met with the tomato growers to try to convince them to soften their stance against the penny-a-pound program. They held firm.

I remember distinctly a staff-level meeting on the subject with representatives of interested Senate offices that sums up what all too often happens in DC. A staffer stated with sincere sadness that she had grown up in Florida, was aware of what was going on in Immokalee, felt that it was horrendous, but believed that it was "never going to change." My internal response was: Bullshit. (I stress it was my internal response. It was the Senate, after all. Gotta be polite.) That was Bernie's sentiment also.

Bernie made sure that workers from Immokalee were invited to testify at the hearing. They were the people suffering, and they should be there to tell their story in their own voice. There were workers who, for a variety of reasons, were reluctant to walk into a federal facility, let alone testify before a U.S. Senate committee. But Bernie assured everyone that they would be safe testifying before the Senate.

The hearing itself was one of the most meaningful I attended in almost a decade and a half working in the House and Senate. Usually congressional hearings consist of a panel of administration representatives who speak and are followed by a panel or two of experts or lobbyists for this or that interest. It is comparatively rare for average people to appear before a congressional committee. But in this case, you had some of the most vulnerable people in the country, from the lowest rungs of the economic ladder, who would make their case to a leading committee of the U.S. Senate. And it was all because of Bernie's dogged determination to help people—in this case, people who were in so many ways far from Vermont.

It is difficult to convey the power of that hearing and what it symbolized. The voices of the marginalized being heard and, importantly, listened to in the halls of power. That is what Bernie Sanders brought and brings to governing—giving voice to the voiceless. It's not quantifiable. But it is as real as, if not more real than, bills or amendments passed. It's something the mainstream media will never get and that the Clinton campaign couldn't or wouldn't understand. But millions across the country would understand it in 2016.

In the end the Immokalee workers won their fight for Penny-A-Pound, against the opposition of the growers. In the years since, the collective wages of Immokalee workers have risen by millions of dollars.

After a tremendous amount of deliberation, I left Bernie's office in mid-2009 to take a break from politics and the Hill. After commuting to Vermont for six months and then two years as his Senate chief of staff, I needed a break. As my time came to an end, Bernie called me into his office and asked me to stay longer. It was difficult to say no but I did.

PART TWO

THE REVOLUTION BEGINS

4

DECIDING TO RUN FOR PRESIDENT

IF THERE'S ONE THING EVERYONE knows about Bernie Sanders it's that, other than his devotion to his family, he is singularly focused on his work. When you are working with him, he is in very frequent contact with you. But when you are not, you are not likely to hear from him very often. The amount of time and focus he devotes to his lifelong efforts to move the country in a progressive direction just doesn't allow for it. I had seen him each year at his annual holiday party, but not much other than that. When I got a call from him in the early spring of 2015 it came as a bit of a surprise.

I was sitting at my kitchen table. "Hi, this is Bernie Sanders," he said. It sounded strangely formal, because I would have known who it was if he had just said "Bernie." (The accent is a dead giveaway.) He invited me to dinner with no other explanation. Of course, I accepted. I knew him well enough that it wouldn't just be a dinner to catch up.

We met at the Thunder Grill in Union Station. I have spent so much time with Bernie that no matter how long it has been since we've talked, it always seems like we pick up just where we left off. I'm sure we talked about Honk-A-Mania and a bunch of old war stories, like the time he was trying to talk to an AP reporter from the phone in my father's pet store while a cockatoo screamed in the background. Or the time we were running late for a radio talk show and the host kept announcing over the radio that he had no idea where Bernie Sanders could be. We were on a rural road racing to the studio and desperately hoping to find a pay phone on the way to explain that we'd be late. That one is always good for a laugh.

He asked about my comic book store. After I left his office in 2009 I had opened the store and actively traveled the comic convention circuit. We talked about that for a while and how great it was going. Then we talked about my boys' Little League teams. When he was the mayor of Burlington, he had helped start a Little League program in the working-class area of the city. The conversation then moved to some Senate shop talk. We were there for quite a while, and, as with any dinner with a friend, the conversation naturally wound its way down. We said good-bye and headed our separate ways.

Now I know that Bernie was getting closer to deciding to run for president. The political commentator and author Bill Press had hosted a few meetings at his house with Bernie and a number of folks just to talk through the possibility. The guests at these meetings had been invited just to be sounding boards, with the understanding that none were committing in any way to Bernie if he did run. One of the attendees, Brad Woodhouse, would later file a bogus Federal Election Commission (FEC) complaint against us as part of his work with a David Brock–affiliated organization. But Bernie and I never discussed any of it that night.

When I got home, my wife asked what Bernie had wanted to talk about. I said, "I have no idea." Over the next couple of months, there started to be more media speculation about Bernie running for president. It became clear to me what our conversation at the Thunder Grill had been about.

Despite his public persona, Bernie is in many ways private and reserved. Born in Brooklyn, he has nonetheless internalized a Yankee ethos. One aspect of this ethos is self-reliance and nonimposition. He finds it hard to ask people for things that he perceives as personal rather than political. If someone is working with him in politics, he expects the same level of commitment that he puts in. But the personal is something else entirely.

When we met at the Thunder Grill, he was looking to gauge my happiness with my nonpolitical life. His takeaway, no doubt, was that I was content, which I was. Given that, he didn't want to ask me to put that aside and join what would be an all-consuming, long-shot presidential campaign.

With all the press speculation about Bernie intensifying, I called Phil Fiermonte. I asked Phil if this rumored presidential bid was real. He told me that he didn't know if it was or not. That, of course, was the truthful answer, because at that time even Bernie didn't know for sure. I told Phil to let me know if that changed.

Bernie called me again at the end of April to meet for dinner. We met again at the Thunder Grill. As we sat down, I asked him, "Are we going to talk about whatever it was we were supposed to talk about the last time we had dinner?" He told me he had decided to run for president.

We discussed me joining the campaign. I said I would obviously have to talk with my family. I knew what a campaign like this meant in terms of time. I also said that I would only be interested in coming on if the campaign was one to win the nomination, as unlikely as winning was at that moment (CNN reported Bernie's support was then at 3 percent). I asked Bernie, "Are you in this to win?"

I told him that if it was just an "educational" campaign, I would be happy to max out and write nice things about him on social media, but I could not upend my life unless we were going to run to win. "Yes, I'm running to win," he assured me. Moreover, he would compete in every contest, regardless of how the campaign was going. "I'm going to run all the way to the end of the process," he said. In hindsight, I'm not sure if he was totally convinced at that moment that it was a campaign to win, but that night he sold me.

He laid out his vision for the campaign. It would be a grassroots, volunteer-centered effort focused on the progressive agenda he had championed his whole life. He asked what I thought. "A grassroots campaign is great, but it's not going to be enough to win," I said. The campaign would have to use every weapon at its disposal, because his opponents would. "We will run a grassroots campaign, but we will also have to use all the modern tools of campaigning. We are going to have to do it all," I said. "Yes, exactly," he said. "We will do it all."

But he lamented how much everything seemed to cost. He wanted someone he trusted to help coordinate that world. "Do you know what the standard Washington monthly consulting fee is?" he asked. "It's 30,000. That's what they all want. It seems to be the going rate inside the Beltway." He did not want the campaign's resources devoured by consulting fees, especially ones that bore no fruit. (Tad's firm was working purely on the basis of ad commissions, so they charged no monthly retainer.)

We talked about my role in the campaign. After a while he got around to suggesting that I should be the manager. Both of us understood that while I had managed his first Senate race, this would be a completely different animal. Hillary Clinton had spent years preparing and had some of the top Democratic talent running her campaign. "Jeff, I would be crazy to offer you this position and you'd be crazy to take it," he said. We agreed to meet the next day after I talked with my family.

When I got home, my wife asked if Bernie wanted me to work on the campaign. I said he did, and she immediately said she thought I should do it. My daughter and two boys were enthusiastic about it also. As my boys encouraged me to do it, I looked at them and told them, "You don't know what you're asking." I knew that dinners home, doing homework together, coaching their Little League teams, and being there for them would be a thing of the past.

The next night Bernie and I met again. Turns out we were both crazy. We were off to the races in a campaign against a candidate who had the backing of the entire Democratic establishment. Their campaign had been years in the making. Ours was starting from scratch.

Putting together the campaign team was going to be a difficult enterprise, and we were way behind. In addition, the ground rules for the 2016 Democratic contest were already set. And a limited debate schedule would soon be imposed on us by the chair of the Democratic National Committee—a schedule worked out ahead of time by the Clinton campaign.

One thing I knew was all the things I didn't know. I had to get as much help as I could from the experienced people around us. I met Mark

Longabaugh, one of Tad's partners, at the Mad Fox Brewing Company in my home town. Mark had a long history of involvement in politics, including working for Bill Bradley in New Hampshire (when Tad was working for Al Gore) and in the environmental movement. He had been hired to run Mario Cuomo's New Hampshire operation in 1992 until Cuomo unexpectedly dropped out. Mario Cuomo had been a hero of mine, and I remembered being very upset when he decided not to run. Had Cuomo become president in 1992, the country and the Democratic Party would have been in a much different and, in my view, infinitely better place. Mark had even been a congressional candidate himself.

Mark became a key adviser to Bernie, and to me. Mark "gets" politics— both the big picture and the nuances. I relied on him in many cases daily. What is important to understand about him is that Mark was himself a candidate for the manager job. And he would have been a great one.

When Bernie hired me, Mark reached out to me immediately to offer to help me in any way possible. Many in politics would have been bitter; Mark and I both knew that in terms of experience and expertise at the time, he was head and shoulders above me. Not Mark. He understood my long-standing relationship with Bernie. He would often say that, given that history, no one else could have run the campaign. I'm not sure that's true. But what is true is that Mark is one of the people without whom I could not have done it. Mark was and is a mentor and a friend—someone who fought by my side and always had my back.

It's not quite fair to say there was nothing in place when I was brought on to manage the campaign. Bernie and Jane had already retained a few key players who would take on critical roles. Devine, Mulvey, and Longabaugh—DML—were already the media consultants. They had also brought on the digital firm Revolution Messaging. Rev, as we called them, oversaw our online fund-raising—which we all knew early on was going to have to be a substantial (or *the* substantial) source of funding for the campaign. Rev also handled online advertising, list management, and all related tasks. Their success made the entire campaign possible.

During an initial meeting with Revolution Messaging's Tim Tagaris, Keegan Goudiss, and Scott Goodstein, Bernie asked how much could be raised online. Tim said, "If it's a competitive primary, thirty million to fifty million." Bernie, not wanting too rosy an estimate, asked, "What if it's not a competitive primary? How about credible primary?" Tim replied, "Probably close to thirty million, then." Tim's $30 million estimate became the basis for all our early budgeting. And his $50 million number became our fantasy target.

In addition, there were Senate staff, like communications director Michael Briggs, digital director Kenneth Pennington, and social media director Hector Sigala, who were moving over to the campaign. A number of Bernie's other Senate staffers helped in the off hours.

But we were woefully understaffed. One person described our situation as running a marathon while you are trying to put on your shoes. That was a pretty accurate description. We were going to have to build campaign infrastructure while we supported Bernie's aggressive public calendar.

Bernie's initial announcement for the presidency of the United States was perhaps the most understated of the 2016 campaign season and maybe in recent memory. There was no fanfare. No crowds, no big event. Bernie called a press conference on April 30, 2015, in the Senate Swamp— outdoors, on Capitol Hill, where senators often hold press events. Usually they are highlighting some bill or legislative initiative. It was a low-key event—ironic, given the explosion of grassroots support his candidacy would receive in the summer. One thing that did bode well for the future of the campaign is that online donations of $1.5 million poured in over the next twenty-four hours from 35,000 donors. That seemed like a huge amount of money at the time, but it was only a small preview of the generous support Bernie would receive over the next year. A hundred thousand people also signed up to join the campaign.

What became clear very early on was that, despite the fact that there was a sitting Democratic president, Hillary Clinton had assumed the mantle of the incumbent in this contest. And in political contests against an incumbent, the path to victory is a two-step process. The first is to convince the voters that they want to look beyond the incumbent. And once they do, you must convince them that you are the better choice, or many of those who have been pulled from the incumbent will drift back.

Hillary Clinton had considerable political strengths. She had an impeccable résumé. She was a seasoned candidate with the experience of running a near-successful primary campaign in 2008. She had the Democratic establishment (and many outside the establishment) in her corner. She would be a formidable fund-raiser. And she was universally known. Almost 18 million people had cast votes for her in 2008, when she ran against Senator Obama. As we were to discover in polling later, her "favorables" with self-identified Democratic voters were extremely high. Given that self-identified Democrats made up the majority of primary and caucus voters—and in closed primary states (that is, those that did not let independent voters participate) all the voters—this was a serious challenge.

On the other hand, she had a reputation for being aloof and not comfortable with unscripted human interaction. In addition, as later polling also revealed, many voters had serious concerns about her trustworthiness. This was particularly true of Democratically aligned independent voters—voters who call themselves independents but dependably vote Democratic and often participate in Democratic primaries where it's allowed. She had played an active role in the first Clinton White House—a strength and a weakness. Hillary Clinton was an experienced leader at the highest levels of government. But that meant she also was an active participant in policy making and policy advocacy in the 1990s. Many of those policies—like NAFTA, harsh criminal justice policies, welfare reform, and the Defense of Marriage Act—were as much hers as they were Bill Clinton's. And these were the very policies that Bernie Sanders had fought vigorously against during this time in Congress.

But before we could make these contrasts, we had to let the people of the country know who Bernie Sanders was and what he stood for. Even as late as November, our polling showed over 40 percent of voters in some places didn't have enough information to form an opinion of him.

There was a strong consensus among Bernie, Jane, myself, and other top advisers that we were not going to run a negative, burn-everything-to-the-ground campaign. The media thought it was just a talking point, but it went to the essence of what Bernie was trying to do. He wanted to inspire the nation, not drag it into the mud. Bernie wanted to win, but not for personal reasons. He wanted to run in a way that uplifted the progressive policy vision that had been his life's work. And, importantly, he wanted to run on concrete policies so that in the event he won the White House, however unlikely it seemed, he would have a mandate to advance those policies in Congress.

In broad terms, we had to introduce Bernie Sanders and that policy agenda to the nation. We had to show them he was a credible alternative to Hillary Clinton so they would give him a good look. And then we had to lay out the contrast between them in a way that was policy-focused and not personal or negative.

The goal, of course, is to acquire enough delegates to win the nomination, or to create such a tidal wave of support that all of one's opponents drop out. The latter would be difficult to do, as Clinton had shown in 2008 that she would fight all the way to the end. Even so, given the expectation that she would dominate the primaries, a series of early wins could create the momentum Bernie would need to win the nomination. Our thinking began to focus on how to make that happen.

I met John Robinson at a café called The Coupe in DC late in May for a meeting. Mark Longabaugh had recruited him. When I arrived, John was already there, sipping some tea. I ordered a glass of wine. John had worked on John Edwards's presidential campaign and had a wealth of other campaign experience. The idea was for him to come on for a few months and get the internal accounting, human resources, and financial processes in order. As part of that, he would train someone to take over those responsibilities for the long term.

He had already met with Bernie and Jane. They liked him. During the interview Bernie asked John, "Do the people on campaigns with you like you?" John replied, "They don't, because I tell them they can't spend all the money they want." Bernie then asked me to meet John. We talked about the various aspects of the job, and John agreed to come on board for a three-month stint.

Job number one was to put together a budget—actually, two budgets. One would be based on Revolution Messaging's $30 million estimate through the end of the first four contests—all of which occurred before March 2016. The second would be based on the $50 million fantasy number. As it turned out, John had the Edwards for President budget from 2004. Coincidently, it was for about $30 million. From my perspective, it was extremely helpful to see the relative allocation of funds to the various spending categories. Little did we know that we would ultimately raise over $230 million. That unknown—that the American people would generously donate nearly a quarter of a billion dollars—shaped the structure of the campaign early on more than any other single fact.

In our many meetings, DML estimated that paid media (television, radio, and digital) for the first four contests would be in the neighborhood of $18 million. In those early days of the campaign, that seemed like an incredibly high number. But I was determined that we not find ourselves in the final weeks of these contests with no money to spend. As Bernie and I had discussed at Thunder Grill, we could only win if we could deploy the tools of modern campaigning in conjunction with our grassroots efforts. The need to squirrel away $18 million would guide my hiring and spending practices throughout the summer. If we only raised $30 million, then the campaign would have to live on $12 million. That was not a lot to spend over nine months' time.

Bernie, for his part, also wanted to keep staffing low and expenses down. He was less focused on the need to keep the $18 million in reserve for paid media in the first four states. He was focused on the long term.

As he and I had discussed at the beginning of the campaign, he was committed to contesting every single primary and caucus. We also knew that if we faltered along the way, our fund-raising could very well dry up. So Bernie wanted a slow "burn rate" so there would be adequate resources to go all the way to the end. He was not confident we would even hit the $30 million number. He reminded me of his experience in 1986, when his campaign had gone through all the money early.

In addition, Bernie is a frugal manager by nature. He is always convinced that the work being done by any ten people could really be done by five. It's an instinct that had served him well as mayor of Burlington—he could accomplish a lot while keeping trust with the taxpayers. He certainly favors an activist government, but he also wants an efficient one.

That view carried over to the campaign. He was determined to do as much as possible with the limited resources we expected to have and so was very cautious about creating a large campaign bureaucracy. We didn't always see exactly eye to eye on how many people were needed for a given task, but it is fair to say that we did far more with far fewer people than most campaigns ever do. His pledge to go to the end was one that was taken seriously. Once we reached $10 million cash on hand in our bank account, we never fell below that amount until very late in the campaign. With a bare-bones staff, that amount would have kept him on the road through June 2016. So, between Bernie and me there was a real effort to keep staffing low and costs down during the summer of 2015—although we may have had somewhat different motives. If we had known how successful the fund-raising would be, we would have set up in more states earlier in the process, and we would have fleshed out our headquarters staff considerably.

The other major factor that would affect the early campaign was Bernie's decision that at least through the end of 2015 he would continue in his role as a full-time U.S. senator. He felt an obligation to the people of Vermont, and he wanted to make sure he was representing their interests in Washington. Republican Marco Rubio had done the opposite, taking to the campaign trail and rarely attending to Senate business. Bernie's position was a controversial one within the campaign, as it meant that he would only be available to campaign on weekends and whenever the Senate was out of session. That was a severe limitation, especially given the fact that we were relying on commercial air travel and not a charter at that point. It also meant that he would be working seven days a week either in the Senate or on the trail.

And he did intend to be on the trail. It is an understatement to say that Bernie is a strong believer in getting out and meeting voters. A central part of his vision of the campaign—maybe *the* central part, for him—was to hold meetings and rallies with people all over the country. That had been the key to much of his electoral success in Vermont. If he could just speak to voters directly, without the filter of the media, he was confident that the power of his ideas would win them over. He certainly recognizes the power of TV, radio, and the internet to reach voters, but in his heart he prefers to campaign the old-fashioned way—going from town to town talking to people face-to-face.

Bernie's view of rallies is different from many politicians'. For most, it is really a media appearance, with the crowd as a prop. For Bernie, the rally itself and his connection with the people who are in the room with him are the most important. That's one of the reasons he feels comfortable delivering his stump speech to crowds over and over again. The people he is speaking to that minute have not heard it before, even if the media has. Of course, he wants the media to cover the event, but his primary goal is to win over the people right in front of him. (None of us could even dream of the possibility that the media would broadcast his speeches from beginning to end the way they did for Donald Trump throughout the campaign.)

In addition to him speaking to voters, the rallies, if successful in terms of their size, would help validate the campaign in the eyes of skeptics. We didn't know then that Bernie's signature rallies would grow to the massive events that they did—and quickly.

With our tight budget and an even tighter schedule, we had three immediate administrative goals: to continue to assemble a small headquarters staff; to begin staffing the first four states to hold contests, with Iowa and New Hampshire being priorities; and to get Bernie on the road.

The other challenge we were facing—although we didn't know the specifics at the time—was the extent to which the rules of the game under which we would compete were already being molded to benefit the Clinton campaign. On May 5, 2015, the Democratic National Committee announced that there would be only six sanctioned debates between the contenders for the nomination. (Contrast this with the twelve that the Republicans held.) They would begin in the fall. Dates, times, and sponsoring media organizations were left TBD. Importantly, any candidate appearing in a nonsanctioned debate would be barred from any of the sanctioned debates. This last provision was particularly onerous. If Bernie and Maryland governor Martin O'Malley had participated in a non-sanctioned debate, they would be barred from the sanctioned debates in which Hillary Clinton would appear. Without Bernie and O'Malley, the sanctioned debates would have been canceled or not covered by the media. That would have worked fine for the Clinton campaign. Bernie needed the exposure. Clinton did not. The DNC had thrown down the gauntlet. Agree to only debate the six times, or there would be no debates against Hillary Clinton.

In his story that same day, CNN's Mark Preston quoted DNC chair Debbie Wasserman Schultz as saying, "Our debate schedule will not only give Democratic voters multiple opportunities to size up the candidates for the nomination side-by-side, but will give all Americans a chance to see a unified Democratic vision of economic opportunity and progress— no matter whom our nominee may be."

In an interview on May 31 with *Meet the Press*'s Chuck Todd, Bernie called for more debates—and earlier debates, to start as soon as July. He followed up with a letter to Wasserman Schultz on June 1 requesting more debates. He pointed out that it would be good for voters and good for the Democratic Party for there to be additional debates. He also called for the additional debates to be held at various locations around the country to increase interest in the election outside the early voting states. In late June, we announced that over 200,000 people had signed our petition calling for more debates. It fell on uncaring ears.

One might chalk this all up to the DNC chair just trying in her own way to help Hillary Clinton. But the 2016 leaks of Hillary for America (HFA) chairman John Podesta's emails showed it was much more. In truth, the debate schedule and rules were hashed out behind closed doors between the DNC and the Clinton campaign.

An April 27, 2015, memo from top Clinton aide Charlie Baker revealed it all. The memo was emailed to Clinton campaign manager Robby Mook, communications director Jen Palmieri, and adviser Ron Klain. (Ron Klain had been Vice President Joe Biden's chief of staff for the first two years of the Obama administration.)

Baker's April 27 email detailed that, since February 2015, Mo Elleithee and Anita Dunn of the DNC had been in communication with the Clinton campaign about the debates. It suggested they might have been in contact with other campaigns, but I can certainly say that they had no contact with the Sanders campaign. Apparently, they did have discussions with the O'Malley campaign, but according to former staffers involved in those discussions, there was little interest in any real input from Team O'Malley. Lis Smith, O'Malley's communications director, described the whole process as "kabuki theater."

As for the substance of the Clinton position on debates, Baker wrote:

> Through internal discussions, we concluded that it was in our interest to: 1) limit the number of debates (and the number in each state); 2) start the debates as late as possible; 3) keep debates out of the busy window between February 1 and February 27, 2016 (Iowa to South Carolina); 4) create a schedule that would allow the later debates to be cancelled if the race is for practical purposes over; 5) encourage an emphasis on local issues and local media participants in the debate formats; and 6) ensure a format that provides equal time for all candidates and does not give the moderator any discretion to focus on one candidate. Through discussion of these goals with the DNC their current plan is to begin a debate schedule that would commence in early October, with one debate a month, one each in the early primary and caucus states, and the remaining 2 post South Carolina (we will need to push them to post March 1

and then the later 2 debates would be cancelled if the race ends). The DNC's current plan is to release the attached press release (which lacks this specificity but confirms the number and start window for the debates). The other campaigns have advocated (not surprisingly) for more debates and for the schedule to start significantly earlier. Mo and Anita believe that this announcement prior to the actual entry into the race of other candidates will strengthen their hand as they lock a schedule in with local media partners and state parties. One remaining issue is the criteria for participation: we believe it is important to the extent possible to keep the debates "multicandidate" and to eliminate the possibility of one on one debates; the most likely standard that would achieve this result is to allow any announced candidate who is: 1) a Democrat and, 2) who meets some threshold of viability (1 percent) in either a national or state specific (e.g. Iowa, NH) to participate.

On August 6, the DNC released further details of its debate schedule. Not surprisingly, they aligned perfectly with what Baker described as "in our interest." The first four debates would be held on October 13 in Las Vegas, November 14 in Des Moines, December 19 in New Hampshire, and January 17, 2016, in Charleston. There would be no debates during the Clinton-proposed blackout period. The last two debates were to be held in Milwaukee and Miami, on dates to be announced (obviously so they could be canceled in accordance with the Clinton campaign's position if the race was not competitive by then). The DNC issued this schedule right after Bernie's announcement and before Martin O'Malley's, no doubt "to strengthen their hand," as the Baker memo notes.

For the record, the October CNN debate used the 1 percent threshold as the qualifier for debate participation. While the Clinton campaign wanted that low threshold to have as large a field as possible on the stage, Bernie himself supported it, because he felt it only fair that all the candidates get to make their case to the voters. During later negotiations, one of the networks was trying to exclude Martin O'Malley, because they wanted a head-to-head between Bernie and Hillary Clinton (something that would have been better for Bernie than a three-way debate). Bernie's response to me was that even if O'Malley was not polling well at the moment, he was a serious candidate running a serious campaign. He told me, "Jeff, you tell them that if Martin O'Malley is excluded, I won't be there either."

Two of the first four debates were scheduled for Saturdays, when viewership would likely be lower. The Iowa debate would be the same night as the annual football game between the Iowa Hawkeyes and the Minnesota Golden Gophers—a rivalry that goes back over a century. The New Hampshire debate was on the last Saturday before Christmas—not likely to draw a large crowd unless it was playing on jumbotrons at shopping malls.

The rigging of the debate schedule would be just an early example of the DNC—and by that I mean Debbie Wasserman Schultz and those acting at her behest—putting a finger on the scales in favor of Hillary Clinton. Not until the release of John Podesta's emails and former DNC chair Donna Brazile's book did anyone realize the full extent of the active coordination between the DNC and HFA. The debate over debates would rage for months, with an interesting turnabout in fair play occurring during the New Hampshire primary, when the Clinton campaign saw itself tanking in the Granite State.

5

THE BIG ANNOUNCEMENT

BERNIE SET HIS FORMAL announcement of the campaign for May 26 in Burlington, Vermont. It would be followed by events in New Hampshire, Iowa, Minneapolis, Denver, and Madison.

First, we had to find a venue and someone to organize the event. It became clear to me that we were at the point in the campaign where we needed experienced advance people to help us. Advance people are the ones who scout out sights, help with the physical design of the event, ensure that all the infrastructure is there for both candidate and press, manage crowds and the press during the event, arrange ground travel between events, and generally ensure that while the candidate is on the road the trains run on time and without incident.

Once you have a traveling press corps, the advance teams make sure that there are adequate hotel rooms for the campaign party and the press. They find the restaurants where everyone will eat. They are also the lead interface with the Secret Service concerning events and event security. They are indispensable to the campaign's successful operation—especially in a campaign like ours, which would rely on a large number of huge rallies.

The integration of the professional advance staff caused a bit of culture shock at the beginning. Bernie had been doing large numbers of events in Vermont for decades. They were generally well attended but done in a low-key way. They were organic; Bernie liked it that way. As the number of campaign rallies and attendance at those rallies exploded in the coming months, the number of advance people necessarily grew a lot. Managing a rally for thousands or tens of thousands of people with all the national media in attendance is not the same as managing a two-hundred-person event in Burlington. And with all these advance people necessarily came more bureaucracy and less nimbleness in the schedule. The bigger ship was much harder to turn.

Person for person, our advance people outperformed any other. Their personal dedication and sacrifice made it possible to do many rallies that would have required two or three times more people in any other campaign. But back in the simpler days of May 2015, we were just looking for an advance person or two to help us pull off a successful Burlington kickoff. Through some contacts in Obama-world, we were introduced to Jean-Michel Picher. He would become one of our most trusted advance "leads" on the campaign. He had extensive experience, including on the Kerry presidential campaign.

In terms of the venue, if the weather was nice, outside would be the best. But committing to an outside venue was risky. For those not familiar with the vagaries of Vermont's weather, let me just say this: Where I grew up, in northern Vermont, people planted their gardens on Memorial Day weekend and then prayed we didn't get any frost.

We set a date: May 26. Our first choice of venue was the Burlington waterfront. The waterfront is not just physically beautiful but an important symbol of Bernie's successful tenure as a people-oriented mayor. During his mayoral tenure, he had fought against a waterfront redevelopment proposal that would have put high-end condominiums right on Lake Champlain's shore. The final project instead created a people-oriented waterfront that the entire community now enjoys.

We had some intense discussions about the risk of being outside after consulting some weather forecasts. Bernie made the call to go with the waterfront. Jean-Michel set about arranging for an elevated stage and a large press riser—an elevated platform or series of platforms built at the same height as the stage. The media sets up their equipment on these risers so they get a straight-on camera shot of the candidate and are not blocked by the crowd. While Jean-Michel got to work, the rest of us prayed for good weather. He also fought for, and finally got approval for, a tent-enclosed media filing center. All the members of the media who could file their stories from the relative comfort of the media tent instead of leaning over the hood of a car can thank Jean-Michel.

As it turned out, May 26 was a spectacular day. Bernie spent the early part of the day with Tad Devine polishing his speech. Like virtually every speech he would give in the campaign, Bernie drafted it himself and delivered it from a stack of handwritten sheets of paper. As the crowd began to assemble, it became evident that we were going to get a great turnout. In total, some 5,000 people made their way to the Burlington waterfront. The city has a population of slightly over 40,000; the county, 160,000. By comparison, Hillary Clinton's June 13 official kickoff event in New York City drew about the same number of people. New York City has a population of some 8.5 million people.

As the hour drew near we got frequent reports about the turnout and prepared to drive there. Bernie and Jane rode with me in a rented Jeep Cherokee. We came down the hill to the waterfront from a side street and tried to park inconspicuously behind the stage. The program began and a series of supporters began their speeches.

It was a warm day, and all of us in the car were a bit nervous. We idled for a short while with the air conditioner on. It was Jane who pointed out the environmental impact of sitting in an idling car. Her point was well taken, so we got out. Once people caught sight of Bernie, there was an audible buzz through the crowd.

He took the stage to the roar of his fellow Vermonters and delivered what became the foundation of his now-famous stump speech. It was shorter than the ever-expanding version he used throughout the campaign, but it laid out in concrete terms what much of the race would be about: In a nutshell, America is facing a crisis. Wealth and income are being concentrated at the top, while working people and middle-income people are seeing their standard of living decline. This dramatic and increasing wealth and income inequality is held in place by a corrupt system of campaign finance. Over time, the speech would expand to include, for instance, articulating some of the ways in which people of color are particularly disadvantaged by this system, but at this first event, Bernie spoke to the commonality of the problem facing people in every zip code in America. America is economically and politically controlled by a few at the expense of the rest.

The response was electric and celebratory. There were many people there who had been with Bernie from my earliest days with him, and many from even earlier. One thing was clear. Whatever happened in this campaign, Vermonters had Bernie's back.

He stepped down the side of the stage and began shaking hands with the crowd, from whom he was separated by a thin piece of rope. He walked around the front of the stage while others of us worked to keep the crowd from surging forward. We finally made our way to the car. But the crowed mobbed us. I could not drive the car without hitting someone.

Jean-Michel had proposed using "bike rack" as a crowd control measure. Bike rack is a rigid steel fencing system that would become a staple at our later rallies and a requirement once the Secret Service started protecting Bernie. Jean-Michel lost that fight on May 26, but his wisdom in suggesting it became apparent as the car was immobilized by the crowd.

Thankfully, the Burlington police came to our aid and created a small space in front of us. We inched forward at a snail's pace. The police moved forward in front of us to keep an opening, but as we passed, the crowd would quickly close up again. After an extremely slow crawl for what seemed like forever, we were out of the crowd and headed away from what we all knew was an extremely successful kickoff. The question that loomed large, however, was how Bernie would be received by voters outside Vermont. We got our answer very quickly—extremely well!

It should come as no surprise that while we were focused on the successful kickoff on a bright, clear May day, there were forces at work who were determined to rain on Bernie's parade. On May 26, the Clinton campaign announced the endorsement of a number of Vermont politicians, including the mayor of Burlington and the governor of Vermont, Peter

Shumlin. Shumlin's endorsement of Clinton was a particularly tasteless move. He was wildly unpopular in Vermont and had been since before his last election in 2014 (Vermont's governors serve a two-year term). During the 2014 governor's race, Bernie had campaigned across Vermont for Shumlin. In the end, he limped to victory with about a 1.25 percent margin. Without Bernie, he would have lost. And everyone including Shumlin knew it.

When we learned some days before the May 26 kickoff that Shumlin was about to endorse Clinton, Jane called him to ask that, as a courtesy, he at least delay the announcement to the following week. I had heard that Shumlin claimed that he could not, because he had personally been responsible for securing Robby Mook's job as Clinton's campaign manager, and so he owed the Clintons. (Mook had worked for Shumlin when Shumlin was in the state senate.) It was a flimsy excuse and based on what I know, untrue to boot.

When Bernie helped secure Shumlin's win in 2014, Shumlin was an advocate for a single-payer health system in Vermont—long a principal policy goal of Bernie's. In December 2014, in a betrayal of those who supported him, Shumlin publicly abandoned the effort. Often, in the presidential race, the Clinton campaign would point to Shumlin's unwillingness to create a single-payer plan in Vermont as evidence that the program was impractical. But single payer was not impractical. Shumlin just didn't have the political capital or courage to push it through. Despite Shumlin's disloyalty to Bernie in endorsing Hillary Clinton on Bernie's announcement day, Bernie never threw him under the bus when asked why single payer didn't succeed even in Vermont. On the few occasions when I was asked about it by the media, I was not so generous.

Bernie immediately and astutely understood why Shumlin had turned on him. In a telephone conversation shortly after, Bernie said to me, "You know what this means?" Answering his own question, he said, "He's obviously not running for reelection." Bernie was right. On June 8, Shumlin announced that he would not seek reelection. His attempt to curry favor with the Clinton organization, no doubt to secure an administration position, would come to naught.

Particularly in the four earliest states—Iowa, New Hampshire, Nevada, and South Carolina—there is a tradition of significant in-person voter contact with the candidate and an intensive field campaign. That means staff and volunteers reaching out to voters one-on-one at their doors, on their phone, and at any place where three people are gathered together for any purpose. If our campaign was going to survive the early contests, we needed to create the organization that could carry out this intensive voter contact. Thankfully, Bernie wanted exactly this type of grassroots effort. Problem number one could be summed up in one question: Who the hell did we know in Iowa?

Iowa was the first contest in the presidential nominating process, so it made sense to start there. Folks in Iowa whom Bernie and Phil had met during earlier exploratory meetings referred us to Pete D'Alessandro. A political director for former Iowa governor Chet Culver, Pete is the most unassuming person in the world. But his down-to-earth demeanor hides a truly skilled political professional.

We hired Pete as our campaign coordinator in May. Campaign co-ordinator was the title we gave the initial organizer in many states until we had a more formal hierarchy established there. Pete set out to help us find a campaign manager for Iowa. As in so many other places, it turned out that many of the most experienced people were either already involved in the Clinton campaign or were hesitant to be associated with a campaign against Hillary Clinton. It was tough to blame anyone. We were 50 points down in the polling, and the Clintons had a reputation for having a long memory for those who crossed them.

It turned out that while we were looking for someone to run Iowa, someone was looking to connect with us to do just that. Enter Robert Becker. Robert Becker had run Iowa for Bill Richardson in 2008. But his real claim to fame was his foreign work. He was part of a group of American and Egyptian democracy workers who were arrested in a crack-down by Egyptian authorities. When the American government arranged for the Americans in the group to be released from jail long enough for a jet to spirit them all out of the country, Becker had stayed behind because he didn't want to leave his Egyptian counterparts to their fate.

His interest in the campaign came to me from a couple of sources, including Mark Longabaugh and Pete D'Alessandro. Mark arranged for me to meet Becker at the DML office. The DML offices were at that time in a Georgetown building originally built as the Iraqi embassy. It was now occupied by a number of tenants. It has the distinction of having the most difficult-to-use front-gate visitor intercom of any building I have ever been to. Despite visiting many times, I generally had to resort to calling the office on my cell phone to get somebody to ring me in.

Waiting to get through the security door was a tall guy wearing all black, with close-cropped hair. It was Becker. He always prefers to go by his last name. And everyone obliges. The one person I know who does not call him Becker is Bernie. Bernie calls him Robert. In Iowa, I once told Bernie that he prefers to go by Becker. Bernie said to me, "Isn't Becker his last name?" "Yes," I said. Bernie looked at me and replied, "Well, I'm not going to call him that."

That first meeting in the DML building went well. Becker understood the unnecessarily arcane caucus process in Iowa. He knew the geography and how to run the type of intensive voter-contact operation that we needed to win there. I left the meeting mostly convinced that we should bring him on. Knowing what I know now, I should have hired him immediately. But I hesitated.

My doubts centered on whether Becker would be a good fit in a rural state like Iowa. (How wrong I was.) In the end, any doubts I had were overcome by this simple fact: If he could stand up to the Egyptian authorities, he wasn't going to be intimidated by the Clinton campaign. That meant a lot. We needed people who were going to be all-in and not worried about their next job in politics or retribution from Clinton-world.

We had our Iowa manager. Becker headed out to Iowa shortly thereafter and began assembling the rest of the team. I had already been to Iowa, and Pete and I had rented a small space in a suburban Des Moines office building. The Clinton campaign was also housed in that complex. Becker decided that the space was too small for the type of intensive field effort we would need in Iowa. He found a large space in a shopping center in a less well-off part of town. It was run-down but cavernous. That would become Bernie Central in the Hawkeye State.

One down, over fifty to go. Phil and I turned our attention to New Hampshire. Our candidate for manager there could not have been more different from Becker. Kurt Ehrenberg had been brought on as campaign coordinator in New Hampshire to get the ball rolling. But we were still looking for a long-term campaign manager. Kurt had been the Run Warren Run staffer in New Hampshire. We quickly decided that the qualified choice for New Hampshire was Julia Barnes, executive director of the Vermont Democratic Party. Julia had substantial experience in New Hampshire politics. She was extremely organized and understood the Granite State. She struck us as a forceful leader, which Phil Fiermonte and I both liked.

We knew that the campaign could devolve into trench warfare, and we wanted people like Becker and Julia, who would hold the line against the inevitable assaults by the Clinton campaign and their establishment allies. Phil and I met with Julia. Our initial conversation went well, but she was a tough negotiator in the terms of her employment. We were not in the strongest negotiating position—the clock was ticking. Julia seemed to be an excellent choice, and we didn't have a lot of (or frankly any) equally qualified alternatives. The truth is there probably wasn't a more qualified candidate.

We offered her the job shortly after, and for personal reasons she decided against it. We were back to square one. Losing Julia was a big setback. Time was running out, and we had to win New Hampshire for Bernie to be a viable candidate for president. Lose New Hampshire and it would be over. We were starting to look for another candidate when Julia called back and said she had reconsidered. We met one more time and hammered out her contract. Having the first two managers in place—and topflight picks at that—was a tremendous relief. Maybe we'd get this plane in the air after all.

6

THE SUMMER OF SANDERS

THE DAY AFTER BERNIE'S May 26 announcement, he was off to New Hampshire. Tad Devine and a crew were following him to capture footage that could be used later in paid media efforts. As would be the case throughout the campaign, Revolution Messaging's video and photo team chronicled Bernie's travels on a day-to-day basis. (A lot of their footage would also find its way into many of the ads that DML would create.) He held events all day. All of them were packed houses. He finished the night in Portsmouth. All of us were relieved. It wasn't just Vermonters who wanted to come and hear Bernie Sanders. Someone we know in Obama-world contacted us to let us know what a great success the events had been. The ball was starting to roll down the hill. What the media would dub the "Summer of Sanders" had begun.

That designation was not entirely, or even mostly, positive. It suggested that, like many insurgent campaigns, his would burn hot through the summer and then burn out by the time voters actually had to cast their ballots. Throughout the summer, there were a lot of comparisons to the past presidential campaign of the libertarian Republican Ron Paul, who had also excited crowds of people—but who was not able to translate that into votes.

The political pundits and the media, as we know now, were missing something fundamental about the 2016 election cycle and about Bernie Sanders. Voters felt a deepening distress about the growing systemic problems in this country—income inequality, racial inequality, environmental degradation. The American promise that all people shared a common dignity and that anyone who played by the rules could get ahead was becoming less and less true. The Summer of Sanders was not a flash in the pan. It was a spark that ignited a powder keg of pent-up disgust with the status quo that continues to burn even to this day.

Because we only had Bernie when the Senate was not in session, his schedule was packed. But getting him around the country took a tremendous amount of planning, because until he flew out of Iowa on the night of the Iowa caucuses, he continued to fly commercial. There are great pictures on the web of Bernie, Jane, communications director Michael Briggs, and the rest of us schlepping our bags through the airport to make the next connection. The cell-phone photos of Bernie sitting in the middle seat in coach as he traveled the country in the summer and fall in pursuit of the presidency of the United States became iconic.

That's not to say that the Summer of Sanders started without a hitch. On the day after Bernie's big announcement in Burlington, *Mother Jones* ran a story about some articles Bernie had written decades earlier. The focus was on one particular piece—"poorly written," as Bernie admitted—challenging traditional gender roles. It begins in a shocking fashion, with quite graphic language clearly designed to yank the reader in, before moving to the substantive discussion of what continues to be a critically important societal issue. The timing of the *Mother Jones* story was interesting. We suspected that it came out of the Clinton campaign's opposition machine, but perhaps its publication reflected an editorial decision made to take advantage of the news interest in Bernie right after his big Burlington event. It could have been both.

Of course, graphic language was enough to get the rest of the media interested. I'm not sure how many of the people reporting on the article actually read it. Clickbait and provocative headlines are more and more valued in our twenty-four-hour news cycle than substantive analysis. The irony is that the media used the graphic first paragraph for the same purpose it was used for in the original article—to draw in the reader with an over-the-top opening.

The *Mother Jones* story represented our first real media rapid-response crisis, and it exposed some organizational shortcomings that we would remedy. Bernie was on the road in New Hampshire with a jam-packed schedule of public appearance. Michael Briggs was with him. I was in Burlington. It created some logistical challenges in getting everyone on the same page message-wise and in responding to the flurry of media inquiries.

Having Michael Briggs on the front lines day to day with the senator was in hindsight the right move for our campaign. Bernie was very much in control of messaging, and having the top communications person with him 24/7 meant that the substance of what Bernie wanted to convey was in fact what was put out. It also allowed our top communications person to be in constant contact with the traveling media corps. Of course, it was also true that we were so short-staffed that Briggs, like everyone else, was performing the functions of four people. That's possible in an environment when the campaign just has to put out its positive message. The quadruple-duty arrangement does not work when you are also taking incoming from opponents or the media.

That the articles had been exposed was not a surprise. We had found them in our self-opposition research for the Senate race back in 2006. Our expectation, though, was that they would surface later, once Bernie's campaign gained real traction. We didn't think that the media would be going for the political headshot right out of the gate. We responded as best we could, and the media lost interest after a couple of days, because the whole point of the coverage was its shock value. And the shock value of any story has a very short shelf life in the age of the internet.

What was important is that dealing with the *Mother Jones* story demonstrated that we had to accelerate our efforts to build up the press office. Briggs had put out the word that we were looking for additional press people. Arianna Jones, then a producer with Ed Schultz's MSNBC show, heard that we were looking and reached out to Briggs. Bernie met with her on June 6. I talked with her on June 7. And she was on staff by June 22.

Arianna took over the day-to-day management of the headquarters press office and built out an operation that could support Bernie and Briggs. When we hired her, we could not have known what a central role she would play in helping Bernie and Briggs get Bernie's message out to the world, and in responding to the inevitable attacks that came later.

Campaigns and the media each need the other to do their respective jobs. And while those jobs require frequent contact between the two, their aims are often not aligned. The campaign wants positive stories about the candidate and the candidate's message, and wants to see stories that support the campaign's larger narrative—all with the goal of persuading people that its candidate is the one they should vote for.

The narrative is the overarching message of the campaign—the elevator pitch for why a candidate is running. Use of the term "narrative" is not pejorative. In our campaign, the narrative was the rigged economy: an economy held in place by a corrupt campaign finance system, which could only be defeated by everyday people standing up and electing a president who would fight against the economic and political elites and for a more people-oriented government and economy.

Campaigns often have multiple complementary narratives, although having too many can leave voters confused. One of our supplemental narratives was that Hillary Clinton's vast experience showed that she would not be sufficiently aggressive with the economic and political elites to bring about the kind of change the nation needed—and voters wanted (not a change agent). Another was that Hillary Clinton's long career showed that her positions on some issues were fluid (as on guns) or too conservative (Iraq War). This latter one played as much to Bernie's strength (consistent principled leader) as it did to Clinton's perceived weakness (what you see may not be what you get).

The Clinton campaign's narrative, or at least my takeaway, was that the country had the opportunity to elect the most qualified person ever who would move the country steadily, but not recklessly, forward and could actually get elected in November (a progressive who likes to get things done). Having the opportunity to elect the first woman president was certainly a positive subnarrative of theirs ("I'm with her"). Their counternarratives included Bernie as wide-eyed dreamer (that's a positive and generous statement of their characterization) who overpromised, was unelectable, and even if he won wouldn't be able to deliver (dishonest Santa Claus). This latter narrative was targeted to people who might otherwise be attracted to Bernie's campaign but would move to Clinton once they realized the futility of the whole exercise ("resistance is futile"). Another was that Bernie was a single-issue candidate who only cared about the economy and not about other issues, such as race and gender (very thinly veiled code for Bernie doesn't give a damn about women and minorities).

From a campaign's perspective, it is always good to get positive press coverage, and almost always good for one's opponent to get negative coverage. But both kinds of coverage have the greatest impact when they align with the campaign's larger narrative. That's why Debbie Wasserman Schultz's shutting down our access to our own data created such a backlash in our favor. It fit exactly with our theory of the case—the political elites controlled a rigged system.

Being able to place or initiate stories that support one's theory of the case or rebut the other's is critical. It is easiest to do when the reporter, columnist, or editor accepts the larger narrative. Trying to pitch a story that goes against a narrative that the media has accepted is tough. Knowing who is sympathetic to one's narrative is key to influencing coverage.

In contrast to the campaign, the reporters' role in the abstract is to write stories, both positive and negative, that they believe are relevant to voters' selection of the candidate. In that regard, there is often strong disagreement between a campaign and the press about what constitutes a story worthy of print or airtime. What reporters cover in the real world is heavily influenced by editorial assignments and what other people in the media are writing about. There seems to be a strong aversion in the press to being the only outlet that is not covering a particular story when everyone else is.

From the media's side, access is a central issue to success—access to the candidate, access to the campaign, access to information. This access is important today in the twenty-four-hour news cycle—the media constantly needs new material, and being first becomes in many cases as important as the substantive importance of what is being written.

One of the pressures on the media is the reality that if a reporter writes too many bad stories, he or she may find him- or herself shut out from contact with the candidate and even in some cases campaign officials. In the most extreme case, Trump's campaign and his White House have famously barred certain reporters and media outlets from access altogether. The Clinton campaign went long stretches during which it held no public press events. Our campaign also was not always accommodating (another generous characterization) of consistently hostile reporters, columnists, and media outlets. (Concern about losing access is even greater when the candidate in question is more likely to be the future president of the United States.)

A reporter's ability to contact well-placed sources quickly to get information others don't have is an invaluable professional asset. You can see that play out on CNN and other cable news networks when there is a breaking story. Often the journalists sitting on a panel will be busily texting and emailing sources with whom the journalist has an established relationship to get as much information as quickly as possible.

Part of that relationship-building is made up of off-the-record meetings between groups of reporters and the candidate or senior staff. We certainly held them, including one I remember quite well in the living room of Bill Press's house. The Clinton campaign held them as well. Theirs included dinners not just with reporters but also top media broadcasters and executives. Smart! It is just human nature that people are much less likely to be needlessly hostile if they have met you and had a conversation with you. That's true in dealing with the media and in almost every other aspect of human life.

There is a substantial amount of off-the-record interaction between campaign staff and reporters at restaurants and hotel watering holes after hours. Both sides have a professional interest in better understanding where the other is coming from and trading information. I remember one evening at the Des Moines Marriott, where the media stays when the

Iowa caucus is going on. It was a who's who of virtually everyone covering the Iowa race from the national media. I stopped to mingle with the press corps in the lobby bar. John Heilemann showed me some clips from the next episode of the Circus, a political program that he was doing for Showtime. I spoke with Peter Nicholas of the *Wall Street Journal*. He suggested we join a circle of people seated at one side of the lobby. "Sure," I said. Turns out it was a group of Clinton press staffers and a big chunk of their traveling press corps. Awkward!

We sat down with the group anyway. You could sense the Clinton folks' guard going up immediately. The conversation became very stiff. To make an uneasy situation even worse, Nicholas quickly left the circle to talk with O'Malley communications director Lis Smith, who had just entered the lobby. I could have gotten up as well, but I was on some level (okay, honestly, on every level) enjoying the clear (and frankly unnecessary) tension. I was in good humor. The Clinton camp appeared not to be. Even the press corps seemed much stiffer than in my prior dealings with them.

After what seemed like hours, Nicholas returned, accompanied by Smith. They both sat down. No relief of the tension in the circle. I guess Lis Smith wasn't any more popular than I was.

On another occasion, I remember sitting with a group of reporters in the lobby of a South Carolina hotel where our campaign was staying. Bernie was meeting with Congresswoman Tulsi Gabbard to discuss her possible endorsement of his candidacy. These conversations were not public yet, and we wanted to keep it that way until it could be properly announced.

One of the reporters in the circle said, "Wow, what a crazy coincidence. I just saw Tulsi Gabbard in this hotel."

Damn, the jig was up.

I said, "Wow, that is a coincidence." And we went back to our former conversation. Crisis averted.

Once staffers have developed a good working relationship with journalists or columnists, it is possible to pick up the phone and have an off-the-record conversation and to pitch a story that the reporter or columnist might be interested in. Because columnists' and editorial writers' politi-

cal and ideological leanings are obvious that they become important contacts. Through their writing and by the nature of their work, they can
amplify their preferred candidate's cause more directly.

Because of the value of these media relationships, having a much larger
press staff is an advantage, because a campaign can take the time to keep in
close contact with reporters and columnists. A bigger press staff should mean
that the campaign has people who already have established relationships
with a broad representation of the media. We were at a disadvantage in 2016,
with a press staff a fraction of the size of the Clinton campaign, even when
we were staffed more fully. In addition to its official campaign press staff,
the Clinton camp also relied on the super PAC Correct the Record (CTR)
to peddle dirt on Bernie without soiling their own hands.

Following New Hampshire, Bernie headed to Iowa for a three-day swing.
Jane was with him, and this was her first trip to the Hawkeye State. At
their first stop, in Davenport, some 650 came out to hear Bernie. The *New
York Times*'s Trip Gabriel tweeted that the "crowd of 500+ . . . may be
largest for an individual candidate in Iowa this year."

On the final day of the Iowa visit, an overflow crowd of some 1,100
people greeted Bernie in Iowa City as he was introduced by local county
supervisor Rod Sullivan—an early backer. Emilie Stigliani, of the *Burlington Free Press*, reported that the auditorium was full, with people
packing the lobby of the local recreation center ("appropriately abutting
Burlington Street").

From Iowa he went to Minneapolis. In Minneapolis, we started
experiencing a phenomenon that took us a while to get used to, and that
was the throngs of people who wanted to see and hear Bernie. We spent
a lot of time early on having to change venues in city after city because
the building crowds outstripped the room size.

We were trying to live by the cardinal rule of political events: Hold
the event in the smallest space that will accommodate everyone. If you
hold a 5,000-person event in a space that accommodates 4,500, it will be

judged a huge success, with an overflow crowd. On the other hand, if the room only holds 2,500, then half the crowd is outside, which is not good—you are only speaking to half the folks you are there to see. If you hold a 10,000-person event in a venue that holds 20,000, the report will be that the room was half empty—no doubt a sign of Bernie's waning support. It's really the Goldilocks rule—not too big, not too small, just right.

We weren't experienced enough with Bernie's rallies to make those calls well in the beginning. We would advertise the events and ask people to RSVP online and then make an initial call as to the size of the room to secure. But as the date would approach, the number of replies in the affirmative would explode, and the room would become totally inadequate. In the case of the Minneapolis event, we had to upsize the location three times.

In addition to the big crowds, there was other good news. Wisconsin Democratic convention caucusgoers in a straw poll gave Bernie 41 percent of the vote, compared to only 49 percent for Hillary Clinton. And this was with no campaigning on our part among the convention delegates. Perhaps more significantly, the executive committee of the South Carolina AFL-CIO passed a resolution urging support for Bernie's campaign. The resolution stated, in part:

> We call on the AFL-CIO, union members and working people everywhere to unite behind Bernie Sanders and elect the President America's workers desperately need, and
> Be it further resolved that: The South Carolina AFL-CIO Executive Board strongly urges the AFL-CIO to support Bernie Sanders 2016 and his campaign to become the nominee of the Democratic Party for president.

In Iowa, Steve Abbott, the head of the State Labor Council and president of Communications Workers of America (CWA) Local 7108 in Waterloo, came out for Bernie. The *Gazette* quoted Abbott: "We need a presidential candidate willing to confront big money and its corrupting influence on American politics. . . . That kind of leadership is not going to come from someone trying to raise a billion dollars from Wall Street banks and other business interests. We need a voice of our own, not an echo of the Republicans." The paper also reported that Abbott expected "a resolution along the lines of one approved by the South Carolina AFL-CIO executive board supporting Sanders and recommending his endorsement by the national labor organization . . . at the Iowa Federation of Labor AFL-CIO annual convention in August."

This "recommendation" for an endorsement, along with the support Bernie received from the Vermont AFL-CIO, the Vermont-National Education Association, and Iowa labor leaders, was just part of an explosion of grassroots support for him among rank-and-file union members and many locals and state labor groups.

National AFL-CIO head Rich Trumka sent a memo admonishing locals and forbidding them from making endorsement separate from the national organization. A *Politico* headline at the time called this an effort to "quell [a] pro-Sanders revolt" within labor. In that *Politico* story, Massachusetts AFL-CIO president Steven Tolman's quotes summed up a lot of what we were seeing among labor around the country:

> "Bernie Sanders has spent his life actually fighting for working people. He's made no secret of it, and he's used it as his mantra. And that I respect very much."
>
> When asked about Clinton's candidacy, Tolman was less effusive: "Who? Who? Please. I mean with all respect, huh?"

Trumka's memo also came shortly after Bernie received the endorsement of Larry Cohen, the recently retired president of the CWA. Larry joined the campaign to head our labor outreach. He offered to work ten hours a week. I laughed inside when I heard it. No one on a campaign works ten hours a week. Neither did Larry. Soon Larry was going full-time and often more. He not only did outreach to the unions themselves but also helped coordinate, with other leaders like Rand Wilson and Carl Shafer, Labor for Bernie, which was comprised at that time of over 10,000 union members and local union officials supporting Bernie.

Things really looked to be firing on all cylinders. Huge crowds were coming out to the rallies and meetings. The grass roots of the American labor movement, including in places like the all-important early state of South Carolina, were standing up for Bernie. And Bernie was already dictating the terms of the political debate. He had pledged to only choose Supreme Court nominees who would overturn *Citizens United*, the case that had deemed corporations people and had eliminated caps on "noncoordinated" campaign spending by corporations and others. *Citizens United* led to the birth of the super PAC, a political entity that can take unlimited contributions and make unlimited expenditures for favored candidates. Clinton was backed by affiliated super PACs. Bernie chose not to be.

Bernie was also taking Clinton on over her support of the Trans-Pacific Partnership, an international trade deal that threatened, among other things, to move even more American manufacturing abroad. While secretary of state in the Obama administration, Hillary Clinton had called it the "gold standard" of trade agreements. The American labor community did not agree. Clinton would be on the defensive on trade throughout the primaries, even after her flip-flop on the TPP, and it would follow her all the way to the general election.

Bernie gave a successful talk at the National Association of Latino Elected Officials (NALEO) in Las Vegas. Speaking about his own story as the son of an immigrant, he laid out his vision for comprehensive immigration reform. He spoke about the plight of undocumented workers, such as the people in Immokalee he had helped a decade before. And he called into question people who had advocated denying entry to children fleeing violence in Central America, as Hillary Clinton had done.

Although Bernie did not call out Hillary Clinton by name, everyone in the room knew who he was talking about when he described those who wanted Central American children to be "shipped back to their country of origin like a package marked Return to Sender." They were strong words. But taking a position that would lead to children being sent into danger was strong and extremely poor public policy.

The same day as the NALEO speech, Bernie held one of the more unusual town hall meetings of the campaign—in Las Vegas, at the Treasure Island Casino. The Summer of Sanders was proceeding well. Neil Young, upset that Donald Trump was using his song "Rockin' in the Free World" without his permission, told Bernie he could use it. And we did at most rallies thereafter. Not even Hillary Clinton's announcement rally, on June 13, could dampen the growing momentum of the campaign. (She had previously announced her candidacy on the internet on April 12.) For many of us on the campaign, in fact, her announcement rally reflected the real weakness of her campaign. Held on Roosevelt Island in New York City, it drew only about 5,000. The event in New York City was heavily choreographed and professionally done. But where were the people? After all, this was the largest city in the country. And Hillary Clinton had been a two-term senator from New York. The fact that she could not draw more people to her announcement than Bernie had on May 26 was a signal to many of us that the Clinton campaign faced a real enthusiasm gap.

Another piece of good news came in June. Efforts to draft Massachusetts senator Elizabeth Warren into the race ended. MoveOn.org and Democracy for America (DFA) had joined together in an effort called Run Warren Run to promote the candidacy of Senator Warren as the progressive alternative in the Democratic race long before Bernie got in. They had hoped to demonstrate support for Warren and hired staff in Iowa and New Hampshire to begin the organizing. Both MoveOn and DFA, along with groups like the Working Families Party and Friends of the Earth, would endorse Bernie during the campaign.

Bernie and Elizabeth Warren had always had a great relationship. They continue to share a deep dedication to fighting income inequality and corporate power. Given the similarity of their economic message, a Warren candidacy could have presented us with a challenge in the primaries. The converse was also true. Bernie's candidacy would have made hers impossible. As the spring of 2015 turned to summer, it seemed less and less likely that Senator Warren would run, but it continued to be a concern as long as there were Run Warren Run staff on the ground.

Even before that, we had hired Kurt Ehrenberg, who was running the program in New Hampshire to be our state coordinator. And we had made a point of reaching out to the much larger Run Warren Run team in Iowa. I had personally visited their offices in Iowa. A lot of people, including the staff on the ground, saw that the draft effort was probably not going to be successful. My view was that we had to bring in the Run Warren Run staff and bring all progressives together in this fight.

In a June op-ed, Ready for Warren campaign manager Erica Sagrans and cofounder Charles Lenchner wrote, "Sanders has captured the imagination and support of people looking for a real progressive challenger in the 2016 Democratic primary." We announced quickly that we had brought on Run Warren Run staff in Iowa. The Run Warren Run Iowa field director, Blair Lawton, became the political director for Bernie in Iowa. We also brought on Susana Cervantes, Beth Farvour, and Margaret Jarosz.

Overall, it was an enormous success. We acquired experienced staff, sent a message to the many supporters of Elizabeth Warren that the people who had been working for her on the ground were with Bernie Sanders, and could rest a little easier knowing that we would not be facing a fellow progressive in the long primary process that lay ahead.

As we neared the end of what I call Part I of the Summer of Sanders, Bernie finished strong, with two wildly successful rallies. The first was in Denver, Colorado. He was greeted by a crowd of over 5,000 at the University of Denver. He was introduced by law professor Robin Walker Sterling, a family friend of mine whose work focuses on criminal justice and juvenile justice issues. A story by John Wagner in the *Washington Post* pointed out the significant fact that the rally in Denver rivaled the number of people that Bernie had had at his announcement in Burlington and Hillary Clinton had had at her kickoff rally in New York City.

The next rally, in Madison, Wisconsin, blew the lid off anything that any candidate in 2015 had yet done—10,000 people came out. The MSNBC headline read, "Bernie Sanders Draws Biggest Crowd of Any 2016 Candidate Yet." The *Washington Post* downplayed the significance of the event by pointing out what a liberal enclave Madison is, but the attendance was a significant milestone as Bernie's campaign continued to gain steam.

The size and frequency of the events was a huge strain on our staff resources. John Robinson had dispatched Arianna Jones to Madison ahead of the rally after we learned that an earlier event had not had the sound boxes that the media need to hook into. He wanted to make sure that this problem was corrected. When Arianna got there, she discovered that there was no lighting beyond the house lights. To TV viewers, it would have looked like Bernie was giving his speech in the dark. She quickly improvised by borrowing lights from the media to create a spotlight effect. It looked great on TV. But having Arianna there doing the job of a press advance staffer meant that she'd had to leave her post in Burlington.

The day after the Madison rally, we announced that Bernie had raised some $15 million since his initial announcement. That amount came from almost 400,000 contributions from over 280,000 donors, 99 percent of which were under $250. We had spent only $2.9 million. That may seem like a lot, but it was a pittance for a presidential campaign. The Clinton camp spent over $18 million during that same quarter, although their campaign operated for a month more than ours did during that reporting period. Even prorating it, the Clinton campaign was spending over $6 million a month, while we were spending less than $1.5 million. And we had over $12 million cash on hand. The frugality was paying off. Small donors across America were stepping up to support Bernie's campaign. Maybe we'd reach $50 million after all. Maybe we'd have the resources we'd need in the first four states.

Bernie then went back to both New Hampshire and Iowa. In Iowa he set a new attendance record for the season when 2,600 people came out to see him in Council Bluffs.

June 2015 was marked by one great tragedy that cannot go unnoted— the murder of nine African American congregants at the Emanuel African Methodist Episcopal Church in Charleston, South Carolina, by a white supremacist gunman who had joined them at a prayer meeting. Their names were Cynthia Marie Graham Hurd, Susie Jackson, Ethel Lee Lance, Depayne Middleton-Doctor, Tywanza Sanders, Daniel Simmons, Sharonda Coleman-Singleton, Myra Thompson, and Clementa C. Pinckney, the church's pastor.

7

ENDLESS SUMMER

PART II OF THE SUMMER OF SANDERS began much as Part I had ended, with signs of growing support. On July 4, Bernie and Jane marched in two different Iowa parades, accompanied by over a hundred supporters. Having marched in innumerable small-town parades in Vermont, Bernie felt right at home shaking hands and posing for selfies.

Two days later, he held a 7,500-person rally in Portland, Maine. The reporting that day showed the scale of his support. John Wagner (*Washington Post*), MaryAlice Parks (ABC News), and Alex Seitz-Wald (NBC News) all wrote stories or social media posts that captured the seriousness of Bernie's threat to the Clinton campaign. Parks tweeted, "My early guess is 8k screaming fans here for @BernieSanders in Portland. Hundreds more couldn't get in."

Wagner and Anne Gearan had recently penned an analysis piece that talked about the growing challenge that Bernie posed. In it, they fairly laid out the obstacles that Bernie faced, particularly the challenge of reaching minority voters and the prospect of being underfunded once the campaign moved to more expensive media markets. But it was clear from the story that many insiders were completely out of touch with what was going on in the real world.

In a *Morning Joe* interview quoted in the Wagner/Gearan piece, Senator Claire McCaskill expressed a view common inside the Beltway at the time: "Any other candidate that has the numbers that Hillary Clinton has right now would be, you know, talked about as absolutely untouchable, and all of a sudden, Oh, Bernie, Bernie, Bernie. It's not unusual for someone who has an extreme message to have a following."

She was an early and vitriolic opponent of Bernie's. Unlike most of his other Senate colleagues who were supporting Clinton, McCaskill took the low road. Having been an early supporter of Barack Obama's presidential candidacy, she was now working overtime to ingratiate herself to Clinton-world with red-baiting attacks.

The Clinton campaign for its part was determined to minimize Bernie. Wagner and Gearan noted that the Clinton policy was to not mention Bernie on the record and hope that her "progressive" policy rollout later in the summer would reassure the large number of Democrats and Democratically aligned independents that she was in sync with them.

The day after the Maine event, Bernie was back in Washington. We held two policy-related conference calls. One was on campaign finance reform, the other on marijuana policy.

Campaign finance reform was already a central issue in the campaign. Bernie was running with the support of small donors and had refused to authorize a super PAC. In every speech, he spoke about the need to overturn *Citizens United*.

But he wanted to go even further. Bernie is a strong proponent of public financing of elections. As he often said on the campaign trail, he wanted any person, regardless of personal wealth or ability to raise money, to be able to run for office. The point of the conference call was to get down in the weeds a bit about the best way to structure such a program. As part of that, Bernie wanted to get an overview of the various public-financing programs already operating in many states and localities, and others that were pending before Congress. One of the advisers on the call was Larry Lessig.

Larry Lessig is a Harvard professor who had been active in campaign finance reform, internet freedom, and a host of other efforts. Bernie asked him to be on the call because of his long-standing commitment and his knowledge of the subject matter.

Imagine our surprise when Lessig announced less than a month later that he was running against Bernie in the Democratic primary. His announcement came with a pledge that, if elected president, he would push Congress to pass his political and campaign finance legislation—and then resign. He pledged to run only if he raised $1 million by Labor Day, a goal he claims to have met. But after a smattering of media attention, his campaign folded in early November, with no impact on the race other than to relieve progressive, small donors of $1 million or more.

It's not clear to this day what his goal really was. Campaign finance reform of the type Lessig advocated was a key component of Bernie's campaign. Maybe it was ego—he wanted to be the messenger instead of just advising on the message. In the end, maybe he just wanted to raise $1 million online. Needless to say, he was not on any future calls about campaign finance reform.

The second call, on marijuana reform, ended up having a tremendous impact on the race and on the national discussion of marijuana policy and drug policy more generally. Bernie was increasingly focused on the need for reform of a broken criminal justice system that disproportionately penalizes communities of color. As he has pointed out, rates of marijuana use are similar across racial lines. But black users are far more likely to find themselves arrested. And with an arrest record comes difficulty getting a job, an education, and housing.

In addition, it struck Bernie as a waste of human dignity and scarce resources that the number of people in jail in the United States is greater than in any other country, including authoritarian countries like China—which has many times our population.

The pressing need to rethink all of this was confirmed when we later learned, in April 2016, that the disparate impact of the war on drugs started by Richard Nixon was intentional. The war on drugs was a conscious effort to give government officials the justification to harass and jail political opponents and members of the black community. An explosive article by Dan Baum in *Harper's* magazine features top Nixon aide John Ehrlichman in a 1994 interview admitting that the Nixon administration's war on drugs was really an attack on the black community and the antiwar movement:

> At the time, I was writing a book about the politics of drug prohibition. I started to ask Ehrlichman a series of earnest, wonky questions that he impatiently waved away. "You want to know what this was really all about?" he asked with the bluntness of a man who, after public disgrace and a stretch in federal prison, had little left to protect. "The Nixon campaign in 1968, and the Nixon White House after that, had two enemies: the antiwar left and black people. You understand what I'm saying? We knew we couldn't make it illegal to be either against the war or blacks, but by getting the public to associate the hippies with marijuana and blacks with heroin, and then criminalizing both heavily, we could disrupt those communities. We could arrest their leaders, raid their homes, break up their meetings, and vilify them night after night on the evening news. Did we know we were lying about the drugs? Of course we did."

It's shocking to read. But even more shocking is the devastation that the war on drugs has caused in communities both in the United States and abroad.

One impact that Ehrlichman may or may not have foreseen was the extent to which the war on drugs would be used not just to harass and jail black people in America but to rip away their ability to fight back politically through disenfranchisement. According to the Sentencing Project, a nonprofit involved in research and advocacy around criminal justice issues, some 6.1 million Americans have lost the vote due to felony convictions. Of those, over 35 percent are African Americans. In seven states, over 15 percent of voting-age African Americans are disenfranchised in this way. The following are the top seven states with the highest percentage of blacks of voting age disenfranchised by a felony conviction: Alabama (143,924; 15.11 percent); Florida (499,306; 21.35 percent); Kentucky (69,771; 26.15 percent); Mississippi (127,130; 15.86 percent); Tennessee (173,895, 21.27 percent); Virginia (271, 994; 21.9 percent), and Wyoming (966; 17.81 percent). But the percentages don't tell it all. Both Georgia and Texas, while not making it into the top seven in terms of percentage, have disenfranchised over 140,000 African Americans.

This intersection between the war on drugs and felon disenfranchisement is a deadly combination when it comes to suppressing the ability of black communities to fight back politically. The impact of this disenfranchisement was powerful in the 2016 general election. Donald Trump beat Hillary Clinton by less than 113,000 votes in Florida. That's a fraction of the disenfranchised black community in the Sunshine State. The war on drugs threatens not only the lives of individual people, their families, and their local communities, but also basic American notions of democratic rule. Bernie would later call for the restoration of all voting rights for felons.

On the July 7 call, however, the issue was how best to address the issue of marijuana and its regulation at the federal level. Despite our opponent's narrative, Bernie was a successful long-term legislator, and the specifics of policy mattered to him. All the reforms to marijuana regulation were happening at the state level. Some two dozen states had approved the use of medical marijuana. And a handful, most notably Colorado, had approved recreational use. All of these policies violated federal law, because marijuana was listed as a Schedule I drug by the federal government. That meant it was classified as having no medical benefit and a strong likelihood of abuse. Marijuana is on the same schedule as heroin. Even cocaine is listed as a Schedule II drug—judged likely to be abused, but possessing value as medicine.

The Obama administration had chosen not to enforce federal law when it came to states that had decided to loosen restrictions on marijuana use. But individuals and businesses still run a huge risk, because a change in administration can quickly lead to a change in policy. While Bernie didn't come to any final conclusions about the way forward, it was clear to me during the conversation that he was leaning toward a policy that would remove federal restrictions on marijuana (although retaining the right to regulate and tax it) and leave it to states and communities to decide whether to allow its use, under what circumstances, and other issues of taxation and regulation. This is consistent with the way alcohol is regulated. Bernie wanted to think over the exact parameters of his position. He and I spoke about it on a number of occasions. He gave it a lot of thought; a final policy announcement would ultimately come in the fall.

He appeared at a Democratic town hall meeting in Arlington, Virginia, on July 9. It was a packed house and Bernie was appearing with Virginia Eighth District congressman Don Beyer. (He happens to be my congressperson.) Longtime Democratic activist Sandra Klassen was moderator. She would lead our Virginia delegation at the convention.

There seemed to be a good number of Bernie supporters in the crowd. There was a disagreement between Bernie and Don Beyer on trade policy, but by and large things were going extremely well. At some point Bernie was asked about his vote for a 2006 gun liability bill. The exchange got a little testy, but it was not a huge part of that evening. It did, however, make it into the *Washington Post* coverage. Bernie detailed his long support for background checks and the assault weapons ban. Note to self at the time: We would need a shorter, more direct response in the future.

July 17 and 18 proved to be pivotal days in the early campaign that would have ramifications both substantively and in the media narrative until the end. Bernie was in Iowa on the eighteenth to attend the Iowa Hall of Fame (HOF) dinner. As in many other states, state Democratic parties hold annual fund-raising dinners at which they recognize some individual or group whose work they want to honor. During presidential election years in early voting states, these types of events take on additional importance, as they are an opportunity for presidential contenders to speak to large numbers of party faithful at one time. They are well attended, and the state parties can raise significant amounts of money.

Such events typically attract those who are most active in the party and those who can afford the admission. More pro-Clinton voters attended than working-class or younger voters who were more open to Bernie—

not to mention the overwhelming number of Democratically aligned independents who flocked to his campaign. But a cool reception to Bernie at the Iowa HOF dinner so early in the campaign would have led to a lot of bad media stories about Democrats rejecting Bernie. Explaining that the audience was more likely to be more pro–Democratic establishment in rebuttal would have violated the cardinal rule of political messaging: If you are explaining, you are losing.

So the campaign bought a bunch of tables, and our Iowa team invited our own supporters to attend. While we would still be outnumbered in the room, at least this would guarantee that there would be some Bernie supporters present. To conserve resources, we bought tables farther from the stage—they were less expensive. Bernie did have one table up front, as did all the other candidates (there were still five at that point); he and Jane and special guests would sit there. The general practice in politics was to fill the rest of those seats at the candidate's table with prominent endorsers or donors. Our campaign did it differently. To illustrate the crushing debt that so many college graduates are forced to bear, the guests at Bernie's table were all Iowa students who collectively had student debt of over $1 million.

But what was most significant about the Iowa HOF dinner was that Bernie—whose political life began when he fought housing and educational discrimination in Chicago—had decided that he wanted to be much more vocal about police violence against African Americans.

He was personally moved by the all too frequent accounts of black Americans being beaten, shot, and killed. He correctly observed that this was not a new problem but one that was being brought out in the open by the proliferation of cell-phone cameras. And he purposely decided to debut this increased focus about the scourge of violence against African Americans in front of a largely white Iowa audience. As those who followed the campaign know, Bernie was never one to "tailor" his message to his audience. Upper-income voters heard the same discussion of wealth and income inequality as did attendees at union rallies. Audiences in more conservative red states heard about the need to protect a woman's right to choose or the need for equality for the LGBTQ community. And rallies that were in some cases overwhelmingly white (although not as white as the Clinton campaign and the media liked to portray) were going to hear about the violence being meted out against the African American community by state actors. Period. That's just Bernie.

During the Iowa HOF dinner, he brought the crowd to its feet when he said,

> And like everybody in this room I want to see an America
> where when young black men walk down the street they will not
> be harassed by police officers; they will not be killed; they will
> not be shot.

He praised President Obama for his recent trip to a federal prison to highlight the fact that America's criminal justice system disproportionately penalizes black men. He closed with one of his most popular taglines: "We need to invest in jobs and education, not jails and incarceration!" The crowd responded with chants of "Bernie, Bernie!"

After the event, a number of people of color in the room came up to Bernie to thank him for raising the issue of police violence—especially in that forum. He felt good about the impact of this increased emphasis, not so much politically but morally. To him, it helped empower those in Iowa and elsewhere who were trying to raise the alarm bells about this issue to people who were not directly affected by it.

Unfortunately, as we were to learn, no one who was attending the political convention Netroots Nation the next day seemed to have watched Bernie's Iowa Hall of Fame speech. (Nor, for that matter, did Hillary Clinton. Unlike all the other candidates in attendance, she chose to leave the room when the other candidates were speaking.) They also had not seen Bernie's June 28 interview with George Stephanopoulos, largely about the economic challenges faced by communities of color.

Despite the limited campaign time Bernie had because of his commitment to attend the Senate during 2015, he agreed to attend the annual

Netroots Nation convention being held that year in Phoenix, Arizona. Netroots Nation is an annual conference of progressive activists and thinkers with a strong connection to those working in the online space. Started in 2006, it features panel discussions, workshops, and presentations by progressive leaders inside and outside government. It is also an opportunity for people working for progressive change to see one another, exchange ideas, and network.

For Bernie, attending meant leaving Iowa when he was already there. And it meant going to Arizona, a state that was voting much later in the process, when we had ground to make up in the first four contests—in some cases a lot of ground. Bernie decided to go for two reasons. The first was that the focus of Netroots Nation that year was on immigration reform. The Netroots site said: "For Netroots Nation 2015, we're choosing to . . . make immigration a central issue to the progressive agenda."

> We've also got a lot to discuss from a policy perspective. It's time to start talking about how militarizing our police forces and borders is problematic, how trade agreements like NAFTA and CAFTA [the Central America Free Trade Agreement] have created the economic conditions for the migration from Central America, and how this issue ultimately comes down to family.

As the son of an immigrant from a non-English-speaking country who grew up in an ethnic neighborhood, Bernie had and has a tremendous amount of empathy for immigrants and the devastating effects of US immigration policy in dividing up families.

The agreed-upon format was that Bernie would give a short version of his stump speech, which always started with a discussion of economic inequality—a problem that he knew affected middle-class and working families across all races. Then there would be a moderated interview and question-and-answer period on the issue of immigration. He prepped a lot for the immigration portion of the program. It would be a great opportunity for him to expand on the themes he had talked about in his NALEO appearance the month before. He was prepared to talk not just about immigration generally but also about the corporate profiteering by the private prison and detention center industry and issues facing specific immigrant communities. Among these issues was violence and abuse faced by undocumented transgender detainees.

Bernie planned to hold a large rally afterward in Phoenix and two the next day in Texas. The media, in its ongoing efforts to discount and dismiss Bernie's success, was now suggesting that he could only draw crowds in blue, Frost Belt states, which carried with it the implication that only white progressives were coming out. To the media, 10,000 people in Madison was now what any vaguely liberal pol could draw. A diverse city like Phoenix, in a red-leaning state like Arizona, was a perfect location to demonstrate the falseness of that narrative.

A side benefit to going to Phoenix became obvious as the date of our planned rally neared. The weekend before us, Donald Trump held a rally at the same Phoenix convention center. Trump boasted of his 4,000-plus crowd at that rally. Bernie and all the rest of us wanted to best him in that regard. We obviously had as priority one beating Hillary Clinton in the primary process, but that did not mean that we wanted a right-wing authoritarian like Trump to have any standing in American politics. If our rally had the unintended consequence of knocking some air out of his balloon, so much the better.

Our 7:00 a.m. first leg to Phoenix—from Cedar Rapids, Iowa, to Minneapolis—had us all up at 5:00. The Iowa HOF event the night before had gone late. Bernie hadn't started speaking until about 9:30 p.m. And it's fair to say that no one in our traveling party got to bed until well after midnight. We would all hit Phoenix pretty low on gas, and Bernie was scheduled to speak at Netroots only forty-five minutes after we touched down.

Tim Tagaris of Revolution Messaging picked us up from the airport and drove us to Netroots. We arrived and were escorted backstage. The scene was chaotic. From the stage area, we heard incessant shouting. Backstage was separated from the main stage by a translucent white screen through which we could see shadows. There were multiple people on stage.

I quickly called over one of our staffers, who had been dispatched earlier in the day to the event, to figure out what was going on.

He told us that a group of Black Lives Matter protesters had interrupted Governor Martin O'Malley's presentation, and that a representative of the protesters, Tia Oso, had come onstage. From our vantage point, we could see that the crowd was very "hot." We learned later that Governor O'Malley made an explosive situation even worse when he said, in a flustered attempt to respond to the protesters, "Black Lives Matter, White Lives Matter, All Lives Matter." To the protesters, it demonstrated that O'Malley fundamentally misunderstood the Black Lives Matter movement.

Black Lives Matter seeks to end the systemic discounting of black lives. While the slogan is "Black Lives Matter," its meaning is really that Black Lives Matter, Too! "All lives matter" may be a truism, but it misses the fundamental point of the movement: that systemic racism as expressed through state actions like police violence and mass incarceration and in the economic and social sphere demonstrate that black lives are not valued as highly as others and in some cases appear not to be valued at all. Given that, the protesters at Netroots were not pleased with Governor O'Malley's comment (for which he apologized later that day).

Even more than our campaign, the O'Malley camp was operating on a shoestring budget. (We had maybe a dozen headquarters staff at the time covering management, scheduling, advance, political, fund-raising, digital, communications, policy, and every other function.) Unlike the Clinton operation, with its legions of headquarters staff, O'Malley's campaign and ours relied on very few people covering work that would ordinarily be done by many. The event had been billed as focused on immigration, so candidate and staff prep time would necessarily have been targeted to the details of immigration-related topics. That said, there are several issues that do overlap—for example, the need to abolish private prisons and immigration detention facilities.

The question facing us at that moment was whether, given the situation, we should just leave or go in and face what would likely be a difficult confrontation. Our concern was not really facing unhappy people or demonstrators. Bernie had a long political career and had faced unsympathetic audiences before. And he had been arrested in a demonstration against racial discrimination (the video would later be unearthed). Rather, the concern was that, under the hyperscrutiny of media coverage in a presidential race, our opponents would weave a false narrative after a difficult encounter.

A decision had to be made. Our staffer on the ground told us that he had been given assurances that Bernie was not going to be protested—that O'Malley had been the subject of the protest because of his policing policies during his tenure as mayor of Baltimore. It made sense. O'Malley had adopted a "zero-tolerance" policing policy that, according to the *Washington Post*, resulted in tens of thousands of arrests for littering and loitering. That same story notes that, in 2005 alone, Baltimore police made over 108,000 arrests. Granted, some of those people got arrested multiple times; even so, that 108,000 figure is equivalent to one-sixth of Baltimore's population at the time.

Bernie made the call. He would go in. He was intent on increasing the focus on the need for police and criminal justice reform and the disproportionate impact of economic inequity on young people, particularly young people of color. His presence at Netroots certainly accomplished that goal, but not in the way any of us expected. Unfortunately, either the intelligence was wrong or the protesters were so angry that whatever assurances may have been given could not be lived up to. Either way, Bernie's Netroots Nation appearance did not turn out as planned.

He took the stage intending to carry out the format of the program. He would give short remarks and then engage in a policy discussion about immigration with moderator Jose Antonio Vargas. A few of us stood on the floor next to the stage in the crowd. There were many Bernie supporters in the room, including a group up front with cardboard signs that featured him in a Robin Hood hat. He got a standing ovation as he came on stage.

Beginning as he always did, he talked about grotesque levels of wealth, and about income inequality. The protesters quickly began shouting at him.

Many of the chants were unintelligible, but most seemed to be focused on the issue of violence against black Americans. Bernie responded to them as reported by the *New York Times*: "Black lives, of course, matter. I spent 50 years of my life fighting for civil rights and dignity, but if you don't want me to be here, that's O.K. I don't want to out-scream people." I thought that wasn't bad on four hours of sleep. The demonstrators didn't seem to share my appraisal.

Bernie also spoke about research showing that youth unemployment and underemployment among high school graduates in the African American community was approximately 50 percent. His view is that economic abandonment of communities contributes to other ills, and that lifting communities economically tends to improve them in other ways as well.

Of course, improving people's economic lives is not the only thing that needs to be done. It doesn't automatically address other manifestations of systemic racial discrimination, like police violence; and Bernie never said it would. Actions have to be taken on multiple fronts concurrently. (This would be one of the false narratives that the Clinton campaign would try to use against Bernie later in the campaign—that he believed addressing income and wealth inequality would solve every other problem facing the country. He never held that view, but it was a convenient way to delegitimize his lifelong fight for economic fairness and to excuse Bill and Hillary Clinton's long-term coziness with economic elites. Regardless, Bernie's discussion of the plight of African American youth didn't seem to resonate at that moment.)

After a few attempts to move the program along, the moderator ended it ahead of schedule. Given the press coverage of the event, it looked like the winner of that morning's news cycle was Hillary Clinton, who had wisely, it seemed, chosen not to show up at all. Having been coldly received at Netroots in 2008, she had apparently learned her lesson. But that was just the immediate read. Secretary Clinton's inability to connect with young voters of color would ultimately be one of the factors in her loss to Donald Trump in the general election.

In the end, Bernie, whose political life had begun when he was dragged away by Chicago police after he and other protesters chained themselves together at a construction site of a substandard school for black students, understood that the protest was not about him. Rather, the event provided a platform for the protesters to bring attention to what was and is unquestionably one of the critical issues facing us as a country. That nuance was not appreciated in the national news coverage, however. And it never was. Anytime a Black Lives Matter action took place at a Bernie event, it was further evidence that black people hated Bernie.

Bernie wanted to give voice to those young protesters and their cause, because they were right about the issues they raised. He wanted the young people of color who were fighting in the streets for their communities and their families to be part of the broader "political revolution" he so often spoke about. But we also wanted to have that happen in a way that did not damage the campaign and lift up the Clinton campaign.

It would prove to be difficult to navigate at times, in part because of the lack of clear organizational lines within the movement. We also disagreed with some people in the movement over tactics. Our campaign, for instance, would never agree that disrupting or "shutting down" our campaign events was a strategic positive. The discussions that ended up happening between Bernie, the campaign, and so many dedicated Black Lives Matter activists across the country in both formal and informal meetings proved, in my personal view, to be some of the most substantive and meaningful of the entire primary season.

As an aside, the Netroots event spawned one of the best Twitter hashtags of the campaign, #BernieSoBlack. It was started by Roderick Morrow. Rod and his wife, Karen, run a podcast/blog called *The Black Guy Who Tips*. He posted #BernieSoBlack as a joke and it took off.

There were those who took it way too seriously, including some of the younger folks in our own campaign who just missed the point of it, as did some of the tweeters. But those who got the real spirit of what Rod said he was trying to accomplish (in a July 20, 2015, *Vox* interview) and who wrote tweets in line with that spirit, should all apply to be satire and parody writers. A bunch of us were howling with laughter. There were some genius tweets.

Rod's *Vox* interview was extremely insightful, especially his thoughts on how the campaign had to speak more directly and with greater specificity about race. He felt that we were working on doing that, and in fact we were. There was a sincere interest on Bernie's part and the campaign's part to communicate more effectively on issues of race. It's never fun to see your team lampooned, even if skillfully by some of the tweets, but Rod's *Vox* interview had an impact on me and, by extension, the campaign and its messaging.

We all left Netroots demoralized—and dreading the spin that would come out of it. Over lunch at a local restaurant, Bernie asked about various slogans that the demonstrators had shouted. He wanted to understand what the specific things they were concerned about. We discussed "Say Her Name" and Sandra Bland. Because Sandra Bland received so much attention during the campaign and in the media, many are familiar with her and her tragic death. But for those who are not: She was a black woman from Chicago who had traveled to take a job with a college in Texas. She was stopped for failing to signal a lane change on July 10, 2015. As dashcam video released on July 21 reveals, an officer dragged her violently from her car and arrested her. Three days later, she was found dead in her jail cell. The officer was later fired for perjury in connection with the case, and a wrongful death suit brought by her family was settled for some $1.9 million.

The death of Sandra Bland brought further attention to police violence and highlighted the fact that it was not limited to men. Bernie wanted the names of black victims of police brutality added to his stump speech. He would say the names of individuals so that they could be remembered as real persons deserving of human dignity, not just statistics.

That afternoon, Bernie authorized a tweet to be sent on the subject. The first version was not drafted as tightly as it might have been. It said *"I will #SayHerName. Sandra Bland, Eric Garner, Freddie Gray and too many others."* With a few punctuation changes, it would have been fine, but as written, it looked like we did not understand that "SayHerName" was focused on black women. So the campaign pulled it down and put out a second tweet: "*Sandra Bland, Eric Garner, Freddie Gray and too many others.*"

By the next day, when Bernie appeared at events in Dallas and Houston, the names of black Americans—including Sandra Bland—who had died at the hands of police or while in custody became a permanent part of the speech he delivered across America for the next year.

And that night, at the Phoenix rally, Bernie rewrote his remarks—by hand, of course, as he always did—to include more explicit references to the need for criminal justice reform, and to address racism: "When a police officer breaks the law, that officer must be held accountable. Let us be clear, while we have overcome a lot of racism, we still have a long way to go."

Before the rally, we attended a Latino Victory Fund event. Bernie was warmly received. It was a good mood-changer after the stressful events earlier in the day.

That evening's Phoenix rally was held in a 123,000-square-foot space that accommodated 10,000 and could be expanded to hold 12,000. The campaign had had to move to this space from two previously booked locations because of the flood of responses we had received. The *Washington Post* reported that the convention center put actual attendance at over 11,000 people. That made Phoenix the largest Bernie rally to date, beating the previous 10,000-person record in Madison, Wisconsin. The crowd in Phoenix was much more diverse than many we had seen in other areas, with a large Latino presence. Bernie had shown that he could draw large crowds outside blue, Frost Belt states.

Importantly, in the red state of Arizona, Bernie's attendance blew away the crowd size of Donald Trump's rally held the weekend before. The *Phoenix New Times* reported that Trump's event was held in a room that accommodated 4,200. Some 7,000 more people showed up to see Bernie than had come out for Trump. Donald Trump likes to boast that he always draws the biggest crowds, but saying you draw the biggest crowds doesn't make it true, whether it's a political rally in Phoenix, Arizona, or Inauguration Day 2017.

The next day we headed to Dallas and Houston. At each rally Bernie was introduced by a local Communications Workers of America leader—in Dallas, Joe Montemayor, and in Houston, Claude Cummings. The afternoon Dallas event drew some 8,000 people. Bernie spoke about the need to take on Republican control of Texas, where childhood poverty exceeded 25 percent. This was and is a core Bernie Sanders theme. The national Democratic Party cannot concede all the red states to the Republicans. Voters in red states are hurting because of Republican policies. Throwing off the yoke of Republican rule in what are in some cases the nation's poorest states must be a priority for the Democratic Party. It's not enough to invest money during election years in battleground states alone. Long-term investments in rebuilding anti-Republican forces must happen even in states that vote solidly for the GOP.

Over 5,000 people packed the University of Houston's Hofheinz Pavilion. As in Dallas, Bernie stressed that the Democratic Party cannot be a successful national party without competing in all fifty states. And he also spoke about criminal justice reform, and specifically about Sandra Bland, whose death had occurred about an hour north of Houston. As reported in the *Texas Tribune*, this part of the speech received the loudest response from the Houston crowd.

It was clear when I got back to Washington that we needed to open a dialogue with Black Lives Matter. They were raising the right issues—issues that Bernie was already committed to. But we faced a practical difficulty. Black Lives Matter is a movement, not an organization. There is no traditional hierarchy, no political office, no executive director. I reached out to one of the initiators of the movement, Patrisse Cullors. The two of us would have a number of conversations over the following weeks, but we were not able to lock down a meeting, even a private one, between the senator and top voices in the movement—which is something Bernie wanted to happen. But we would keep trying.

On July 21, the authorities released the dashcam video of Sandra Bland's violent and unnecessary arrest. I watched it and drafted a statement, emailing it to Bernie. He called a few minutes later, having watched the video. "This is outrageous," he said. "And I've read your draft statement. It's not strong enough. Let me rework it and get it back to you." He was noticeably upset by the video.

As reported in *Salon*, he wrote:

> This video of the arrest of Sandra Bland shows totally outrageous police behavior. No one should be yanked from her car, thrown to the ground, assaulted and arrested for a minor traffic stop. The result is that three days later she is dead in her jail cell. This video highlights once again why we need real police reform. People should not die for a minor traffic infraction. This type of police abuse has become an all-too-common occurrence for people of color and it must stop.

In December, when a grand jury refused to indict, Bernie released a statement: "There's no doubt in my mind that she, like too many African Americans who die in police custody, would be alive today if she were a white woman. We need to reform a very broken criminal justice system."

In early August, Bernie planned to do a West Coast tour. Starting on the eighth, he would attend a Social Security rally, followed by an event of his own. Then he would hold rallies in Portland and Seattle. As it turned out, two young women who identified with the Black Lives Matter movement planned to shut down the Social Security rally. And they did. As they took over the stage, Bernie stepped away and let them have the microphone. He stood by respectfully for a bit and then waded out into the crowd who had come to see him.

Donald Trump would later attack Bernie at a press conference. As reported by CNN, Trump said, "That will never happen with me. I don't know if I'll do the fighting myself or if other people will, but that was a disgrace. I felt badly for him. But it showed that he's weak." In fact, Trump did incite his supporters to attack protesters at his rallies on more than one occasion. Trump, of course, has never understood leadership or respect for others, so his comments were not surprising. So much about him was and is a mask for what appears to be deep insecurity and low self-esteem.

No one on the campaign was happy about the shutdown. In more recent times, Bernie has rightly been praised for the respect he showed to the protesters and the issues they raised. But in the twenty-four-hour news cycle of a presidential campaign it was a problem. It fed the Clinton campaign's false racial narrative. Plus, we had a large and expensive rally that evening and more in the coming days that had to be protected.

While two women of color had taken the stage in Seattle, two other women of color had stepped up to help. The first was Symone Sanders. Coincidently, Symone had been hired days before as the campaign's press secretary. She had worked at Public Citizen's Global Trade Watch and had been an activist for juvenile justice. Symone was scheduled to arrive in Seattle that same day in time for Bernie's evening rally. She opened the rally for Bernie that night. We were getting reports from various quarters that other protests were possible. So as part of her presentation, Symone instructed the crowd that in the event of a protest everyone chant, "We stand together!"

She was a natural in front of a crowd of some 20,000. Bernie would later call me, very impressed. "Jeff, can you believe that a young person just gets up in front of 20,000 people and delivers like that?"

The other woman was Teressa Raiford, lead organizer of Don't Shoot Portland. Our advance staff on the ground had come into contact with Teressa in Portland. I spoke with her by phone. She supported Bernie and did not want to see his Portland event shut down. We talked a couple of times that day about rumors of protests. Later that day she led a demonstration in remembrance of the killing of Michael Brown, and she was arrested. (She was acquitted unanimously by a jury in April 2016.) I called Bernie and updated him.

"Make sure they know we are watching to make sure she is okay," Bernie said to me about the police. The campaign contacted the local police to inquire about Teressa. Word started to spread that she had been arrested because she was connected with a planned protest of Bernie's Portland rally. Of course, it was untrue. I knew that in fact the opposite was true.

In the end, there was no attempted shutdown of the Portland rally. After the event, Bernie, Jane, and Symone Sanders met with Black Lives Matter activists to discuss their concerns. The next day, Teressa was released from jail. She called me because she was getting criticized on social media and in phone messages over the false rumors that she was involved in a protest of Bernie.

I thanked her again and assured her that I would take care of things. I sent our social media team a text to be distributed far and wide:

> A special thanks to Teressa Raiford Mazique of Portland who reached out to the campaign in solidarity and friendship. Her help in Portland is greatly appreciated. As she said, "We stand together." And she's right. All of us fighting for justice must stand together if we are going to win for all communities. We are all relieved that she is safe.

I called Teressa back a few hours later. She said that the social media post we'd placed had ended all the criticism. I asked her to let me know if she had any more problems in that regard. As I had said to the social media staffer in my email, I wanted to be sure that people who stood with us knew that we would stand by them.

One of the most promising events of the summer was Bernie's appearance at the Iowa State Fair in mid-August. It started inauspiciously, when I put the wrong address in my GPS and we ended up in a residential neighborhood. Thankfully, we didn't end up too far away.

When we finally arrived, there was an instant crowd around Bernie. It was hard even to walk around. Our first stop was a previously scheduled interview with the late journalistic icon Gwen Ifill. It was one of the most pleasant and upbeat interviews of the campaign. Bernie and Gwen sat at a picnic table while the huge crowd of fairgoers stood around them in a big circle.

We headed next to the *Des Moines Register* soapbox. The soapbox gives presidential candidates an opportunity to speak to the fairgoers. The crowd around Bernie kept growing and growing. It was an incredibly hot day. Bernie's shirt was dripping with sweat. As he was speaking on stage, one of the organizers of the event asked Robert Becker what we had done as a campaign to attract so many people. "Nothing," he replied. And in fact, we had not. The people just wanted to hear Bernie.

We squeezed through the crowd after the speech for an interview with Bloomberg's *With All Due Respect* political show. It was short, but the hosts concluded by getting Bernie to do the "monster"—a routine involving a scary face and accompanying growls that amuses Bernie's young grandson. He had told them about it in an earlier interview, and they often had him repeat it. Bernie was happy to oblige.

It became almost impossible to move after we left that interview. After a quick visit to the Bernie booth in one of the exhibit halls, we headed for the exit. Bernie ordered a draft root beer from one of the sellers on the way to the exit so the media could get their obligatory photo of Bernie eating fair food. In truth, had the crowds been more manageable, he would have had quite a bit of it. It was a far cry from the 1980s, when Bernie and I campaigned regularly at county fairs across Vermont and ate a lot of fair food. As we drove away, we lamented our inability to eat more of it that day—that and not getting to see the famed Iowa State Fair butter cow.

OF BERNIEBROS, HILLBOTS, THE RUSSIANS, ALT-RIGHT RACISTS, AND A WHOLE LOT OF REALLY GREAT PEOPLE

It bears stepping away from the chronological account for a minute to discuss the incredibly important role played in the campaign by the internet in general and social media in particular. It is more than an understatement to say that Bernie 2016 would not have been possible without the internet. Coupled with other modern means of communications, such as texting, it provided almost all the funding for the campaign. It provided a means for the campaign to communicate with, organize, and persuade people from one end of the country to the other. It also had a darker side. The internet in its anonymity can be a rude and unpleasant place, and a place where not everyone is who he or she appears to be.

In terms of fund-raising, no other campaign has been able to raise the amount of small-dollar contributions online as Bernie Sanders' did. The generosity of millions meant that for the first time in modern American history a truly progressive candidate had the resources necessary to go toe-to-toe with a well-funded establishment candidate. Without that funding, the campaign would certainly never have gotten off the ground. There were times—at the end of fund-raising quarters, for example—when contributions were coming in two per second for hours.

At particular moments in the campaign, people expressed their support in enormous ways. In his speech following the New Hampshire primary, Bernie asked all those watching to go to his website and donate. The result was some $6.5 million over the next twenty-four hours. After a bird landed on his podium at an Oregon rally in late March 2016, we asked for any donation to receive a "Birdie" sticker. In the few days after the bird landed, people responded with over $3.5 million. There is no way to thank properly all of those who gave to support Bernie and his run for the White House. But everyone who donated should know that they truly changed politics forever—not because every candidate will be able to fund his or her race the way that Bernie did, but because we now know that at least at the presidential level it can be done.

In total, through the hard and effective work of Revolution Messaging, we raised over $218 million online from over 8.2 million contributions. We reached our first million contributions in September, our second in December. It only took a month to get to 3 million and another month to get to 4 million. In March, we went over 6 million contributions. April saw us over 7 million and in May we reached 8 million. The $30 million budget that John Robinson and I painstakingly drafted had to be thrown out the window.

That's more contributions in a presidential primary than any candidate ever, and more than President Obama had in his 2008 campaign in total.

The web also allowed us to organize the huge rallies that Bernie held across the country. Texting and the internet allowed us, after the Madison rally, to build crowds with no paid online advertising at all. Hustle—which is a peer-to-peer texting program—was invaluable in crowd building for rallies. We also saw Bernie supporters across the country using the internet, and particularly Facebook, to keep in touch with one another.

There was a proliferation of Bernie-supporter Facebook pages during the campaign.

In terms of social media, Bernie 2016's numbers were impressive:

YouTube videos: *over 30 million views*
Facebook videos: *over 42 million views*
Videos produced: *over 550*
Facebook: *4.3 million page likes*
Twitter: *2.4 million followers*
Instagram: *1.3 million followers*

The campaign, again due to the success of Revolution Messaging, was responsible for a number of "firsts" online:

# of digital ads: 1,185
First presidential candidate to use Instagram ads
First candidate to sponsor multiday Snapchat filters
First in 2016 election to sponsor a national trend on Twitter
First candidate to secure a NYTimes.com takeover ad

Bernie had a tremendous following on Reddit. The folks on Reddit raised over a million dollars for the campaign. The discussions on Reddit helped keep our most active online supporters engaged and up-to-date on campaign developments. They may not know it, but they also provided a big morale boost to those of us on the campaign. My daughter especially liked "Beast Mode Weaver Is Best Mode Weaver" and the comparison of me to Henry Knox, a Rhode Island bookstore owner who became one of George Washington's generals.

Reddit users also spawned what became a tremendous asset to the campaign—Coders for Bernie. It was originated by Kyle Pierce, who, according to the *New York Times*, started a Coders for Bernie thread in June 2015. Coders for Bernie, like Daniela Perdomo and over 120 others, were responsible for the issues-based site FeeltheBern.org.

Coders for Bernie—which billed itself as "a loose collective of developers, designers, and creatives working to elect Bernie Sanders for President"—built apps and programs that allowed people to find events, places to stay, voters who needed calling, and a host of other tools. Their devotion to Bernie and the campaign allowed us to do things online that would otherwise have been hugely expensive.

The internet also had its downside. The first was the Berniebros meme advanced by the media and echoed by the Clinton campaign. The phrase was coined by *The Atlantic*'s Robinson Meyer in a condescending piece published on October 17, 2015. It described a subset of Bernie supporters: young, male, educated, and rabidly pro-Bernie. Among the faults ascribed by Robinson to the Berniebros: their belief that Bernie could win (apparently Meyer's establishment crystal ball didn't reveal Bernie winning twenty-three nominating contests or the consistent polling that showed Bernie beating Trump) and their support for "pie-in-the-sky" proposals such as free college tuition and the $15 minimum wage. Both proposals are now included in the Democratic platform and are gaining widespread support across the country in the wake of the 2016 presidential campaign. By the time of the Democratic convention, Hillary Clinton supported both.

What started as a negative meme meant to belittle a group of Bernie supporters turned much darker. Throughout the fall and early spring, there was a proliferation of articles on a presumed wave of rude Bernie supporters—all supposedly testosterone-crazed, twenty-one-year-old misogynists—taking over the internet and making it unsafe for anyone who was not as fanatically for Bernie as they were. Leaked DNC emails had top communications staff labeling a reporter a Berniebro just because he wanted to ask the DNC chairwoman about the questionable operation of the joint fund-raising agreement that the Clinton campaign and the DNC had signed. Soon it was being said that all Bernie supporters were racist, misogynistic twenty-one-year-old men. There were no women, no people of color. Just Berniebros.

Before we get too far into this discussion, which could consume a book of its own, let me say that there is no doubt that there were some supporters who posted offensive and hateful content. It was not welcome or encouraged by the campaign. And we worked to tamp it down. On the other hand, there was and is tremendous support for Bernie Sanders online. People can and did complain that his supporters were too zealous in supporting him online when he was being ignored in the media and defamed by paid agents of the Clinton campaign such as David Brock and by the hired online trolls—the Hillbots—that Brock employed. Often this ardent support for Bernie was conflated with legitimate concerns about offensive posts. To the extent the complaints were really about zealousness and not offensive content, those were not complaints that found any resonance with the candidate or any of the senior staff. If folks in the media or on Twitter expect only praise from the world, they are in the wrong playground.

While I don't embrace every conclusion and observation in it, Glenn Greenwald's January 31, 2016, *Intercept* article laid out many of the problems with the Berniebro meme, including the abuse of the term by Paul Krugman, who not only disliked Bernie supporters but also was a public hater of Obama's 2008 supporters. There's no room in the ivory tower for the unwashed masses who actually want to see progressive policies implemented rather than just jawboned about in the paper.

In fact, President Obama's online supporters faced identical criticism in 2008, being dubbed at the time "Obama boys." On April 14, 2008, Rebecca Traister wrote an article in *Salon* called "Hey, Obama Boys: Back Off Already!" She wrote, "A growing number of young women are struggling to describe a gut conviction that there is something dark and funky, and probably not so female-friendly, running below the frantic fanaticism of their Obama-loving compatriots. . . . I was horrified by the frequent proclamations that if Obama did not win the nomination, his supporters would abstain from voting in the general election, or even vote for John McCain. I was suspicious of the cultlike commitment to an undeniably brilliant and inspiring man."

The reality is that Bernie's supporters were disproportionately young, and therefore disproportionately represented in the online community. The sheer imbalance between the number of Bernie supporters online and

Clinton supporters meant that the majority of those discussing politics on the internet and commenting on stories at any given time were going to be Bernie supporters.

Naturally, the Clinton team was busy selling the Berniebros meme to reporters. *New York* magazine's Olivia Nuzzi tweeted, "Maybe I would buy into 'bernie bros' more if I hadn't been pitched a story about bernie bros by Hillary's camp." Many others did buy in, however.

The meme was an element of the political messaging designed to paint the campaign as hostile to women and people of color and to make people who were part of those constituencies feel ashamed for supporting Bernie. This fiction that all of Bernie's support was coming from young, white males incensed many of the people of color and women who supported Bernie. This manifested itself in the most public way with #BernieMadeMeWhite, started by Leslie Lee III and comprised of people of color who supported Bernie and who expressed their sense of frustration and outrage that the media was making them invisible—that somehow supporting Bernie Sanders had made them white. Lee and people of color supporting Bernie were right to be offended.

As NPR reported in March 2016, Randy Brown of Edison Research, after conducting exit polls in twenty states, said, "Among African-Americans, who are 17 through 29, Bernie Sanders is actually leading that group, 51 to 48 [percent]. Among 17- to 29-year-old Hispanics, Bernie Sanders leads Hillary Clinton 66–34." "I think the big takeaway," Brown said, "is that whether it's among whites or African-Americans, Bernie Sanders does significantly better among the youngest voters in the Democratic primary." In truth, Hillary Clinton was winning older voters of all races, and Bernie Sanders was winning younger voters of all races.

While exit polling was capturing this reality, public polling and polling paid for by the media did not. It was extremely frustrating to see the media provide all kinds of breakdowns of white voters (age, education, and so forth) while lumping all black voters into one pot. This was all about money. Getting enough black voters to provide statistically valid breakdowns requires oversampling. That means more phone calls must be completed for each poll; and that, in turn, means more money. I don't know if the media ever spent that money.

In addition to the media's failure to make the investment needed to truly understand the complexity or nuance within many minority communities, there was certainly Clinton-world messaging that verged on both race-shaming and gender-shaming against people who supported Bernie. It was not just people of color who were upset. Young women supporting Bernie registered their outrage online when Madeleine Albright said that there was "a special place in hell" for women not supporting Hillary Clinton, and when Gloria Steinem said on Bill Maher's show that young women were only supporting Bernie so that they could meet "boys."

A young Vermont woman interviewed by the *New York Times* put it best: "'Shame on Gloria Steinem and Madeleine Albright for implying that we as women should be voting for a candidate based solely on gender,' Zoe Trimboli, a 23-year-old from Vermont who supports Mr. Sanders and describes herself as a feminist, wrote on Facebook. 'I can tell you that shaming me and essentially calling me misinformed and stupid is NOT the way to win my vote.'"

When pressed by CNN's Carol Costello about whether Hillary Clinton should disavow these statements, campaign spokesperson Karen Finney said, "These are women who are passionate advocates, they support Hillary Clinton. We can't control what they say." In the eyes of her campaign, Secretary Clinton apparently lacked the mystical powers that Bernie Sanders—like Barack Obama before him—possessed, but refused to use, to control what each of his supporters wrote or said.

Of course, unlike the Clinton campaign, Bernie himself did disavow unacceptable comments from supporters. When asked in an interview with CNN's Jake Tapper in early February about inappropriate supporter posts, Bernie responded in his usual circumspect manner: "We don't want that crap." He added, "Anybody who is supporting me and who is doing sexist things, we don't want them. I don't want them. That is not what this campaign is about." If only he hadn't issued such a vague denunciation, or if he had used his behavior-altering mental control superpowers, all the bad online conduct would have stopped.

While Berniebros got a lot of media attention during the campaign, what did not get coverage were the over-the-top attacks online coming from Clinton supporters. It is impossible to know if these were hired trolls or real people. As I discuss below, the Clinton campaign–controlled super PAC Correct the Record admitted to hiring online trolls—something, for the record, our campaign never did.

Here are just a couple of the many enlightened Twitter posts by supporters of Hillary Clinton:

DavezNotHereMan @daveznothereman tweeted · May 2, 2016: #HillaryOrBust I will never bote for Bernie fucking Asshat and his detestable, disgusting, POS lying-bitch wife. #fleethebern #fuckBernie

Jo Ann @Catslawrence tweeted · June 7, 2016: I wish Nina Turner would shut the fuck up!

Deng @Hayabusa_19 tweeted on · June 2, 2016: @VinnyTimNJ Sniveling Weaver tries to weasel his way out. #FuckJeffWeaver #FuckBernieSanders.

Sexist attacks by the Hillbots (or Hillbros or Hillbullies) against Jane Sanders became so frequent, as documented by Patrick Curl's pro-Bernie pivotamerica.com in early April 2016, that Bernie's supporters on Reddit rallied to defend her. If you read some of the threads, it is also clear that some Clinton supporters defended Jane as well.

The aggressiveness of Clinton's online supporters is reflected in the findings of a poll done in early March 2016 by Craigslist founder Craig Newmark, Lincoln Park Strategies, and Rad Campaign. The poll found that 57 percent of respondents described Trump supporters as very aggressive online; 13 percent believed they were somewhat aggressive. Coming in a strong second were supporters of Hillary Clinton, at 30 percent very aggressive and 18 percent somewhat aggressive. Cruz's devotees came in third, at 21 percent/18 percent. Lagging in fourth place were supporters of Bernie

Sanders. Only 16 percent felt Bernie's supporters were very aggressive on social media; another 16 percent felt they were somewhat aggressive. *Politico*'s Hadas Gold reported these results in May 2016. Oddly, I can't find the story in the rest of the mainstream media, but I may have missed it.

This story of ugliness on the internet is not limited to the bad behavior of random Sanders and Clinton supporters. While I do not intend in any way to distract attention from unacceptable, albeit organic, social media conduct, it is important to recognize that there was also organized political warfare taking place in the anonymous world of the internet among super PACs, the racist alt-right, Trump supporters, and interests outside the United States. They all contributed to turning what would otherwise have been zealous and at times unacceptable internet discourse into a political cesspool. Let's look at some of them.

1. HILLARY CLINTON'S SUPER PAC CORRECT THE RECORD AND ITS PAID TROLLS

The head of CTR, David Brock, revealed in April 2016 that the group was spending $1 million on paid trolls to attack its opponents online. Whether it was happening even earlier than he admits is not verifiable at this point and probably never will be, given his tortured relationship with the truth. But Correct the Record's own statements, reported by Ben Collins on April 21, 2016, in the *Daily Beast*, indicate that they did, in fact, start earlier. Collins reports that CTR's own press release stated that they had already "addressed more than 5,000 people that have personally attacked Hillary Clinton on Twitter." He further reports, "Correct the Record's communications director, Elizabeth Shappell, told *the Daily Beast*, 'The expanded task force was established in anticipation of the general election.'" Expanded task force? How big was the task force before it was expanded? It could have been very big; Correct the Record had already spent $4.5 million when it made this announcement.

Correct the Record played a distasteful role in the Democratic primary campaign, using what some describe as a campaign finance loophole— or, as others allege, engaging in outright improper behavior—to fully coordinate with the Clinton campaign, something that super PACs are not supposed to do. The *Los Angeles Times* reported in November 2016: "Campaign finance reformers were appalled." The assessment was not confined to people outside the campaign. In that same *Los Angeles Times* story:

> Even Clinton's allies worried that the unprecedented setup has gone too far, the hacked emails show. "This does seem shady," Clinton friend Neera Tanden wrote to Podesta. His response was brief: "Brock $ machine!"
> "That's fine," Tanden wrote back. "But skirting if not violating law doesn't help her."

The questionable legality of CTR was matched by the questionable character running it, David Brock. Brock started his career as a defamer for the right, viciously smearing the reputation of Anita Hill and others during the Clarence Thomas Supreme Court confirmation process. The *Los Angeles Times*'s Evan Halper described Brock this way: "a Clinton confidant who once made a career of spreading such misinformation and misogynistic attacks against her and Bill Clinton."

Brock confessed to having conducted full-out attacks on women who were detractors of Justice Thomas. In one instance, as reported on June 27, 2001, in the *New York Times*, he used information leaked to him about the details of one woman's divorce to blackmail her into silence. "Mr. Brock wrote that he used the information to intimidate her into recanting her account, threatening that he would 'blacken her name, just as I had done to every other woman who had impugned Thomas's reputation.'" The article quotes Brock as saying: "I demonized Democratic senators, their staffs, and Hill's feminist supporters without ever interviewing any of them." He had also been a big promoter of attacks on Bill Clinton's personal life.

Brock claims he had a road-to-Damascus conversion while writing a book that was supposed to be a hit piece on Hillary Clinton. While he was never viewed, and is still not, as a person with an ideological compass of any kind, he dropped the far right's flag and became a crusader in the Clinton army. They readily adopted him, despite his long history of defaming anyone it was politically convenient to defame—even the Clintons themselves. What did Bernie think of the Clintons' associating themselves with Brock? He summed it up this way in a May 2016 interview he gave to *Time*: "I don't think you hire scum of the Earth to be on your team just because the other side does it."

Correct the Record's stated purpose was to protect Hillary Clinton from the expected barrage of right-wing attacks they were concerned about. In truth, CTR's principal function was not the defense of Hillary Clinton but rather the smearing of Bernie Sanders while allowing the Clinton campaign to keep its hands clean. In our campaign, the group became known as Distort the Record. Brock admitted, as reported by Jonathan Swan in a mid-February story for *The Hill*, "One of the roles of Correct the Record is to do things that the campaign shouldn't do or won't do or can't do, and one of those things is being more out front with some of the more pointed criticisms of Sen. Sanders."

CTR's primary tactic was a steady stream of attacks on Bernie that it provided to the media only if they agreed to accept such attacks "off the record." However, Brock's under-the-radar smear campaign was exposed by the media at various times. The *Huffington Post*'s Samantha Lachman and Ryan Grim reported in September 2015 that, despite the Clinton campaign's claim that they were not attacking Bernie, Correct the Record circulated an email trying to tie Bernie to positions of Hugo Chávez of Venezuela and UK Labour Party leader Jeremy Corbyn. CTR had apparently expected the email to have been an off-the-record transmission but didn't get the authors' agreement in advance. Okay, from a professional point of view, that's just sloppy.

The *Burlington Free Press*'s Emilie Stigliani exposed more details about how CTR's smear machine worked: "Hillary Clinton's super PAC has tried to 'flag' stories about Bernie Sanders, but the group does not want its name attached. Daniel Wessel, Correct the Record press secretary, contacted the *Burlington Free Press* by email and phone to offer 'off the record' story pitches." Stigliani reported further that during a phone conversation,

"Wessel said that his organization prefers to be named only when speaking about Republican candidates. He offered to have his organization named in certain cases if the *Free Press* requested permission. The *Free Press* declined to agree to Wessel's terms."

Reporters acknowledged to me privately that they were receiving anti-Bernie attack emails from CTR but couldn't speak about it—because they had agreed to receive the material off the record. When I would confront a reporter who was chasing a negative story and ask whether the source was Brock, he or she would generally look away in silence. That told me all I needed to know.

It is common for reporters to take off-the-record story tips or pitches from campaign staff, including me. What is unusual here is that the Clinton campaign was running its dirty tricks through a wholly owned subsidiary funded by unlimited donations far exceeding the federal campaign finance limits. Considering that Brock was admittedly operating his defamation factory in full coordination with the Clinton campaign and therefore was just an arm of the campaign, his activities did not receive the kind of attention they warranted from the press—a press Brock held in such contempt that he told Glenn Thrush, in a December 2016 *Politico* interview, "The press are animals and they need to be treated that way." In fairness, many in the media felt the same way about him. On two separate occasions, reporters independently told me that they felt like they needed to take a shower after interviewing Brock.

Brock also used vehicles other than CTR to attack our campaign, including the website Blue Nation Review (BNR), originally established as a progressive blog that featured positive stories about Bernie and other progressives. According to the *Daily Beast*'s Lloyd Grove, David Brock, with the help of BNR board member and pro-Clinton telecom magnate Leo Hindery, orchestrated a takeover in November 2015 that resulted in Brock's owning an 80 percent share. The founder (and much of the staff) were unceremoniously kicked to the curb, replaced by Peter Daou, a militant Clintonista and Brock lackey—the perfect combination for his role as internet Bernie hater in chief. BNR thus became yet another part of the network of Brock-controlled smear vehicles unflatteringly known as the Brocktopus.

Brock's tactics in attacking Bernie were so over-the-top that they even raised alarm bells in Clinton-world. When Brock went after Bernie's age and health before the Iowa caucus, Clinton campaign chairman John Podesta publicly tweeted that Brock should "Chill Out." Top Clinton adviser Neera Tanden emailed Podesta opining that Brock was doing them so much damage that he might be a Republican plant.

So why was Brock allowed to run amok if top Clinton advisers thought he was doing them harm and they believed, through some campaign finance loophole, that they could fully coordinate with him? That's a good question, and we may never know the answer. In an email to John Podesta, Neera Tanden suggested that Hillary Clinton or Bill Clinton was giving him the green light. In that same email, she suggested that Bill Clinton approved Clinton 2008 campaign manager Mark Penn's attempt to insinuate that Barack Obama was a cocaine abuser.

In January 2017, Brock publicly apologized to Bernie and his supporters for his conduct during the 2016 race. People will have to judge for themselves whether he's sincere. For context, the apology did come shortly after I wrote an opinion piece for *The Hill* imploring large Democratic donors not to waste more money on Brock's failed electoral efforts when that money could be more effectively deployed in other ways to help elect Democrats.

For his part, Brock acolyte Peter Daou harbors so much venom toward Bernie that he continues to attack him online to this day. Daou reminds me of the World War II Imperial Japanese soldier who was left behind on an island only to learn decades later that the war is over.

We cannot know for sure what Brock's paid troll task force was doing online throughout the campaign. As the *Burlington Free Press* documented, they went to great lengths to hide their tracks. How many anti-Bernie commenters in threads complaining of Berniebros were Brock operatives with multiple Twitter or Facebook handles having a conversation with themselves? Wired.com reported in December 2007 that Clinton presidential campaign staffers were caught creating fake accounts to appear as grass-roots Clinton supporters on the progressive Blue Hampshire blog.

Or was the troll task force just putting out fun, positive facts—like how much Hillary Clinton loves puppies and kittens? Given Brock and Daou's conduct during the campaign, are they in part responsible for ugly social media attacks targeted at Clinton supporters by supposed Bernie-bros? That kind of thing doesn't happen, you say? As you will see below, there were many parties doing it in 2016. Kind of hard to believe the Brocktopus would have been so far behind the curve in the dirty tricks department.

2. ALT-RIGHT RACISTS

In addition to the paid Brock trolls, another group was maliciously in-jecting itself into the discussion between Bernie and Clinton supporters online. Alt-right racists organized on sites like 4chan to go out onto the web posing as Bernie supporters to harass black Clinton supporters with overtly racist attacks. I personally saw those boards, long since erased to hide their tracks, as did others on the campaign. They featured photo-shopped images of Bernie standing next to a bed on which lay an interracial couple. They described African Americans as "apes" and "animals." They were particularly incensed by Bernie's refusal to attack Black Lives Matter activists after some of his events were interrupted. They described Bernie as "cuckolded" by the Black Lives Matter movement.

It was painful to see real political debate hijacked by such racist filth. I cannot say how much of a role these disgusting individuals played in ramping up the coarseness of the dialogue online during the primary sea-son. But certainly their posts were incendiary and repulsive.

3. TRUMP TROLLS, FOREIGN AND DOMESTIC

The *Huffington Post*'s Ryan Grim and Jason Cherkis documented, in a lengthy article in March 2017, that as the primary season wound down there was a wave of activity by trolls on Bernie-friendly Facebook pages from a couple of different sources. This has been verified anecdotally by people active on pro-Bernie Facebook pages. The trolls in May were strongly anti-Bernie. The *Huffington Post* article posits that the trolls were from David Brock's expanded program.

Grim and Cherkis note that in June 2016 the trolling changed. It switched to anti-Clinton messaging by supposed Bernie supporters who had decided to support Donald Trump or Green Party candidate Jill Stein. And it became more intense and vitriolic as the general election neared.

The authors document the efforts of the administrators of pro-Bernie pages to alert the Bernie online community about the trolling and to shut it down. Aleta Pearce, an "administrator of half a dozen pro-Sanders Facebook groups and a member of many others . . . , posted a memo to various Facebook groups about the fake news issue, warning of bogus sites." According to Pearce, "The pattern I'm seeing is if a member is repeatedly posting articles that are only from one URL that person is just there to push advertising. . . . They probably have a sock account with little to no content. They are often from Russia or Macedonia."

Another administrator, Bev Cowling, saw a surge in people trying to join her group. "It came in like a wave, like a tsunami," she told Grim and Cherkis. "It was like a flood of misinformation."

According to the authors, these trolls were joining multiple sites and were pushing over-the-top anti-Hillary stories, including ones about made-up illnesses, collusion with ISIS, and more. The article notes that efforts to eradicate this infestation were complicated by Brock's public announcement of his troll army. Legitimate Bernie supporters became wary of anyone promoting a vaguely pro-Hillary position—including the message that pro-Trump trolls were the ones infecting the Bernie pages with anti-Hillary venom. In that way, Brock's initiative actually helped create an environment of distrust that allowed anti-Hillary trolls to flourish.

The *Daily Beast*'s Gideon Resnick revealed that, like the alt-right racists, more garden-variety Trump supporters were also using 4chan as a place to organize efforts by Trump supporters to go online posing as pro-Bernie or pro-Clinton so they could sow discord between the two Democratic camps. One poster to 4chan laid out a line of attack:

They are going all out to paint Bernie supporters as non-Democrats and selfish "white people." . . . This is an excellent wedge that you can exploit by finding Bernie supporters and calling them privileged and entitled white men from the point of view of a Hillary supporter. . . . Your main goal should be to mock and humiliate Bernie supporters while leaving subtle but unmistakable hints that you're voting for Clinton. . . . Remember, if they hate you and you support Clinton, then they will hate Clinton.

Another 4chan poster quoted in Resnick's article noted the opportunities presented by Brock's announcement of his troll army to create divisions between Bernie and Clinton supporters. "Correct The Record is the greatest gift to Trump ever, let's use it to our advantage and make both sides lose credibility with each other."

Were the June trolls that invaded pro-Bernie social media sites part of the Russian effort to help elect Donald Trump by turning off Bernie supporters from voting for Clinton? The proliferation of links from Russia and Eastern Europe certainly suggest it. But like so much of what happened online, it is impossible to lock down 100 percent.

Taken together, foreign trolls, Trump trolls, Clinton's paid trolls, and organic supporters of each of the campaigns who behaved inappropriately make it impossible to know who was doing what on the web. As bad as it was in 2016, it is sure to only get worse in the years ahead. One hopes that the media will take note of this and resist buying into false narratives.

A MOMENT OF PERSONAL INDULGENCE

Due to campaign appearances on television news programs, I personally acquired many "fans" during the campaign, particularly Twitter followers. Although many close to me felt bad about it, I would occasionally enjoy a glass of wine at my dinner table and read aloud some of the many mean tweets. The more creative and outrageous, the more I would howl. For the record, I do want to clear up a couple of memes. I am not related to

Karl Rove, by marriage or otherwise. I did not make $800,000 a month on the campaign. And I do still like Cher, even if she's not, as the following tweet suggests, my biggest fan:

SANDERS MANAGER,IS SCUM.HIS"HILLARY IS RESPONSIBLE 4 ISIS"IS PURE TRUMP!! #JEFFWEAVER IS 🔥 ASSHOLE, BUT HE SAYS THE 💩.BERNIE"WANTS 2 SAY.

8

STARTING TO RISE IN THE FALL

OCTOBER PROVED TO BE a difficult month in terms of messaging. There were several events that the media viewed as significantly buoying the Clinton campaign—which necessarily hurt ours. The contest was clearly becoming a two-person race.

The first event was the Democratic debate in Las Vegas on October 13. It represented an important moment for Bernie's campaign for the Democratic nomination. Polling at the time showed that in some states as many as 40 percent of the voters either did not know who Bernie Sanders was or did not have enough information about him to form an opinion. That's the reality of politics.

Bernie had held rallies across the country to crowds of thousands, in some cases tens of thousands. He had been in the news for months. While people consumed with work on a campaign are sure that every word is being carefully considered by every voter, the truth is that people have real lives, with innumerable things competing for their time and attention. Hillary Clinton was known to virtually everyone. She had run for president in 2008. She had been secretary of state and had served as first lady.

The fact that we were unknown to so many people created a challenge in terms of the debate. Creating a lot of "contrast" with one's opponent in a debate when the voters don't even have an opinion of you is generally a risky strategy. In our case, all the data showed that the more people got to know Bernie and his agenda, the more they liked him. We had tons of room to gain support just by introducing Bernie to more voters and without engaging Hillary Clinton at all.

That reality drove our debate strategy. The CNN debate would be viewed by millions of people. From our point of view, we did not need or necessarily want to spar with Hillary Clinton. We just wanted Bernie to articulate his progressive vision to the nation. A lot of the talking heads on the political shows either didn't understand that or pretended they didn't understand it. In any case, this would be the chance for Bernie to get the kind of national exposure that the media was already giving to Donald Trump on a regular basis.

In a debate, however, it is not always possible to avoid exchanges, because your opponent may well want to engage you. Or the media may initiate an exchange. Hillary Clinton had shown herself to be a skilled debater in 2008. She could give as well as she got, and in most cases she could give more than she got. She was a dangerous opponent.

We also had to consider Governor O'Malley. He had hoped to position himself as the progressive alternative to Hillary Clinton. But Bernie had "occupied that lane," as the politicos like to say. O'Malley was trailing badly in the polls. Would he use the debate to go after Bernie? Or would he go after Clinton in hope of attracting voters who were not keen on Clinton and who were not Feeling the Bern?

The preparation required for this debate would necessarily be different from that of any Bernie had ever had to prepare for. He had a lot of experience debating. But he had not had a real contest since the 2006 U.S. Senate run—fully ten years before. And those debates had gotten "hot" in terms of tone and volume—not that Rich Tarrant didn't deserve the heat, given the despicable attacks he had launched against Bernie in the paid media.

Hillary Clinton, on the other hand, had a lot of experience from 2008 debating at the presidential level. Most pundits at the time had given her high marks in her appearances against Barack Obama, who himself was great on stage.

Our research head director Edward Chapman and his team prepared all the debate-related research materials. They were extensive—Bernie, Clinton, and O'Malley all had long political careers. Bernie could be called out for votes cast twenty-five years before. Or some statement connected with his mayoral tenure from thirty years ago could be thrown at him. Of course, the others faced the same challenge.

Having all the details of your candidate's record and those of the other candidates is just a first step. The records have to be combed over to find each candidate's strengths and weaknesses, including your own. Then that information has to be imparted to your candidate, who is the one who must stand on stage in front of millions of viewers and deliver. It is an exercise that requires important political judgment calls in terms of divining what will be the questions asked and the attacks made. It also requires discipline by the candidate, who must internalize a lot of information.

We decided to get Bernie to the West Coast days before the debate so that he and the rest of the crew could be acclimated to the time zone. He left Washington, DC, on October 9 and headed west for the rallies in Tucson and Boulder. The Tucson rally was one of the most memorable of the campaign. It was held in a large park with a stage. It was a 5,000-plus event, with an overwhelmingly Latino audience. Congressman Raul Grijalva—one of our earliest endorsers—helped organize the event and introduced Bernie. There was a tremendous sense of community as we heard the stories from young Dreamers whose families had been torn apart by a broken immigration system. No one who heard the stories that evening of parents and children being separated could have left unmoved by the tragedy so many were facing. Today, under Trump's presidency, the tragedy is more severe.

Boulder was scorching hot the next day. Bernie spoke to thousands at an outdoor rally; people were fainting from the heat. The National Nurses Union was there in force and provided medical assistance. The union ran an independent expenditure campaign in support of Bernie's run. Their bus traveled the country, and their membership seemed to be everywhere—Their work was an example of the impact that an independent grassroots effort can have.

That evening we arrived in Nevada. We stayed in Henderson, rather than in Las Vegas itself. It put us away from the huge media presence, but that was the point. This was Bernie's first presidential debate. He needed to prepare and focus. Being a bit farther out made that all the more likely.

Supporting a candidate in a presidential debate is a big logistical undertaking that requires a big team. In addition to the actual debate prep team, there are surrogates, family members, staff covering communications and research, and advance staff to support them all. The ever-frugal Bernie felt greatly overstaffed. We definitely had more staff at the first debate than at any of the subsequent ones. But this being our first debate I wanted to be sure that we had what we needed. I took Bernie's far-too-serious teasing about this in stride.

Debate prep is intense work. Bernie was provided with voluminous briefing books on past positions and votes, and on issues that we anticipated would come up. It is not all that difficult to anticipate what the universe of media questions will be. I would estimate that we were well over 90 percent accurate in figuring out which questions would be asked. By this time, the campaign had come to be defined in terms of issues and divisions between the candidates. Bernie dove into the materials. His years as a legislator gave him a lot of experience digesting material on various topics quickly.

We also had formal debate prep sessions. For the first time in his career, Bernie would be prepping with other people standing in for his opponents. Michaeleen Crowell, his Senate chief of staff, stood in for Hillary Clinton. Mark Longabaugh played Martin O'Malley. In addition, the prep would take place in what for us was a very crowded room of people—Tad, Mark, Jane, some other family members, the research team, the policy team, and state senator Nina Turner and her husband, Jeff.

Bernie had traditionally prepped for debates from written materials only, so this was a big change. When he asked whether we needed this many people in the room, Tad assured him that it was not too many. "I guarantee you there are at least forty people in the room prepping Hillary," Tad said. "This is really a skeleton crew."

Tad played the moderator. He would read questions from a three-ring binder. Bernie had an excellent grasp of the issues already because his candidacy was so policy-focused.

Because Hillary Clinton had been secretary of state, we spent a considerable amount of time on foreign policy issues even though we knew they would be a relatively small part of the debate. Her strength was her extensive experience. We had to focus on her judgment, which led her to support the Iraq War and the intervention in Libya.

Aside from filling in a gap here and there on substance, there was also a focus on the intangible aspects of debating. No one wanted to have a Rick Lazio moment. (During a U.S. Senate debate between Rick Lazio and Hillary Clinton, Lazio had walked from his podium to hers to deliver a document. It was widely panned as too in-your-face, particularly against a female opponent.)

We put the podiums fairly close together. Bernie, who talks with his hands, got some practice being close to an opponent. "So, I shouldn't do this," he joked, waving his hands in front of Michaeleen's face.

Much of the prep was dictated by our overall strategy of using the debate to introduce Bernie to millions of Americans rather than as an opportunity to spar with Hillary Clinton. We knew that the issue of Clinton's emails would be the subject of a question. Bernie expressed his view that he was not going to focus on it. He felt that the obsession with the emails was robbing voters of a real debate on substantive policy issues. The one thing we did not rehearse was the response he would give when asked about Hillary Clinton's email troubles. That was all Bernie.

Hanging over everyone was whether Vice President Joe Biden would decide to make the CNN debate his first presidential campaign appearance. CNN even had a podium ready in the wings in case he jumped in. Because Biden was a maybe, and the other candidates had such long public records, we really did not do much "Biden prep." If he had decided to show, we would not have been as prepared against him. As debate time approached, it became clear that he would not be there.

Right before the debate, the DNC leadership showed itself to be thin-skinned and petty even to questioning from the inside. Two DNC vice-chairs, Congresswoman Tulsi Gabbard of Hawaii and former Minneapolis mayor R. T. Rybak of Minnesota, had the audacity to question why there were so few debates. Of course, as we now know, the debate parameters were written by the Clinton campaign and implemented by DNC chair Debbie Wasserman Schultz.

Congresswoman Gabbard reiterated her concern in an MSNBC interview just days before the debate. Wasserman Schultz's staff called Gabbard's office and effectively withdrew her invitation to attend the debate. Everyone at the time thought it was just pettiness. Knowing now how the debate calendar was deliberately rigged, it wasn't pettiness. It was arrogance—to retaliate against someone who is questioning your decision making when you know you have deliberately rigged the process. When asked about it on CNN's *New Day,* I said that if the DNC wouldn't give Representative Gabbard a ticket, our campaign certainly would. She ultimately did not attend, but she would later become one of our most effective surrogates.

The debate itself went very much as we had planned. Bernie delivered his message of combating wealth and income inequality, reforming the campaign finance system, breaking up big banks, and advocating for criminal justice reform. There were a few exchanges. On debate points—not sincerity—Clinton won the exchange on guns. Bernie's position does not fit on a bumper sticker. Hillary Clinton's 2016 position did. There was no room on that bumper sticker for her long and tortured history of being on all sides of the gun control debate.

On many other issues, Clinton showed some of the vulnerabilities that would plague her down the road, including flip-flopping on support for the Trans-Pacific Partnership trade agreement and the Keystone XL pipeline.

Bernie delivered the most memorable line of the night. When the moderators brought up Secretary Clinton's emails, Bernie said to a standing ovation, "Let me say something that may not be great politics, but I think the secretary is right. I think the American people are sick and tired of hearing about your damn emails." Clinton loved it.

The point that Bernie was making—a point that was lost on the media even though he clarified his remarks in an interview with CNN's Chris Cuomo immediately after the debate—was that the media was covering the Clinton email debacle to the exclusion of almost any other issue in the Democratic primary. Bernie wanted to talk about trade policy, the minimum wage, the crisis in college affordability, climate change, and the rest of his progressive agenda. His point was not that there was no merit to the controversy. His position was that the legal process should take its course and that the media should broaden the scope of its coverage of the primary to include substantive policy issues.

To the extent anyone in the media or the viewing audience caught that point, Larry David's subsequent *Saturday Night Live* portrayal of Bernie completely blew it away. (Bernie thought that the Larry David portrayal, while over-the-top, was hilarious.)

Bernie did one other thing that should be mentioned. He invoked Sandra Bland's name in the debate. No one knew at the time that in doing so he was keeping a promise he had made to Sandra Bland's mother, Geneva Reed-Veal. He had by chance recently met her at the East Street Cafe in Union Station in Washington, DC. I did not know about the meeting until after the debate, when I read an account of it on soulunbound.com written by the Rev. Hannah Adair Bonner, one of the people accompanying Geneva Reed-Veal that night:

> I was completely blown away by the unexpectedness of it all, the sacredness of the moment, and the sincerity of all involved. You do not often get to witness moments like that. Moments when agendas are laid aside and people who might not otherwise ever have the chance to connect without cameras watching can simply honor one another's pain and humanity.
>
> "What happened to your daughter is inexcusable," he said. "We are broken, and this has exposed us." He then continued by promising that he would continue to #SayHerName #SandraBland and would not give up in the pursuit of justice.
>
> The spontaneity of the moment lent sincerity to words

unrehearsed, phrases unplanned, in an interaction that was never supposed to take place.

We asked Senator Sanders if we could take a picture with him and he consented. He did not impose upon Ms. Geneva to ask for a picture of his own. He did not use the moment as an opportunity to promote his campaign. He took no record, he made no statement. He did not try to turn it into a publicity stunt. He simply made space for a sacred moment, and then let it pass without trying to gain anything from it.

For that, I respect him. For that, I am grateful. That choice may not have made him a very good politician, but it made him a better man.

This meeting almost more than any other sums up Bernie Sanders. Yes, he's loud on the stump, sometimes impatient, and extremely driven. But he also feels a deep and sincere connection with the people he meets in his travels. That's a side of Bernie so few get to see. When I later asked him about the meeting, he said, "It was a personal meeting." It all became clear. To Bernie, Saying Her Name at the CNN debate had become personal.

The Netroots protesters months before had wanted him to Say Her Name at the conference. He had been saying Sandra Bland's name and the names of other victims of police violence before tens of thousands of people ever since. Now he had said her name to almost 16 million viewers sitting at home watching the Democratic debate.

The media almost universally hailed Secretary Clinton as the winner of the debate. They praised her poise and presidential demeanor. There never was any doubt that Hillary Clinton was a candidate of great intelligence and poise, with a presidential demeanor—and that she was good at debates. But everyone knew that before the debate even started.

From our point of view, the debate was a tremendous success. Bernie had delivered the most memorable line of the evening, and the issues that he brought to the campaign dominated the discussion on stage—as they would throughout the campaign. Our goal had been to have him make his case to the nation. He had. And the nation was interested. Philip Bump's analysis in the *Washington Post* that evening showed that Bernie generated huge online interest in terms of Google searches whenever he spoke during the debate. And the interest continued postdebate. Bernie also bested Clinton on Twitter that night.

Following the debate, Tad Devine and I and our other surrogates went down to what is called the spin room. We had watched the debate from our work room—in this case, a small two-room hotel suite. Inside the suite were jammed our press, research, and advance staff and our surrogates. Part of the function of the work room is rapid response. In anticipation of the debate, we had well over a hundred fact sheets prepared on aspects of the various candidates' records and positions. These can be sent out to all the media in real time to either reinforce an attack leveled against an opponent or to defend your own candidate.

Many in the media just ignore them. But there are others who find the background information useful. When a topic came up in the debate that was the subject of one of our prepared sheets, the press staff would put it up on a screen and I would yea or nay it. This was our first go-around with this type of rapid response, but it worked pretty seamlessly. We also monitored social media to see the reaction to the ebb and flow of the debate.

Before the close of every debate, we huddled to condense our talking points for the spin room. Tad usually took the lead in compiling them, but it was a collaborative process that a small group had input into. It was usually a list of the top five talking points. We would then leave the suite before the closing statements so we could be first in the spin room. I didn't see the closing statements of any of the debates during the campaign.

For those who have not been to one, which I expect is most readers, the spin room is where all the media is set up to conduct interviews with surrogates. And because this was the first debate, ALL the media was there. The television networks have set locations around the outside walls of the room, but most reporters are just wandering around. As different surrogates enter the room, they are mobbed by the reporters. Because a spin room is so crowded and chaotic, each campaign surrogate is trailed by a staffer carrying a sign—called a lollipop—with the surrogate's name on it, so the media knows who is available.

The reporters shout out questions. No prescreening. No filter. Cameras, recorders, and notepads take down your every word. It's a stressful environment. The press team is there, setting up times for television "hits" with the various networks. They also can help pull you away from any situation that does not seem to be going all that well. I was rescued more than a few times over the course of the campaign by Arianna Jones, Sarah Ford, or Symone Sanders.

Bernie had asked if he should make an appearance in the spin room. Tad assured him that the only time candidates come to the spin room is when they have had a disastrous performance and need to do something desperate to rehabilitate themselves.

Everything seemed to be going well until Bernie was contacted by MSNBC's Andrea Mitchell to do an interview. His plan was to slip into the spin room and go to the MSNBC booth and then slip out again. Oh, the best-laid plans! The second that Bernie (accompanied by Michael Briggs, Phil Fiermonte, and Shannon Jackson—carrying the "Bernie Sanders" lollipop!) stepped into the room, the media swarmed him. I was across the room and saw a tremendous amount of commotion. But it was impossible to see what was going on through the throngs of reporters and cameras.

In the rush to get to Bernie, the press corps was essentially trampling Andrea Mitchell. She started to go down and Bernie took over. Here's the Yahoo! News report from Hunter Walker:

> In the wake of his debate performance, Sanders' arrival in the spin room led to a near-stampede as reporters and cameramen rushed over to speak to him. The pack of press followed him as he walked out of the spin room.
>
> Yahoo News was standing right behind Sanders as the human surge began to knock Mitchell off balance. Sanders threw his hands out and pushed the crowd away as he shouted for people to move back. As the crowd began to part he reached over to Mitchell, who was still regaining her footing.

"You all right?" Sanders asked. "Are you OK?"

After checking in with Mitchell, Sanders continued admonishing the crowd to move back.

"All right! You know, excuse me! Please move back! You've almost injured—" Sanders said before trailing off and turning back to Mitchell.

"Are you all right?" he asked again.

"Yeah," Mitchell confirmed. "I'm OK."

Sanders continued to wave his hands and urge the crowd to back up.

"All right now! Stop it!" he declared. "Will the cameras slow it down?"

Sanders then reached out and touched Mitchell's shoulder. Seemingly relieved, she took a deep breath.

"Are you all right?' he asked.

"I'm sorry," Mitchell said. "That was a dangerous situation. I apologize."

Sanders waved off Mitchell's apology. She went on to describe the incident as a "terrible situation."

"You don't apologize. These people," he said trailing off and pointing to the surrounding crowd.

He then proceeded to grant Mitchell an interview. She began by acknowledging the huge crowd Sanders brought into the spin room.

"There's a lesson in this," Mitchell said to Sanders. "Obviously, you did very well. You've been on fire tonight."

Bernie had rescued one of the nation's top journalistic talents from her own media colleagues. Walker's account, while detailed, doesn't begin to capture the genuine interaction between Bernie and Andrea Mitchell. Thankfully, the video of the event is widely available on the internet.

Mitchell's remark that "There's a lesson in this" was true. Bernie never went near a spin room again.

The next morning, he appeared at the American Postal Workers Union

National Convention in Las Vegas. And then he was off to the West Coast. Over the course of the rest of the month, he made appearances on numerous national shows: with Ellen DeGeneres, Bill Maher, Tavis Smiley, Jimmy Kimmel, Jesse Jackson, and on *The View*. Much of the rest of the time was spent in Iowa.

Of course, politics is not an endeavor where you just go your merry way without outside events interfering. The third week of October brought us important events completely out of our control. The first was the decision by Vice President Joe Biden to pass on the presidential race. Throughout the summer and fall there had been a tremendous amount of political speculation about whether he would jump in. It was obviously a difficult and very personal decision for him, given the loss of his beloved son Beau on May 30, 2015. Joe Biden had been a U.S. senator and was vice president, but he is known equally as a deeply loving and devoted father. Given his loss, many thought that understandably he would not be able to dedicate his entire being to a competitive run for president.

There had been news stories for months; people were trying to read the tea leaves. A majority offered evidence that he would in fact run. As widely reported in the media, there were meetings with DNC officials, labor leaders, and big-dollar donors. There were public statements by people who had spoken with the vice president that indicated he would run.

As detailed by Glenn Thrush in *Politico* in the summer of 2016, President Obama during this time was working behind the scenes to dissuade Joe Biden from running and to bolster Hillary Clinton's campaign. President Obama's interest was in preserving his legacy, and the powers that be viewed Hillary Clinton as the strongest general election candidate. Thrush notes that the president's political director fed the vice president "a steady diet of polls showing a steep uphill climb," while longtime Obama aide David Plouffe warned the vice president that his candidacy could place third in Iowa behind Bernie Sanders.

An October 14, 2015, email suggests that Ron Klain, the vice president's former chief of staff, also played a role in torpedoing a run by Joe Biden. Klain emailed John Podesta, "Thanks for inviting me into the campaign, and for sticking with me during the Biden anxiety. You are a great friend and a great leader. It's been a little hard for me to play such a role in the Biden demise—and I am definitely dead to them—but I'm glad to be on Team HRC."

In our campaign there was a division of opinion about whether a Biden candidacy would be a positive or a negative for us. On the positive side, the vice president's entry into the race could split the Democratic establishment that was lining up behind Hillary Clinton. That split would be seen in terms of endorsements and money. If the vice president was successful enough, the split in the establishment could push Hillary Clinton into third place (which would have set off a mass panic on the part of the establishment forces that were dumping big-dollar contributions into her campaign and pro-Clinton super PACs). It could have also propelled Bernie Sanders to the top in many contests.

On the other hand, Biden's strong connection with working-class voters could have created competition for rank-and-file labor votes—although the vice president's support of the Trans-Pacific Partnership would have weighed against him. There was also a concern that, had the vice president run, the president would have felt compelled to support him in a more public way than he had Hillary Clinton, and earlier in the process.

Bernie, for his part, was not going to change his game plan based on speculation. He wanted whatever information was available, but he did not waste a lot of time trying to guess what the vice president would do. In his mind, Joe Biden would either run or he would not. Bernie Sanders would continue doing what he was doing regardless of who was in or out.

Of course, Vice President Biden did not run. On October 21, 2015, Tad and I were waiting to meet reporters for lunch. They called Tad and canceled. The vice president had an announcement. Tad and I decided to stay, have lunch at the bar, and watch the vice president on the TVs there.

When we saw Vice President Joe Biden standing at a podium on the White House grounds with the president at his side, we knew that he was not going to run. That in and of itself was not all that surprising. What was surprising was the speech he gave. He decried income inequality, called for free college tuition, criticized the political establishment, and on and on. As Thrush reported, Tad looked at me and said, "Holy shit! That's our message. That's what we're running on." Indeed it was. The most interesting part of Joe Biden's speech was that it was clearly made from a draft of remarks meant to announce his candidacy for president. If you took the word "not" out of it, it was his announcement speech.

The media went into a frenzy anointing Hillary Clinton the nominee almost immediately after. CNN reported that Joe Biden's decision put "Hillary Clinton in a stronger position to capture the Democratic nomination." In my personal view, it did benefit her campaign. But it didn't help to hear it echoing through the media. And there was virtually no coverage that the vice president of the United States had endorsed the platform that Bernie Sanders was running on.

Vice President Biden's decision to not run was followed on the twenty-second by Hillary Clinton's eleven-hour appearance before the U.S. House select committee investigating the deaths of four Americans in Benghazi, Libya. The Republicans showed up in force to take on Hillary Clinton. Let's say it wasn't even a fair fight. She demolished them.

There were certainly aspects of Hillary Clinton's tenure as secretary of state that could be criticized from a policy perspective—and during the campaign we did criticize her in that regard. She was a military interventionist who holidayed with Henry Kissinger. She had promoted fracking technology internationally, and she had said glowing things about the Trans-Pacific Partnership. But laying the tragic deaths in Benghazi at her feet personally came across as the unprincipled political attack it was.

The positive impact of that hearing on her campaign with Democratic voters could not have been greater if she had choreographed it herself. There she was, going toe-to-toe with a gaggle of Republicans who could barely throw a punch, let alone land one. The Republicans' position was made all the worse because House majority leader Kevin McCarthy had admitted on Fox News only a few weeks before that the purpose of the Benghazi hearings was to hurt Hillary Clinton politically.

Well, the Republicans' ham-fisted overreach backfired. As Reuters wrote, "This partisan battle became an opportunity for Clinton to display her leadership skills. As her Republican congressional opponents got into screaming matches, she sat back, smiled and shook her head at the divisiveness and pettiness of Congress."

From our point of view, the Republicans had played right into Hillary Clinton's hands. They had unified Democrats behind a candidate they rightfully perceived was the subject of a political inquisition and had given Hillary Clinton an opportunity to show her mettle. And she did not disappoint.

In the aftermath of her annihilation of the Republicans on the Benghazi committee, the Clinton camp began to go aggressively on the attack against Bernie. The goal of the new attack was to paint Bernie as a misogynist for his comments on gun control during the CNN debate. In discussing his record on gun control, he had said, as reported by NPR:

> As a senator from a rural state, what I can tell Secretary Clinton [is] that all the shouting in the world is not going to do what I would hope all of us want, and that is keep guns out of the hands of people who should not have those guns and end this horrible violence that we are seeing.
>
> I believe that there is a consensus in this country. A consensus has said we need to strengthen and expand instant background checks, do away with this gun show loophole, that we have to address the issue of mental health, that we have to deal with the strawman purchasing issue, and that when we develop that consensus, we can finally, finally do something to address this issue.

As Tamara Keith reported in the same story, Bernie had used similar language months earlier, in August 2015, to describe the gun debate in America during a CNN interview:

> Coming from a rural state, which has almost no gun control, I think I can get beyond the noise and all of these arguments and people shouting at each other and come up with real constructive

gun control legislation, which most significantly gets guns out of the hands of people who should not have them.

In fact, Bernie's statements represented his view. Since he had come to Congress, the issue of gun control had become an increasingly partisan issue. Before, it had been largely a rural/urban issue. This, in part, allowed the Republicans to make huge inroads into rural America, while Democrats lost there. Even so, there is a large consensus among voters—both rural and urban—on a number of gun safety measures, such as universal background checks. But in Bernie's view, there seemed to be more interest in fighting than in solving the issue, more interest in making partisan points than in making progress.

The reality is that in Vermont, during deer season (the two weeks ending the weekend after Thanksgiving), hunters can be seen everywhere with firearms. No one feels unsafe; you drive by dozens of people on country roads carrying loaded high-powered rifles. From my own experience growing up in a rural area, often the most prominent item in someone's house is a glass case with the guns on display and ammunition stored right below. No doubt that is the case in rural communities across America. By bringing regular people together, rather than the lobbies on both sides, a national consensus for keeping guns out of the hands of people who shouldn't have them could be crafted.

But the day after the Benghazi hearing, and fully ten days after the CNN debate, Hillary Clinton turned her perceived disagreement with Bernie on gun control into a charge that he was sexist. Tamara Keith quoted Clinton: "I've been told to stop, and, I quote, 'shouting about gun violence.' Well, first of all, I'm not shouting. It's just, when women talk, some people think we're shouting." Ten days after the CNN debate, the Clinton campaign—through the candidate herself—had fired the first volley in their Bernie-is-sexist narrative. I unfortunately would walk into the same line of fire about a week later in Iowa after the Jefferson-Jackson Dinner—the "JJ."

The JJ is in most ways the premier political event in the Iowa caucus process. It is an event attended by thousands, with a stage in the round where all the Democratic Party's candidates address the crowd. Around the stage is a seated area where dinner is served. Beyond that are rows of chairs where dinner is not served. And beyond that the walls are lined with bleachers. The bleachers are divided by candidate, which has the effect of creating cheering sections. The event is a huge fund-raiser for the Iowa Democratic Party; tickets must be purchased to attend. As we had done in the past, we bought only a few seats in the more expensive area up front and many more tickets in the bleacher area.

To make their splash, the Clinton campaign had Katy Perry perform a free outdoor concert before the JJ. That was pretty hard to top. Our plan was to hold a rally and then march across a bridge with a mass of supporters to the doors of the hall where the JJ was being held. It ended up being a powerful visual, with throngs of people crossing and with Bernie in the lead. As CNN reported, Hillary Clinton broke with the long-standing tradition that candidates march with their supporters to the dinner. Her supporters had to walk to the JJ without her.

We did have a little fun that day. After months slogging it out in Iowa, the local team and I decided to try a little creative campaigning. Katy Perry's Super Bowl performance back in February 2015 had created a sensation because one of the two costumed dancing sharks that accompanied her seemed to be out of sync with the dance routine. Appropriately, from our point of view, it was the "left" shark who seemed not to be with the program. Pete D'Alessandro got the idea that we should have a Bernie left shark attend the Katy Perry concert, so he ordered a shark costume. Our own left shark then went to the concert wearing a Bernie t-shirt and danced out in front of the event.

In addition, we wanted to reach all the young people who were going to the Katy Perry concert. We knew it would be a big hit—some of our own volunteers were going to see the show. Handing out literature or standing around with signs would have been inappropriate. So I decided we would take to the air. Not the airwaves but literally to the air. During the concert we hired a small plane with a Bernie banner trailing behind to circle the area. The banner read, "Revolution Starts Now Feel the Bern." It was a great morale booster. The Bernie Air Force was flying.

Antics aside, the JJ was an important night, as it always is in Iowa. That meant that Bernie's speech had to be great. A group of us including Jane, Tad, and Briggs met with Bernie to talk through it. The tone between the candidates was beginning to get testier. Bernie had gone high instead of low during the CNN debate when asked about Hillary Clinton's emails. She had returned the favor by suggesting he was a sexist ten days later. There were sharp differences between the two on substantive policy.

On issue after issue, Hillary Clinton was late to the party, whether it was the Trans-Pacific Partnership, the Keystone pipeline, gay marriage, mass incarceration, or gun control. Her positions over time "modulated" to reflect the mood of whatever electorate she was trying to win over. Bernie's record, on the other hand, had a marked consistency over the course of decades. In addition, she was still out of sync with Democratic voters on important issues like fracking and her interventionist foreign policy leanings.

The trick was finding a way to articulate those differences, and the fact that Bernie was there when it was not politically popular, without directly calling out Secretary Clinton. Tad suggested using the rhetorical device of political forks in the road. When confronted with difficult political choices, Bernie chose one direction. Others took the alternate, easier path. That then became the foundation for the speech.

In addition, we suggested that people could depend on Bernie as president even when things got politically difficult: "I pledge to you that every day I will fight for the public interest, not the corporate interests. I will not abandon any segment of American society—whether you're gay or black or Latino or poor or working class—just because it is politically expedient at a given time." This alluded to several of the policy differences between the two, where Hillary Clinton had taken the wrong fork in the road: on the Defense of Marriage Act, the punitive aspects of the Crime Bill, turning back unaccompanied minors from Central America, the Welfare Reform Bill, and unfair, antiworker trade bills.

The speech was written as we drove the byways of Iowa. Now for the delivery. Bernie likes to give his speeches standing at a podium with his handwritten notes. The issue was that the stage at the Iowa JJ was in the round. A large part of the audience would be behind him. In addition, there were teleprompters at floor level around the stage. Bernie decided he wanted to give his remarks in his traditional way regardless, so we conveyed that to the Iowa Democrats.

All the candidates were held in an area separate from the crowd. Bernie made a point of introducing me to Secretary Clinton. Robby Mook, her campaign manager, was also there. It turned out that he and I were wearing the exact same outfit. When I say identical, I mean identical. We were even wearing the same Johnston & Murphy shoes. (I just bought another pair of them recently. I call them my "Robby Mooks.") The other staff and some of the media got a big kick out of it.

The candidates were called in and introduced to the boisterous crowd. They then went to their respective tables as the party chair and various candidates running for other offices spoke first. I made my way back to the bleachers, where our supporters were amassed. A little while later a staffer came up and said that Bernie wanted to see me right away. I headed over to his table.

Bernie said that the event was in the round and that his normal way of speaking from behind the podium with notes wasn't going to work. He wanted us to load his speech into the teleprompter. He said, "Jeff, I am going to use the teleprompter, but I'm not going to follow the script exactly. I am going to add some stuff and move some of the parts around. Then I might go back to some parts I skipped. Can you work with the teleprompter person so they keep up with me?"

I got an electronic copy of his speech to load in the teleprompter and to meet the teleprompter operator. I brought her the copy of the speech, apologized, and asked if I could sit there and guide her. She was a real trouper and extremely proficient. I was feeling bad about this last-minute imposition when a Clinton aide ran up and said he had the final version of Clinton's speech to be loaded in. This obviously created even more work for the teleprompter operator, but I did feel some consolation that at least we weren't the only ones changing things up at the last minute.

When Bernie took the stage, his supporters exploded with chants and cheers. He had kept his printed notes with him, and he placed them on a music stand that had been provided. He always liked to have the printed notes with him as a backup, even on the rare occasions he used a teleprompter. He began by making the point that the Republicans seemed to forget the disastrous state of the economy when President Obama took office. None of this was in his prepared remarks.

Then he went to the script; but he jumped down a few paragraphs from the beginning. Because I was part of the speechwriting process, I was very familiar with the material. The teleprompter operator told me to just tell her where to move things. We were off and running. We jumped back and forth through the speech, waiting at times as Bernie added new material. Both the teleprompter operator and I were more than a little stressed. If she didn't have the right material up at the right moment, the flow of the barn-berner of a speech he was delivering would be interrupted. Well over twenty minutes later he finished, to thunderous applause. No one watching knew about the stressful teleprompter operation going on behind the scenes.

Hillary Clinton spoke after Bernie. Many of our people who had been standing in the bleachers for hours without food started to file out. Clinton supporters tried to paint them as rude or as false Democrats. I think they were just tired and hungry.

After the event was over, the presidential candidates and their families took the stage. Bill Clinton came over to Bernie and Jane, put his arms around each of them, and said how "proud" he was of both of them. It came across as wildly condescending.

Following the JJ Dinner, Tad, Briggs, Phil Fiermonte, and I had a scheduled interview with John Heilemann. We met in a hotel room in the DoubleTree hotel by the Des Moines airport. We usually stayed at that hotel when we were in town. It was convenient to the airport and was sufficiently far from the downtown Marriott, where most of the media stayed, that there was a modicum of peace. Heilemann sprang for the pizza. Little did I know as we started talking that I was about to walk into the crosshairs of the Clinton campaign's "Bernie and his people are all sexists" narrative.

Heilemann's article is readily available online, but the critical moment came when he asked me if I thought that Hillary Clinton was "a craven hypocrite and opportunist." His article reports my response this way, " 'A craven hypocrite?' Weaver replied, grinning slyly. 'That's a little bit harsh, don't you think?' Then he added, with a chuckle, 'Look, she'd make a great vice president. We're willing to give her more credit than Obama did. We're willing to consider her for vice president. We'll give her serious consideration. We'll even interview her.' "

Admittedly inartful. But there was a sincere point there. The Clinton campaign was increasingly trying to position her as an Obama loyalist whom the president had chosen to be secretary of state. The tactic of trying to stand in the Obama glow was one that they would employ throughout the campaign, especially when we were competing in states with a lot of African American voters. Everyone apparently forgot the acrimonious campaign that the two had engaged in in 2008, and that President Obama had, as a matter of fact, chosen Joe Biden to be vice president rather than Hillary Clinton. In my humble opinion, she was overplaying her closeness with the president. My sarcastic reply was meant to convey that. Others took it as a sexist attack on Hillary Clinton's qualifications.

At this point in the campaign, we had only really begun to engage the Clinton campaign, having spent the summer and the first debate introducing Bernie to the country. The pile-on from the Clinton campaign and their surrogates was impressive following my VP remark. It included a full-court press in the media and a major tweetstorm. It was effective, and our response, which was to more or less let it die down, was not. Lesson learned.

If this exchange had happened in the spring of 2016, when we were in a more forward posture, the response would have been simple. If my half-joking comments, as misinterpreted as they were, represented sexism, what "-ism" did Bill Clinton's serious suggestion that Barack Obama drop out in 2008 and become Hillary Clinton's vice president represent? At the time, Bill Clinton made those remarks, Barack Obama was ahead in the delegate count.

The social media response was not good. There was a push from parts of the campaign for an apology, an idea that no one at the top of the campaign supported. Bernie did end up referring to the comments as "inappropriate" when pressed in a television interview. It didn't bother me. We had a crisis, and it had to be overcome.

The rest of a very hectic October was dominated by two events. The first was a National Student Town Hall meeting at George Mason University in Fairfax, Virginia. The event was streamed online to some 250 other locations on campuses in all 50 states. It was a remarkable event for a couple of reasons. Bernie announced his position that the federal government should remove marijuana from the list of prohibited drugs under the Controlled Substances Act. This would leave regulation of marijuana to the states. It was the position he had been leaning toward throughout the discussions in the campaign. And before thousands—attending in person or via livestream—Bernie put it on the table. The second came during a spontaneous moment during the question-and-answer period. Remaz Abdelgader, a Muslim student, expressed concern about growing Islamophobia in the United States. Bernie was moved by her question. He brought her on stage and embraced her. And then he described his commitment to fighting racism, invoking the killing of his own family members at the hands of the Nazi regime. That kind of personal response was rare from Bernie. He hates to talk about himself. It's only about the issues. His personal story was made only more powerful by the image of an older Jewish man standing with a young Muslim women united against racism.

My two boys were with me that night at George Mason University. I don't think they understood the significance of that moment, but I was proud that they were there. Bernie's concern for the plight of American Muslims would earn him broad support in that community throughout the primaries.

Another significant event at the end of October was a meeting between Bernie and Vice President Biden. I cannot reveal all the details of the meeting, but I think it is fair to say that the vice president was not unsympathetic, as anyone who had heard his nonannouncement speech would have figured out. It's an understatement to say that he was not a fan of the Clintons.

That would be confirmed when, in a CNN interview with Gloria Barger, he praised Bernie: "Bernie is speaking to a yearning that is deep and real, and he has credibility on it. And that is the absolute enormous concentration of wealth in a small group of people." About Clinton, he said, "It's relatively new for Hillary to talk about that." It was widely viewed as a swipe at Hillary Clinton, despite his effort to massage his remarks the next day. He also spoke favorably about Bernie's position on gun safety—something that Hillary Clinton was trying to make an issue.

As reported by CNN's Dan Merica in March 2017, Biden continued his criticism that the Clinton campaign failed to focus on the kitchen-table issues facing middle- and working-class Americans during the 2016 election: "This was the first campaign that I can recall where my party did not talk about what it always stood for—and that was how to maintain a burgeoning middle class. You didn't hear a single solitary sentence in the last campaign about that guy working on the assembly line making $60,000 bucks a year and a wife making $32,000 as a hostess in restaurant. And they are making $90,000 and they have two kids and they can't make it and they are scared, they are frightened."

You tell 'em, Joe!

9

FROM INSURGENCY TO VIABILITY

AS THE SUMMER OF SANDERS turned into the eventful fall, we had succeeded in demonstrating the tremendous energy and enthusiasm there was for Bernie all across the country. And the public polling in the first two states confirmed it. The *Des Moines Register* poll taken at the end of May had Hillary Clinton leading by 41 points. Their poll done at the end of August had Clinton's lead down to 7 points. The mid-July NBC News/Marist New Hampshire poll had Hillary Clinton up 10 points. The same poll at the end of August had Bernie up by 9 points.

Despite all the attempts to minimize or marginalize the huge summer crowds, Bernie's campaign had caught fire from one end of the country to the other. Unable to dispute the thousands and in some cases tens of thousands of people coming out to hear him, his critics argued that crowds were one thing, but getting votes was quite another. On that point they were certainly right. Organizing the huge numbers of people that Bernie had mobilized was a daunting task.

But even though there was still a tremendous amount of skepticism publicly, the Clinton campaign wasn't buying its own spin, even if the media was. They knew they were losing ground. On August 3, they began spending millions of dollars on television advertising in Iowa and New Hampshire. They would be on the air in both those states until their respective February contests—approximately six months' worth of un-interrupted advertising in the first two states.

The Clinton campaign's decision to go on television so early put us in a difficult position. Should we respond in kind? Or were they wasting a bunch of money that would eat into their financial advantage? We were hampered in our decision making by our lack of a pollster. Without one, it was impossible to know for sure how voters were responding, because we had no way of asking them directly, either with polls or focus groups. We were flying without instruments.

Bernie resisted hiring a pollster at that time. He was concerned that a pollster would try to change his messaging for political advantage. Bernie already knew what his message to the American people would be, so he certainly didn't need a pollster for that—in his mind, he didn't need one at all. I think it's fair to describe his position as adamant.

Bernie did understand the power of television, however. We met to discuss how to respond. Bernie wanted to hear people's views. He was of two minds on the issue. I was leaning toward going on the air. We had a problem with name ID, and television ads would help fix that (as they did later in the campaign). Television ads, for all their limitations, also would have allowed us to deliver a message straight to voters without filtering by the media or spin by our opponents. Given all the media focus on Clinton's emails, I'm sure the Clinton campaign felt the same way.

Tad Devine was the one who ultimately prevailed, with his view that we hold off. He viewed the Clinton campaign's move as one of weakness. Tad thought that we should keep our powder dry, given the resource imbalance between the campaigns. He preferred that we maximize the impact of our advertising when voters would be paying more attention closer to the election.

It turned out to be the right decision. I had doubts at the time. We were relying on instinct, experience, and judgment without the benefit of concrete research about the effectiveness of the Clinton ad campaign. For now, we would end up relying on public polling to monitor the race.

That would change on October 1, when we brought on Ben Tulchin to do our polling. Ben's team included senior analyst Ben Krompak and analyst Kiel Brunner. Ben Tulchin first met Bernie back in March, in the lobby of a boutique hotel in San Francisco. Tulchin had heard that Bernie was going to be in town and had asked Tad and Mark to set up a meeting.

Amid the art deco décor, Bernie spent most of the time asking Tulchin why he should hire a pollster at all. Bernie asked, "Ben, explain to me why I should spend money from my supporters, who may be living off of Social Security, on polling?" Tulchin made the case then that I and others would make in the summer and early fall, and which Bernie ultimately found persuasive. The point of polling was not to craft Bernie's message or measure the horse race. Rather, it was key to understanding the race in a way that would allow us to target what was becoming a substantial amount of resources. For instance, it would help us figure out what parts of Bernie's already existing message should be highlighted in television ads. Bernie, after all, had an almost two-hour stump speech. We couldn't put it all on television. Only Donald Trump had the luxury of having almost every speech broadcast on television in its entirety. Polling data would also let us target resources among the states. We were raising money in the summer and fall, but still we would not be able to spend with equal intensity everywhere. Hard choices had to be made, and they could only be made with research. It was this efficiency argument that really made the most sense to Bernie. It appealed to his Yankee frugality. Now that we were raising money, it had to be spent wisely.

In October, we polled the first four states and also Georgia. There was good news in the polling, but there were also some serious warning signs. Almost all the polling (except in South Carolina) was done after the CNN debate, because we wanted to make sure we captured any bump (or decline) that the debate would cause. In Iowa, our polling showed us down 18 points (53 to 35). That was a huge deficit, and it showed some erosion in support from earlier public polls. Because Vice President Biden had not dropped out yet, we also polled with him in the race. In that scenario, it was Clinton, 45; Sanders, 33; Biden, 13. Clinton's margin was cut by a third. In the Hawkeye State, Biden was taking far more from Clinton than from us.

In New Hampshire, the poll had Bernie up by 5 points (48 to 43). This was very similar to the public polls at the end of the summer. With Biden in the race, the result was Sanders, 42; Clinton, 37; Biden, 12. Biden took about equally from each candidate.

Nevada was a much tougher state for Bernie. Hillary Clinton was ahead by 33 points (61 to 28). As in Iowa, Biden's entry into the race would have helped Bernie. The result in that case was Clinton, 48; Sanders, 23; and Biden, 20—a deficit of 25.

South Carolina was even worse. Clinton was ahead by 52 points (69 to 17). Adding Biden helped somewhat, with Clinton taking 51 percent, Sanders at 12 percent, and Biden at 25 percent. That lowered Bernie's deficit against Clinton to 39 points but pushed him into a solid third place. Regardless of whether Biden was in or not, South Carolina was going to be a tough state for the campaign.

Because the polling in South Carolina was not positive, we decided to test another southern state to see if we might find one that was more favorable. We wanted to make a stand somewhere in the South, but we wanted to invest resources where they would most likely produce results. We decided to test Georgia. It was better, but only barely. Clinton was ahead, 69 to 20—still a 49-point gap. With Biden in the race, the outcome was Clinton, 51; Biden, 28; and Sanders, 16. That was a 35-point gap with Clinton. Ouch!

Given that South Carolina and Georgia were very similar, we decided to fight in South Carolina because it was smaller and less expensive. The South Carolina primary was only a couple of days before most of the other southern states voted. If we could improve there and have a respectable showing, it might produce a bump a couple of days later.

Overall, our situation was precarious. In Iowa, we were down almost 20 points. Hillary Clinton erased Barack Obama's lead and won New Hampshire in 2008, even though he had finished solidly in first place in the Iowa caucus. If we really stumbled in Iowa, our single-digit lead in New Hampshire could very well evaporate. Our weakness in Nevada and South Carolina gave greater weight to the need for momentum coming out of the first two states. In addition, it was clear we had to increase our support among African American and Latino voters.

One issue that weighed on voters' minds was Bernie's electability. It is a sad irony, given the outcome in November 2016, that a year earlier we were spending time and resources trying to figure out how to convey to voters that Bernie Sanders was more electable than Hillary Clinton. As early as the summer of 2015, public polling consistently showed that Bernie Sanders was a stronger candidate against Trump (and most of the other Republicans) than Hillary Clinton would be. The media minimized and dismissed these polls as soon as they reported them.

As part of his presentation to get retained by the campaign, Ben Tulchin prepared a memo at the end of July showing that Bernie was the only major contender who had net positive ratings with voters. Ben's data came from public polls. Bernie was beating all the Republicans tested, even though only 45 percent of voters in a CNN/ORC poll conducted in late July had enough information to give him positive or negative ratings. Hillary Clinton, on the other hand, was underwater with voters (as were all the Republicans tested) and looked to be slipping with voters since her announcement.

Our internal polling did reveal a number of bright points, which Ben Tulchin laid out in an October 30 memo. The first point was that, despite still being behind, Bernie had made considerable gains with voters since his announcement with no paid media whatsoever. He was even winning in New Hampshire. The Clinton campaign had been on TV in New Hampshire and Iowa since August 6. The other important fact was that the two central issues of Bernie's campaign—wealth and income inequality and a corrupt campaign finance system—were the top issues for Democratic primary voters.

The information from Tulchin's polling would guide the program of paid television and radio advertising that the campaign began in November. To continue the process of introducing Bernie to voters in Iowa and New Hampshire, we would present a biographical ad that tracked him from his childhood, through his years in college fighting segregation, to being mayor of Burlington, to his time in Congress. We would follow that up with a pair of ads that combined the two most powerful elements of Bernie's platform—a rigged economy held up by a corrupt system of campaign finance. The third piece would be an effectiveness ad that highlighted his record of accomplishments in Congress and as mayor of Burlington. Finally, we decided to run testimonial ads, including one from a dairy farmer and one from a nurse—both Vermonters. There is no better validator than your neighbor. We wanted people in Iowa and New Hampshire to see that Vermonters sincerely supported Bernie.

This new research also allowed us to flesh out the state-by-state road map to the nomination that Mark Longabaugh had developed and was continually refining. Winning a presidential nomination is not a single contest like a Senate race. It is fought out serially in every state and territory and in the District of Columbia and with Democrats abroad (American Democrats living abroad who vote in a worldwide primary).

Our early focus was the first four states. As an insurgent campaign, we had to win early. We knew Bernie would not get support from most of the establishment without a strong show of strength. Early wins would also demonstrate to the media, our small donors, our volunteers, and voters that this was a campaign that could go the distance. That strong focus on the first four contests meant that the vast majority of Bernie's time was spent in those states.

The strategy fit well with his idea of how Bernie wanted to run. The first four states rely heavily on the person-to-person grassroots organizing that he prefers. He saw his national rallies as a complement to our work on the ground in the early states. "The people in Iowa watch the national news," he would remind us, whenever we suggested that he spend more time on the ground in the early states. To him, the large rallies he would hold throughout the fall all over the country were a key element to doing well in the first four.

A heavy focus on the first four was in line with my thinking on creating local superiority against the Clinton juggernaut. In military terms, local superiority is achieved when a smaller force concentrates its numbers on one part of the battlefield, or in one battle, to gain a numerical advantage that allows it to defeat one part of a larger force. This can be followed up by defeating the larger force piecemeal or by inflicting enough damage that the larger force ultimately loses the will to fight. Because we were outmatched organizationally, the only way to prevail, in my view, was to institutionally and financially achieve local superiority.

We could be as big as they were, if we were focused in terms of resource allocation and Bernie's time. In these smaller states, the Clinton resource advantage would be irrelevant. We could bring as many forces to bear as they could—or more than they could.

Of the first four states, New Hampshire seemed like the most likely place for us to score a victory. It was our "must-win" if we were to have any chance at the nomination. New Hampshire was next door to Vermont. Vermont television bled into western and northern New Hampshire, so the voters there had seen Bernie on TV for decades.

We would also have to make an early play for Iowa. We were behind in Iowa, and we would have to contend with the state's complicated caucus process. But much of Iowa is small towns and rural communities— places like those in which Bernie did very well in Vermont. And unlike New Hampshire, Iowa had never taken to the Clintons. Hillary Clinton had lost in 2008, as had Bill Clinton in 1992.

Nevada and South Carolina, as our polling revealed, would be tougher. Tad, in particular, was of the view that victory in the first four states would constitute a knockout blow from which the Clinton campaign would not be able to recover. That seemed like a forbiddingly ambitious goal, but we would play for the early knockout. Tad's resolve strengthened at the end of the third quarter, when we came within $2 million of Clinton's fund-raising total. Given our lower burn rate, driven in part by our decision to not follow Clinton when she went up on TV, we could potentially achieve an overall resource advantage.

Tad's thinking went this way: The Clinton campaign was relying primarily on larger donors—many of whom had given the federal maximum. They were under pressure to find new donors. We, on the other hand, were relying on many more small donors who had the capacity to give repeatedly. Our gaining a resource advantage would spook her prospective donors. The Clinton campaign could find itself in a money pinch. Winning the first four states could spell the end of their campaign. Achieving a win in the first four seemed very unlikely, but everything that we had accomplished up to that point had been unlikely—at best.

In the event that didn't happen (and unfortunately it did not), the path would be a long slog to the convention using Mark's road map. We would still have to do well in the early states. We would have to win New Hampshire and beat expectations in Iowa. We would have to avoid being "killed" in Nevada and South Carolina. Then we would fight for wins every week thereafter when there was a contest.

Mark's go-the-distance road map also identified key battleground states. Very early on, we knew Michigan would be one. It was relatively early in the calendar (March 8). It was a diverse state, and one that had been devastated by the very trade deals that, over the years, Bernie had opposed and Clinton had supported. If we were doing well at the time of the Michigan primary, it would confirm Bernie's momentum. If we were not, it would serve as a reset going into delegate-rich March 15, when Missouri, Illinois, Ohio, North Carolina, and Florida held their contests.

During the fall and early winter, we accelerated our staffing so we could compete in the first four and beyond. At the end of July, we had only twenty-nine staffers nationwide. We started adding state directors in many of the eleven states that held primaries and caucuses on March 1.

By February 1, the date of the Iowa caucus, we reached a peak of some 1,200 staff and paid canvassers. It was a herculean effort to recruit, vet, and deploy that many people in only a few months. In terms of vetting, we checked criminal backgrounds, social media usage, and other sources. All campaign staffers have to go through a vetting process, and the vetting of so many candidates bogged down considerably in the fall.

I made a conscious decision that our campaign would practice what it preached in terms of helping people who had had encounters with the criminal justice system reintegrate into civil society. Domestic violence and crimes against children were automatically disqualifying. No one else was automatically disqualified. If anyone's vetting revealed any other criminal conviction, I personally reviewed the case. In virtually every case, the otherwise qualified applicant was hired. By magnitudes, far more people were not hired because of the content of their social media activity than because of a criminal conviction. On a campaign of our size, it goes without saying that there were a number of problems that arose. However, I am not aware of a single instance in which the hiring of a staffer with a criminal record was the source of any of them.

10

THE TABLES BEGIN TO TURN

MANY PEOPLE HAVE WONDERED WHEN the campaign really returned to the momentum it had throughout the spring after the setbacks in October. To my mind, it really began in November and was propelled by four critical events. The first was our entrance into the paid media market. The second was the CBS presidential debate. The third was the heavy-handed misplay by the DNC in December when the chairwoman tried to shut down the campaign. And the fourth, which was crucial, was Bernie's ability to campaign full time.

Having ceded the Clinton campaign control of the airwaves for three months, we finally aired with our first ads in Iowa and New Hampshire. We finally could speak directly to voters without the media filter—to introduce Bernie as a person and to present to the nation his powerful message of building a more equitable society.

There is a lot of criticism that television ads (too often negative) are used as a substitute for a grassroots campaign that has a real message and an authentic messenger. I share that criticism, to the extent that campaigns devolve into air wars with little substantive debate or involvement by the people who actually are going to have to vote for one of the candidates.

Bad candidates may have the appearance of strength because their monetary advantage convinces the political and media establishment that their ability to dominate the airwaves will assure victory.

But I can also say that television advertising—when used as a complement to, rather than a substitute for, a grassroots campaign—is extremely powerful in communicating with voters. In fact, empirically, it is the single most powerful tool. Some in the progressive movement have become so disgusted with the role of big money (a feeling I most certainly share) that they advocate abandoning television. It is hugely expensive. This cost is seen as one of the drivers of the constant quest for campaign dollars. That's a great position, if you want to make a point. It's a horrible position if you want to actually win an election.

As we were to learn, being wildly overmatched on television cannot be overcome with a ground game. You have to do it all. You have to build a grassroots effort and you have to be on television. And online and in the mail and a bunch of other places. You don't need to have the greatest number of ads, but you have to have enough. What is enough depends upon the contest; and is not always clear before the voting takes place. In a presidential campaign, enough is a lot.

Of course, the real answer to this problem is reforming the campaign finance system by overturning *Citizens United* and implementing various public matching or public financing proposals. This will create a more level playing field in terms of candidates' ability to speak to voters, because more candidates will have access to TV and a host of other media. Big money won't monopolize the airwaves. Candidates who can mobilize a grassroots following will be able to compete.

The second big turning point was the second Democratic presidential primary debate, held at Drake University in Iowa, although it certainly didn't seem like that was going to be the case the afternoon before the debate. Enter the White Rabbit.

Before every debate there is a large media contingent waiting at the debate location for the event to begin and to interview people in the spin room afterward. During this time the campaigns try to pre-spin the press. Tad describes it as releasing a white rabbit in the room—and then the media chase it around for a few hours before the debate. If they chase your white rabbit, you influence the pre-debate story line. If a campaign is unscrupulous, it can put out a half-baked story that will get pushed out by the media online and on social media before the debate, and there will never be a chance to correct it. Coverage of the debate itself will overtake the media's interest.

On November 14 our opponents released their white rabbit, which the media proceeded to chase. Here's how it went.

The format of each of the debates was negotiated extensively by the campaigns and the sponsoring media organizations beforehand. The media organizations have the ultimate say, but all the campaigns have input. In each of the negotiations, it was our view that the candidates should have an opening statement and a closing statement. The longer the better—it gives each candidate more time to speak directly to the people who matter: the voters.

The media hates the statements, preferring the give-and-take of the debate because it makes for "better TV." They tend to push back on lengthy statements, particularly opening statements. From their perspective, there should be blood on the floor almost immediately.

In the case of the November 14 CBS debate, all the parties involved, including CBS, agreed that each of the three remaining Democratic candidates would have a ninety-second opening statement. Now, ninety seconds is not really that long, but getting the media to agree to statements of a minute and a half each was a huge success.

On November 13, ISIS terrorists launched a cowardly attack on the people of Paris. It dominated the news, and of course we knew that it would become a huge part of the discussion during the debate. In a conference call the afternoon before the debate between the campaigns and CBS, the network informed the campaigns that it was going to eliminate the ninety-second opening statements and replace them with a ninety-second open-ended question about the Paris attacks.

Mark Longabaugh, who was representing our campaign on the

call, pushed back. Of course Paris would be a topic of discussion, but it didn't have to happen at the expense of the opening statements. The moderators could just substitute a Paris-related question for one of the other questions they intended to ask. After all, the campaigns didn't have the questions ahead of time (at least not at this debate; more on that later), so the networks could always change up what they were going to ask.

After the call, one of our opponents promptly picked up a small cage in their work area, walked to the media room, and opened the cage door. Out darted the fluffy, long-eared allegation that Mark was in fact trying to limit debate discussion of the Paris attack—because of course Bernie was wholly unprepared to talk about foreign policy. For the record, the O'Malley people would later blame the Clinton campaign. The Clinton people blamed the O'Malley campaign.

The media immediately went into a frenzy trying to grab the little creature. I had the misfortune of being in the spin room when it was let loose. Annie Karni of *Politico* asked me about it. I told her what I understood from Mark—that we had pushed back on the attempt to eliminate the opening statements and had been successful. However, what was being put out online was that I'd said we were successful in limiting discussion of the Paris attack. C'mon, people. You didn't think we knew we would be talking about Paris the day after the attack?

Social media lit up, and not in a positive way. Our media team saw it immediately. Symone Sanders and Sarah Ford arrived on the scene to extricate me. I called Mark to confirm the details. Meanwhile it was spreading like wildfire. Once one person puts up the story everyone else in the media is compelled to follow suit.

Our defense came from an unlikely source: the DNC. Erik Smith had been given the unenviable job of being the DNC's point person between the campaigns and the sponsoring news organizations over debate logistics issues. Mark called Erik, who had also been on the conference call, and asked him to help set the record straight, which he did.

Some of the media—for instance, CNN's Brianna Keilar and Dan Merica—incorporated Erik's comments in updates to their stories:

But a DNC debate coordinator tells CNN that the argument on the call earlier Saturday was not about whether the debate would focus on Paris, adding that it is unfair to say Sanders' campaign did not want to debate foreign policy.

"No, no," the coordinator said when asked about whether Sanders' aides were worried about debating Paris.

"What happened was that we have had the format of the debate finalized for several weeks," the coordinator said. "CBS wanted to get rid of the opening statements and start with a 30-second answer on Paris. . . . It was never a conversation of whether we talk about foreign policy or not. They just wanted a longer opening comment."

Annie Karni, who was more responsible than any of the rest of the media for creating the scramble for the white rabbit that day, left her story uncorrected. Mission accomplished by our opponents.

The big lesson is that even reputable journalists may stand by stories pushed by unnamed partisans of a campaign well after those stories are debunked by a neutral third party. They might just turn it into a "one person said this and the other person said that" story. The allegation is still hanging out there. Journalists more focused on clickbait don't even bother.

This is the environment in which Donald Trump thrives. He consistently lays out one untrue statement after another, and the media then goes about finding people to say it's not true—turning a false claim into a "President Trump says this and these other folks say the opposite" story. The result is that those predisposed to believe Trump do, and those predisposed to disbelieve him do. But his original outlandish statement gets amplified over and over again as it is repeated on cable news.

It's fair now to ask how, given these developments, the CBS debate gave our campaign new momentum. As the afternoon ended, the scoreboard read: Untrue and Discredited Attacks: 100; Truthful Information for Voters: 0. But social media giveth as well as taketh away. As the debate got under way, it became clear that we had only partially won in the conference call. The candidates got only sixty seconds to open. John Dickerson invited the candidates in that time to "share your thoughts about the attacks in Paris, and lay out your vision for America." In the context of the earlier allegations, talking about anything other than the Paris attacks during the opening remarks (which Bernie did) invited all the talking heads to say that he was avoiding foreign policy. In the Clinton work room, no doubt, staff were busy adding that criticism to the talking points to be taken up in the spin room after the debate.

The debate at Drake was much more contentious than the earlier CNN debate in Las Vegas. The candidates sparred over foreign policy, the minimum wage (Hillary Clinton came out against raising the federal minimum to $15 an hour), and guns (with O'Malley going after both Clinton and Sanders). But the critical moments came when the debate turned to the issue of money that Secretary Clinton had received from Wall Street in the form of speaking fees and campaign dollars.

Bernie and Hillary started to debate the relative merits of their financial reform plans. Then Bernie made the point that large financial interests make contributions because they believe there's a benefit:

> Here's the story. I mean, you know, let's not be naive about it. Why do—why, over her political career has Wall Street been a major—the major campaign contributor to Hillary Clinton? You know, maybe they're dumb and they don't know what they're going to get, but I don't think so.

(All the quotes from the CBS debate are from the transcript published by the *Washington Post*.)

Bernie's articulation of the fact that big corporate donors don't give out of pure generosity threw Secretary Clinton completely off her game. Her response was unbelievable:

> So, I represented New York, and I represented New York on 9/11 when we were attacked. Where were we attacked? We were attacked in downtown Manhattan where Wall Street is. I did spend

a whole lot of time and effort helping them rebuild. That was good for New York. It was good for the economy and it was a way to rebuke the terrorists who had attacked our country.

The only real answer would have been to say that Wall Street can expect whatever they want, but they are not going to get it from me. (That's essentially the line that President Obama's people used.) It's not a great response, but it's the only one there is. Instead, Secretary Clinton used the "9/11 made me do it" defense.

What should have been a political ground rule double was turned into a grand slam when CBS's Nancy Cordes later asked a follow-up to Secretary Clinton based on the following Twitter post from an Iowa voter, which was displayed on the screen: "I've never seen a candidate invoke 9/11 to justify millions of Wall Street donations until now."

I looked over to Tad. "That was devastating," I said. Hillary Clinton would never use the 9/11 defense again, but the questions surrounding her Wall Street ties, particularly the high speaking fees and her refusal to release the transcripts of her speeches, became a real and lingering liability. Later, leaked emails revealed all too clearly why the Clinton campaign preferred to take the political hit for not releasing the speech transcripts rather than just making them public.

As we headed to the spin room, we knew that there would be some media focus on the question of foreign policy chops, but we all knew that the Wall Street gaffe would be the one that voters remembered. It completely validated the central message of our campaign: Americans were hurting because of a rigged economy held up by a corrupt system of campaign finance.

December 16, 2015, started as any other crazy Wednesday in Bernie Sanders' run for the Democratic nomination. That is, until the misdeeds of a few staffers thrust our campaign into what looked like a serious crisis. By the end of the week, the bumbling intervention by DNC chairwoman

Debbie Wasserman Schultz against the campaign gave us perhaps the biggest positive bump to that date.

The crisis first came to my attention when Rich Pelletier, then national field director, called me to let me know that a data firewall failure had occurred in the DNC's voter file, and that other campaigns' information was made available to some of our staff. I instructed Rich to investigate and to inform all staff that they were not to make use of any other campaign's data. At the time, I believed this to be a repeat of a data firewall failure that had occurred back on October 7.

The next morning, in a fit of anger, the chairwoman unilaterally, and in violation of our contract with the DNC, shut off our access to the voter file we had purchased and all the data that our campaign had put into it. As I described it two days later at a national press conference, Debbie Wasserman Schultz had imposed the death penalty on our campaign. Here's why the voter file was so important.

The DNC maintains a central file of all voters in the country by state. The file contains voters' contact information and a wealth of other data—including in which past election the voter has participated, issues that a voter is interested in, and, in many cases, whom the voter supported in various past elections. The file is a critical asset that allows candidates who pay to access it for the purpose of obtaining this information. It is particularly important in early primary and caucus states because it allows you to target voter communications being sent by staff and volunteers. And it is important for modeling—more on that below.

One of the important conditions of using the file is that the voter information you input will become incorporated into it and made available to future candidates once your election is over. This keeps the file fresh for future users. During the course of a campaign, when a campaign identifies that a voter is supporting one or another candidate, that information is loaded into the copy of the voter file that the campaign is using. However, these voter IDs are not shared with anyone else while the campaign is ongoing.

Voters are rated on a 1 to 5 scale, with 1 being a strong supporter,

2 being a leaner, 3 being undecided, 4 being a leaner toward another candidate, and 5 being a strong supporter of another candidate. In a two-person race between Sanders and Clinton, a Sanders 1 was a Clinton 5. This information is used to efficiently manage expensive communications to voters, such as mail and telephone calls. No matter how much money a campaign has, it cannot reach every voter with the same level of intensity. Voters who are a 1 do not need to receive communications designed to persuade voters but certainly would be targeted for Get Out the Vote (GOTV) efforts. On the flip side, a 5 would not receive either persuasion or GOTV communications. Those who are 3s would be obvious targets for persuasion communications—to move them to a 2 or a 1. And one person's 3 is every candidate's 3, so that person can expect to receive a lot of communications from all the campaigns.

A single outside vendor, NGP VAN, provides the software necessary to access and manipulate the Democratic voter file process, and almost all experienced campaign field staffers are familiar with using "the VAN." This voter identification data is also at the heart of a campaign tool called modeling. Modeling is a process by which every single voter in a state's voter file is assigned a score based on how likely it is that he or she will support a given candidate. The modeler starts with the actual results of voter identification. The modeler then combines this known information about some voters with polling results and commercially available data about all voters, but only information that the modeler believes is predictive of how someone will vote.

This is where the true judgment of the modeler becomes important. There is endless information available about all of us in commercial data banks, like what kind of car you drive, where you shop, what magazines you subscribe to, what you buy, and so forth. Some of that—for instance, the fact that you own a blue car—may be irrelevant to your voting patterns. But the fact that you own a minivan may be highly relevant. (For the record, I am not a modeler, so I have no idea whether owning a minivan is relevant or not. I'm just trying to illustrate a point.)

In a general election, whether you identify as a Democrat or as a Republican is highly predictive of how you will vote. Independents who voted in the Democratic nominating process (in those places where it is allowed) overwhelmingly supported Bernie.

The modeler then combines all the information from the various sources and assigns a predictive score for all the voters in the file, even Republicans. This again allows the campaign to target votes. The campaign will focus on contacting voters (for whom it has no actual information) with a high score, because the model predicts that they will be more open to supporting your candidate. As more actual voter ID data comes in over the course of the campaign, the model is updated.

The modeler can also produce predictive models of behavior other than voter preference. They can score everyone on such factors as how likely they are to talk with a volunteer caller on the phone, how likely they are to answer their door in the evening, or whether they will even show up to vote at all. This last determination is critically important. Voters who score high in their support for your candidate, but low in the likelihood of voting at all, need special attention to ensure they show up at the polls.

When the model is run against the voter file, it produces a list of tens of thousands or hundreds of thousands of voters and their respective scores. It is this resulting list and the attached scores that are the useful product of the modeling and allow campaigns to put them to use.

In many cases, campaigns will use the modeled results to turn out voters who have a high score, even if the campaign does not have actual information about a particular voter. In a perfect world, models are about 70 percent accurate. In a best-case scenario, 30 percent of the calls to turn out voters are going to supporters of one's opponents.

Of course, if the modeler is not sufficiently skilled, he or she will include a lot of data in the model that is not predictive of voter behavior at all. And, as a result, the model will not produce more efficient use of campaign voter outreach assets like phone calling or door knocking. Worse even than that, the campaign's GOTV calls based on modeling will reach greater percentages of an opponent's supporters. Our modeling was done by Ken Strasma, Andrew Drechsler, and others at a firm called HaystaqDNA—the best in the business.

This background is not meant as an exhaustive discussion of the voter file and modeling. Rather, it is important to understanding the drama in mid-December. Following my conversation with Rich Pelletier about the data breach, I received an email from the DNC at 6:25 that evening. The email stated that the DNC was suspending the VAN access of five of our employees. The email was copied to the DNC's legal counsel. I discussed the issue by telephone with Lindsey Reynolds, the DNC's chief operating officer. We agreed that the Bernie 2016 campaign would assist the DNC with a complete review of the matter. But I wanted to have time to consult with our counsel, as the DNC was already involving its counsel. We agreed to communicate the next day. Our final conversation occurred after 8:00 p.m. These discussions were perfectly calm and businesslike, with no hint of distress on the part of the DNC. (It did raise a red flag, however, that the DNC was already bringing in their legal counsel—counsel who happened to be at the same law firm as the Clinton campaign's.)

As the day ended, as far as I was concerned, the matter was under review. We had agreed to cooperate completely. The five staffers who were under suspicion had their VAN access temporarily suspended. And I knew that no Clinton data would be used by our side. It's one of the advantages of a leaner, less bureaucratic organization. If this information—and at the time we had no idea what it was—was going to be used for any real purpose, I would know about it.

The next morning began like every other on a presidential campaign. Seemingly endless phone meetings, a huge pile of emails, and a ton of action items that had to be dealt with. The data breach was certainly on the list, but given that it was under active review internally, it didn't require my personal attention that morning until more information was available. Apparently Debbie Wasserman Schultz felt otherwise.

Wasserman Schultz called Bernie personally. She also took it upon herself to suspend access to the VAN for the entire Bernie 2016 campaign— an action directly at odds with the express language of our contract with the DNC. After talking with Bernie, I called Wasserman Schultz myself. Amy Dacey, the top DNC staffer, was also on the phone.

Wasserman Schultz informed me that a new incident report was being created by NGP VAN about what they believed had happened. I asked to have that document to help with our own internal investigation. I contacted her by email at 2:58 p.m., asking again for the new report. At 3:25 I emailed again because it had not arrived. It finally arrived at 3:53. While the DNC staff were obviously eager to hear from me, they were in no hurry to communicate in the other direction. At 5:08, I emailed Amy Dacey a full report of the actions we had taken and the status of our investigation.

I spoke to Amy by telephone, and she said that it would be hard to get in contact with Wasserman Schultz to discuss the report, and that Amy had no idea when our access to the VAN would be restored.

The impact of the VAN shutdown was immediate. Volunteers were showing up all over Iowa and in other states to make phone calls to voters. But it was impossible for them to do their work without access to the VAN. Volunteers had to be sent home. Particularly in the complicated caucus environment in Iowa, direct voter contact is the lifeblood of the campaign. Shut it off and the campaign dies. The Iowa caucus was a month and a half away. Debbie Wasserman Schultz was giving the Clinton campaign extra days of voter contact at a critical time. If our VAN access was not restored, our Iowa efforts would die.

Meanwhile, information about the data issue was leaked to the media by either the DNC or the Clinton campaign. Needless to say, the Clinton spin operation kicked into high gear. My counterpart on the Clinton campaign, Robby Mook, engaged in some hyperbole, saying that Sanders' staffers "had access to the fundamental keys of our campaign." Some in the media who knew less than the reader of this section now does about modeling and the voter file were quick to pile on to the Clinton "aggrieved" narrative, often completely misstating the type of data at issue or its relevance. The story was just too complicated for the modern internet news cycle. Not the media's finest hour.

What every review of the matter concluded, including our own internal review, the preliminary results of which were detailed in my December 17 email to Amy Dacey, was that no information had been downloaded.

What did happen was that the firewall that is supposed to exist between the various campaigns' data came down briefly. During that time, some staffers were able to access Clinton models, but not the underlying voter ID data. The staffers saved this modeling data on the NGP VAN system itself but did not download it to their computers—except for an index, which listed the names of the models. A list of model names is valueless, because models produce lists, as we have seen, of tens of thousands of names when run against the voter file. It's not the name of the model that has value, it's the search results. Each of the searches in this case was done about a minute apart. It would have required superhuman ability to memorize a list of that size in a minute's time. And the lists created were deleted by NGP VAN itself shortly thereafter and never exported.

Moreover, we would not have used information from the Clinton campaign's modeling if we had had it. I was convinced then and am now that Ken Strasma, Andrew Drechsler, and all the folks at HaystaqDNA who had done the modeling for Barack Obama's 2008 primary campaign were producing far more accurate models that the Clinton campaign. Why in the world would we have substituted the professional judgment of our modelers for an inferior product? My confidence in Haystaq and pollster Ben Tulchin would be confirmed during the Iowa caucus, when our projections proved right and the Clinton campaign missed the mark substantially.

That's not to say that we took the matter lightly. We quickly fired the most senior staffer involved and put two others on administrative leave and forbade them from coming into the office or having any contact with the campaign. Even though no information had been downloaded, their snooping across the firewall was unacceptable.

Yet Debbie Wasserman Schultz refused to restore our campaign's access to the VAN. This was not some broad-based conspiracy at the DNC. Later, Donna Brazile told us that DNC executive committee members had urged the chairwoman to restore our access. Wasserman Schultz refused.

We had done everything we could do. We fired people. We provided a complete report of our findings. We agreed to cooperate with any further reviews. But none of it mattered. Soon the weekend would be here. Weekends were important and busy times for our volunteer-based campaign. If we did not have our data back before the weekend, we would have lost almost 10 percent of the days remaining before the Iowa caucus.

It became clear to us that this was a deliberate attempt to torpedo our Iowa efforts. Our contract with the DNC required them to give us ten days' notice to cure any breach. Certainly, they had not done that. The fact that either the DNC or the Clinton campaign leaked the incident was further evidence that what they wanted was political points and not a real resolution.

This was galling. Back in October 2015, our modelers had discovered that when they downloaded Sanders voter ID data into the models, the VAN also downloaded Clinton data. They had immediately segregated the tainted downloads into a password-protected file and notified the DNC about it. We started modeling in October. The Clinton campaign surely started earlier. Did they have access to our voter IDs throughout the summer and early fall? The DNC said no. I would say there's better than even money they did.

But we may never know. Despite express promises to investigate this October incident, it has never been done, to my knowledge. The point here is that we never ran to the media in October. We tried to resolve what we believed to be a technical issue in good faith, without taking unfair advantage. Turns out we were the only party operating on that basis.

Staffers who had much more experience with the VAN alerted me that firewall problems were common occurrences. One staffer who had worked for a state party told me that often when NGP VAN did a software update, they received voter file data from other states. Another reported that on a statewide campaign, the opponent's voter ID information had always been available.

I called Robby Mook personally during this flap. I wanted him to hear from me that we did not have any information and that we would not use it if we did. I was blunt. "We want to beat you, and beat you badly," I told him. "But not like that." I didn't expect him to believe me or to say that he believed me even if he did. They thought they had an advantage and they were going to fully exploit it. I get that.

Beyond the tremendous impact the DNC's improper withholding of our data was having on our field program, we viewed it as a form of theft. We had paid the DNC and state parties an enormous amount of money for access. Each of the first four states in the process sells access to its voter file individually. The Iowa voter file costs $110,000. The other three in the first four ranged in price from $65,000 to $95,000. The voter file for each of the rest of the states is purchased from the DNC at a discount if you buy them all. The cost in 2016 for the rest of the states was $250,000.

The Clinton campaign had an advantage over us in being easily able to afford the $250,000 DNC tab. The $250,000 can be satisfied by writing the DNC a check or by raising $250,000 for the DNC from other sources. This allows well-heeled supporters of a candidate to write the DNC a big check and have it credited against the amount the candidate would otherwise have to pay for the voter file—even if the supporters have already maxed out to the candidate under federal election law.

We had informed the DNC that we didn't have large donors who would pony up the cash for us to have access to the voter file. They offered to set up a joint fund-raising committee with us (which we did) and to organize DNC fund-raisers. Bernie would only have to appear, and whatever the DNC raised would be credited against his bill. The DNC never set up a single event. In the end, we wrote them a $250,000 check straight from the campaign. As we would later learn, these joint fund-raising agreements were used to funnel large sums of money for the benefit of the Clinton campaign—money that was falsely solicited for state parties.

It was bad enough that we had to pay for the voter file directly when our opponent did not, but now to have the file withheld—including the data that we had entered as a result of our volunteers' effort—was unacceptable.

Our backs were against the wall. We could not afford to lose a whole weekend of organizing. The Clinton campaign and the DNC were pounding us in the media—a media unable to digest the technical aspects of the story and too willing to accept the Clinton narrative. This was one of

THE TABLES BEGIN TO TURN · 165

the cases in which the Clinton folks really tested the line in terms of providing false information to the media—and the press bought it hook, line, and sinker.

If we had learned anything from the drubbing we took over my "vice president" comment, it was that we had to get off the defensive and take the fight to them. Bernie, Tad, and I consulted with our attorney Brad Deutsch. I advocated going to court to win back our access to the data. If our case was successful, not only would we have access to the data but we would have the implicit validation of a federal court that the DNC had acted inappropriately. This was not a strategy without huge risks. If the court ruled against us, the other side would have the same validation. So we decided that we would hold a press conference and lay out our case, giving the DNC one last opportunity to restore our service.

There was a lot of hand-wringing by the younger, less experienced staffers on the campaign. They were pushing for a conciliatory tone and a formal apology—from us. That would have been a disaster, because we would have been apologizing for the "alternative facts" put out by the DNC and the Clinton campaign and validated by the media. The next morning, Friday, our press shop put out a very short advisory that there would be a 2:00 p.m. press conference in front of our Washington, DC, office, a row house on Massachusetts Avenue. Bernie, Tad, Briggs, Brad Deutsch, and I met at Bernie's small DC house. Bernie, Tad, and I had each prepared draft remarks, and we went to work creating a single document. The big question that remained was who would deliver them.

There was certainly a strong case for Bernie delivering them. He was unquestionably the person in the room with the most credibility. It would also ensure that the statement would be extensively covered by the media. On the other hand, it would put him personally in the middle of the maelstrom. We had avoided that up to this point.

We finally decided that I would deliver the remarks. If the whole thing went south, I would be the public face of the disaster.

We walked over to the office and went in through the back. The front lawn was packed with reporters and cameras. The press corps spilled over into the front of the next building. Many of the reporters expected the campaign to come out and apologize. That was definitely not our game plan, and we took them by surprise.

I walked out with Brad Deutsch and Michael Briggs. I immediately gained a new appreciation for what Bernie does on a regular basis—step in front of a wall of cameras that capture every word and every movement. There are no do-overs. I delivered the prepared statement. Then I took questions. After about half a dozen, I gave the press conference "thank you" and stepped back inside. It seemed to have gone well. Now we waited to see if the DNC would blink.

They didn't, and neither did we.

That afternoon we filed for immediate relief in federal court. The judge brought the parties together on a 7:00 p.m. conference call and asked if this could be worked out. The problem was that the DNC would still not agree to our central demand—give us back access to our data. Hours went by. Finally, the judge said that she would hold an 11:00 p.m. hearing.

The DNC capitulated. If we would agree to cooperate with an investigation (which we already had), and if we would provide a statement about the chronology of events (which I had done the day before), they would turn the data back on.

The impact of this confrontation was considerable, and it provided a valuable lesson going forward. Reports came in from our offices in Iowa that during the press conference our staff and volunteers were cheering. (In our Iowa offices, the whole incident became known as VANghazi—a play on the Republicans' trumped-up attacks on Hillary Clinton around Benghazi.) Similar reports came in from other states. Our willingness to challenge Debbie Wasserman Schultz had energized our people. Even though we did not make a direct appeal for money, over $2 million was donated in short order.

Attendance at our events over the following days swelled. A reporter would later relate that a key Clinton staffer told her that they expected the crisis to hurt our campaign, but that we had beaten them to a draw. If they were admitting, even privately, that we had beaten them to a draw, it meant that they felt we had won decisively.

Back in October, we had responded defensively to the Clinton campaign's attacks over comments I had made that she should be vice president. No more. To win, one had to be on offense.

Despite this victory, Debbie Wasserman Schultz didn't back down in her efforts to hurt Bernie's campaign. We learned that the DNC had leaked activity logs related to the data issue to the media. We had asked for this type of information to help us in our own internal investigation. It was not until late Saturday, after a DNC staff meeting convened to decide whether they would even give us the information that the media already had, that they decided to give it to us. When we complained to the media that we had not been given the same access to information that was being distributed to the Clinton campaign and to the press, Debbie Wasserman Schultz relied on a tried-and-true tactic in politics. She told the media that we had in fact been given the information when everyone else had received it. In other words, she lied.

Debbie Wasserman Schultz's conduct during VANghazi confirmed what so many people believed already—that the party establishment was putting its fingers on the scale for Hillary Clinton. For those who still had doubts, the leaked emails from the DNC and Clinton chair John Podesta and subsequent revelations by Donna Brazile made it crystal-clear months later.

PART THREE

SWEEPING THE NATION

11

STALINGRAD, IOWA

By December we had some eighty people in Iowa. The design of the Iowa caucus is such that it requires considerable staffing and organization to be successful.

On voting day, caucusgoers are in fact electing delegates to go to a convention at (usually) the county level. That county convention then elects delegates to a congressional district–level convention. And then those present at that convention elect delegates to the statewide Democratic convention—which in turn picks the delegates from that state who will go to the Democratic National Convention. There is some variation between the various caucus states—something that desperately needs to be made more consistent from one state to the next—but that's the basic process.

A campaign not only has to turn out caucusgoers on election day but also must make sure that at each convention the previously elected delegates actually show up. It is possible to win the greatest number of delegates at the first level but to then lose that advantage at the county convention if a large number of those delegates don't show up.

In Iowa, there are almost 1,700 precincts at the local level. Each precinct is assigned a number of "state delegate equivalents" based on Democratic voting performance in that precinct in the last two statewide elections. That number of state delegate equivalents in each precinct is then converted to a whole number of county convention delegates. There can be any number of county delegates, as long as they are in the right proportion. Confused yet? It gets better.

Some precincts are very small and are worth a fraction of a state delegate equivalent. Others are much larger and could be worth, for instance, seven state delegate equivalents. The system is designed to ensure that a candidate have support in precincts across the state to be successful—because even if you triple the turnout in a certain precinct over its past performance and win 100 percent of the vote there, you cannot win more than the allotted number of state delegate equivalents. In practice, the system means that it is far from a one-person, one-vote process. Because turnout fluctuates, a person's vote in one precinct may represent much more than a person's vote in another precinct.

This is a problem that could easily be remedied by assigning state delegate equivalent values to precincts based on the actual relative turnout between the precincts on caucus day itself—rather than relying on historical performance. But doing so would require a much more well-run caucus process than we experienced in 2016.

Assigning state delegate equivalents after caucus day would also remedy another problem created by the Iowa caucus system. The assignment of state delegate equivalents ends up helping to dictate the candidate's schedule and the campaign's resources. That's because the process becomes one of accumulating state delegate equivalents rather than votes.

And here's why. In a precinct where only one county convention delegate is being chosen, the winner in an essentially two-person contest is the person with the majority. If you are ahead by 10 points or behind by 10 points in that precinct, field resources are less likely to be allocated there. In a precinct with two delegates, you are guaranteed to split the delegates with your opponent if you get over 25 percent of the vote.

A candidate must get over 75 percent of the vote to capture both. So if you are at 49 percent of the vote in that precinct, you are not likely to fight to go over 50 percent, because there's no benefit. You are 26 points away from another delegate. However, in a three-delegate precinct, a candidate who breaks 50 percent gets two delegates, while the opponent gets one. As the number of delegates in a precinct gets larger, the number of percentage points needed to get an additional delegate goes down. For instance, in a ten-delegate precinct, moving from 44 percent to 50.1 percent gives you an additional delegate.

And that is where the margins are made in the Iowa caucus—in precincts with odd-numbered delegates and those with the greatest number of delegates. Aggregating precinct results for purposes of state delegate equivalent allocation to create pools with larger numbers of delegates and preferably odd-numbered totals would give each precinct a greater equivalency in terms of having campaigns reach out to them. This would be true even if you did not lower the overall number of precincts.

Unlike most other states with caucuses, the Iowa Democratic Party refuses to release the raw vote counts. (Iowa's Republicans do.) The Iowa Democratic Party only reports the relative performance in winning state delegate equivalents. You could lose the popular vote by thousands of votes in Iowa and be declared the winner (more on that later).

This refusal to release the popular vote totals also severely disadvantages candidates whose campaigns have not yet taken off—because of the caucus night process for assigning delegates. As in most states with caucuses or primaries, the Iowa Democratic Party requires that a candidate arrive at a certain threshold in order to receive statewide delegates. That's not unusual, and in fact the national Democratic Party rules require it. What is unusual is how that process is carried out in Iowa, coupled with its refusal to release the popular vote totals. This process doomed Governor Martin O'Malley's campaign.

When caucusgoers show up, they are separated into preference groups (including "uncommitted"). The numbers in the various groupings are then compared. This is followed by a process called "realignment." During realignment, if a candidate has not reached the threshold in the first round (which varies depending on the number of delegates at stake, but for larger precincts is 15 percent of the votes cast), then that candidate's supporters are asked to join the group supporting another candidate— and a new round of counting takes place. When the evening's results are posted from that precinct, the "nonviable" candidate is reported as having received 0 percent from that precinct. In theory, a candidate could get 14 percent in every precinct in the state and have his or her performance reported on caucus night as 0 percent.

In addition, realignment leads to gamesmanship on caucus night. This clearly has nothing to do with the will of the voters. Because of the way the math works, it is sometimes advantageous to push some of your own supporters into another candidate's group during realignment; the delegate that would thus be won would come from an opponent. On caucus night, our precinct captains had an app on their phones that allowed them to plug in the caucus counts for each candidate and calculate what the correct move was to maximize delegates—how many new people were needed to win an additional delegate, or how many people had to be asked to stand with another candidate's group and which candidate that would be. The Clinton campaign used a similar app.

Realignment also adds considerably to the length and complexity of the caucus. Campaign supporters not only have to show up to caucus, but they must stay through all the proceedings, then be counted, then stay through realignment, and then be counted again. For working people, these extra hurdles are considerable.

This process of realignment should be abolished. It lengthens the caucus tremendously, leads to mathematical gamesmanship by the campaigns, and underreports the strength of less successful campaigns—thereby hiding the true intent of caucusgoers. The Iowa Democratic Party could still have viability thresholds for assigning delegates, as do other states, but the counting would be limited to one round. Coupled with releasing the raw vote totals, you wouldn't hide the true intent of Iowa caucusgoers in an unnecessarily complicated system that's great for political pundits, consultants, and insiders but not great for Iowans.

I do not mean this as a wholesale indictment of caucuses. Caucuses have many advantages. They allow people in a community who are interested in politics to come together all at the same time. Their iterative convention system ensures that presidential campaigns stay engaged in the state long after the original caucuses are over. Their open process, whereby in most cases a voter can change his or her party affiliation at the caucus itself, allows an easy way to grow local party organizations. Caucuses are not burdened by the voter suppression laws being passed by so many states. But real reform is needed.

By December, Bernie's numbers in Iowa showed him moving up. But we were still behind with those voters who were most likely to go to the caucus. It became clear that to do well in Iowa, we not only had to work on persuading those voters, but we had to add additional voters on top of those most likely to attend. Our polling and modeling showed that as the number of people attending the Iowa caucus went up, the additional voters were disproportionately likely to support Bernie Sanders over Hillary Clinton. Our goal, therefore, was to win by changing the composition of the electorate on caucus night.

Even with eighty people on the ground in Iowa, we needed more. I called Becker and asked him how many more people he could absorb into his organization if I authorized them. He said he could use 150 people. I gave him the go-ahead. If we were going to bring out less likely caucusgoers—who by definition would need more attention to get them to attend—we had to have more people on the ground. We also wanted to make sure we had the capacity to recruit and train Iowans to be precinct captains at the almost 1,700 caucus locations—with emphasis on those where a re-alignment was more likely to take place.

In addition, because Bernie did so well with younger voters, I asked the Iowa team about reaching out to those seventeen-year-olds who would be eligible to participate in the Iowa caucus because they would be eighteen by the time of the general election. Their initial response was that there was no way to contact those potential caucusgoers. They would not be on the voting rolls, because they had not previously been eligible to participate, and we couldn't get a list of them because they were minors.

I wasn't convinced. It is a sad reality of the modern era that it is big business to meticulously track the buying habits of Americans. High school seniors buy many things that identify them as such: class rings, caps and gowns, high school yearbooks, college admissions and testing materials. That's not to say that I knew that the purveyors of any one of these products had a list on the market. But I was confident that a list did exist somewhere. Someone had one.

We began asking list brokers whether a list of high school seniors was available. It took some digging, but in fact a mailing list did exist. It was not for sale, but it was for rent. The distinction is that when you buy a list, the list is turned over to you for your use. In a rental situation, the list is generally for a onetime use, and it is actually never delivered to you. Instead it is sent to a mail house, which then addresses whatever materials you want sent to people on the list. If you want to send subsequent mailings, then the list must be rented again. (For the couple of Iowa parents who called the campaign asking how we got their son or daughter's name, I can assure you that we never had the names or addresses—but there are commercial list companies that do.)

We rented the list and prepared some targeted mailings. In this case, because the people on the list were minors, the list broker had to preview our materials to ensure that there was nothing inappropriate.

I know that there is a political mail professional reading this right now and scoffing at us for sending mail to high school seniors. The conventional wisdom is that young people don't read their mail, and that it is a waste to try to reach them in this way. Much better to use online advertising (we did that, too). But my theory was that, while it might in general be true that as a group younger voters do not pay a lot of attention to mail, high school seniors living at home with their parents are different. In fact, in that environment, receiving personally addressed mail would be more significant. In the end, we mailed the people on the list three times. We paired it with a web page that encouraged the young voters to defy expectations by attending the caucus.

Senator Obama did well with young Iowa voters in the 2008 primary. But because of jockeying among the states that year, the Iowa caucus was pushed so early that Iowa colleges were still on winter break. That meant that the students (the vast majority of whom are Iowa residents) would be voting in their home precincts rather than at college. Given the need to do well everywhere to prevail in Iowa, having college-age voters spread across the state rather than in a smaller number of college precincts was a huge advantage. Our outreach to high school seniors was an attempt to overcome that fact that colleges would be back in session during the 2016 Iowa caucus.

We had considered a program to transport college students back to their home precincts on caucus day—a program known internally as Go Home for Bernie. Our modeling showed that moving a relatively small percentage of students to their home precinct would significantly affect the allocation of state delegates in our favor. But the logistics were daunting. It would have meant diverting a tremendous amount of staff time away from other voter outreach. The Iowa staff was not enthusiastic about the prospect. While the program moved far along in the planning stages, including development of various college-themed web pages and research into transportation options, it was never put into operation. In the end, it might not have succeeded anyway due to the bad weather in parts of that state that day.

As time went on, the Clinton campaign started incrementally increasing the number of points it had on television. Points are a measure of how much an ad is viewed. An ad run for 100 points will be seen by the average viewer once; an ad run at 1,000 points will be seen by the average viewer ten times. Television programs with more views have a higher point value (and cost) than programs with a lower viewership. You can put a lot of ads on very cheaply in the middle of the night, but you won't reach many people.

In Iowa and New Hampshire, we generally tried to match the point value of whatever the Clinton campaign buy was in the effort to achieve local superiority. Let's not forget that they had a three-month head start on us in terms of television advertising. Whenever the reports came out that the Clinton campaign was raising its buy, we would follow. (The converse was also true. There was a period in New Hampshire when the Clinton campaign lowered its buy, which we also matched. Julia Barnes, our New Hampshire state director, was not pleased. When they pushed it back up, so did we.)

Over the course of a three-day period in Iowa, Hillary for America pushed its ads up each day—not by huge amounts, but it was significant.

On day one, I told Tad to match it. On day two, I said the same. On day three, I told him to exceed it. They stopped raising their buy. I can't know if the decision to top them on day three convinced them that they were in a race they didn't want to engage in or whether it was pure coincidence.

I told Tad that we were all in in Iowa. "It's Stalingrad, Tad," I said. Stalingrad was the World War II battle that marked the turning point of the war on the eastern front in favor of the Soviets. Both sides poured personnel and resources into the fight in a no-holds-barred bid to win the city, with the Soviets ultimately surrounding and destroying the German Sixth Army. Tad asked jokingly, "Are we the Russians or the Germans?" "I'll let you know on caucus night," I replied. (For the record, on caucus night I reminded Tad of the conversation and answered his question. We were the Russians. It's a bit ironic in hindsight, because it turns out that the Trump campaign was the Russians, but in a very different sense.)

The other important move we made was to reach out to Iowans, particularly rural Iowans, on the issue of the Bakken oil pipeline. It had first come to my attention as an issue as we were driving into Iowa from Minnesota. I saw a sign on some farmland made from two 4×8 foot pieces of plywood: "Don't Take Our Land." After inquiring I found out that many rural Iowans were upset by the use of eminent domain to force property owners to allow the Bakken oil pipeline to be put across their land.

Bernie and I talked about it. We both understood its importance. Allowing big companies to come in and essentially take land is the kind of thing that enrages rural communities. It is felt deeply as a violation of something fundamental to the rural way of life: the relationship of people to their land. In this case it was especially problematic: An oil pipeline not only occupies one's land but has the potential to damage it severely in the event of a leak.

Bernie was calling for a green energy revolution as part of the larger political revolution. He came out against the Bakken pipeline as he had the Keystone XL pipeline. Hillary Clinton had been late to the party in opposing Keystone, and she never came out against the Bakken pipeline. We ran television ads against the Bakken pipeline and sent targeted mailings to voters in counties along its proposed route. Bernie held a town hall meeting focused solely on Bakken. Iowa, it should be noted, is a leader in the green energy revolution. It is one of the leading producers of wind power in the country, and home to many wind power–related manufacturing facilities. At the end of the day, given the resonance of Bernie's anti-Bakken message, we should have highlighted it even more.

By the end of December, all the pieces in Iowa were in place. The leadership team—Robert Becker, Pete D'Alessandro, Rania Batrice, Justin Huck, Brendan Summers—were executing on the ground. The field staff was growing. Bernie continued to be enthusiastically received everywhere. We were competitive on the airwaves. We were advertising in small weekly papers around the state. Our Iowa mail program—handled by Maverick Strategies + Mail's Jessica Vanden Berg and Kristian Denny Todd—was proceeding well.

One of the themes that we used in Iowa mail, which never really became as big a part of the broader messaging in the campaign as it should have, was the connection of Bernie's transformative agenda to President Franklin Delano Roosevelt's. In truth, what Bernie was advocating was merely the logical progression of what FDR had accomplished and what FDR acknowledged had been left unaccomplished during his tenure.

In his 1944 State of the Union speech, as the world was still engulfed in a global war, the president spoke strongly in favor of a new Bill of Rights that would fulfill the promise of our country's founding. (Note: This is dense quoted material I have been warned you won't read. I have more faith in you. Plus, far more so than all my musings, this speech is critical to understanding our campaign, the unfinished business of the modern Democratic Party, how far the party has strayed from its modern roots, and Bernie's place in the continuity of the party and American political thought.)

> It is our duty now to begin to lay the plans and determine the strategy for the winning of a lasting peace and the establishment of an American standard of living higher than ever before known. We cannot be content, no matter how high that general standard of living may be, if some fraction of our people—whether it be

one-third or one-fifth or one-tenth—is ill-fed, ill-clothed, ill-housed, and insecure.

This Republic had its beginning, and grew to its present strength, under the protection of certain inalienable political rights—among them the right of free speech, free press, free worship, trial by jury, freedom from unreasonable searches and seizures. They were our rights to life and liberty.

As our Nation has grown in size and stature, however—as our industrial economy expanded—these political rights proved inadequate to assure us equality in the pursuit of happiness.

We have come to a clear realization of the fact that true individual freedom cannot exist without economic security and independence. "Necessitous men are not free men." People who are hungry and out of a job are the stuff of which dictatorships are made.

In our day these economic truths have become accepted as self-evident. We have accepted, so to speak, a second Bill of Rights under which a new basis of security and prosperity can be established for all regardless of station, race, or creed.

Among these are:

The right to a useful and remunerative job in the industries or shops or farms or mines of the Nation;

The right to earn enough to provide adequate food and clothing and recreation;

The right of every farmer to raise and sell his products at a return which will give him and his family a decent living;

The right of every businessman, large and small, to trade in an atmosphere of freedom from unfair competition and domination by monopolies at home or abroad;

The right of every family to a decent home;

The right to adequate medical care and the opportunity to achieve and enjoy good health;

The right to adequate protection from the economic fears of old age, sickness, accident, and unemployment;

The right to a good education.

All of these rights spell security. And after this war is won we must be prepared to move forward, in the implementation of these rights, to new goals of human happiness and well-being.

America's own rightful place in the world depends in large part upon how fully these and similar rights have been carried into practice for our citizens. For unless there is security here at home there cannot be lasting peace in the world.

One of the great American industrialists of our day—a man who has rendered yeoman service to his country in this crisis—recently emphasized the grave dangers of "rightist reaction" in this Nation. All clear-thinking businessmen share his concern. Indeed, if such reaction should develop—if history were to repeat itself and we were to return to the so-called "normalcy" of the 1920s—then it is certain that even though we shall have conquered our enemies on the battlefields abroad, we shall have yielded to the spirit of Fascism here at home.

Is there much difference between President Roosevelt's call for creating a new set of rights that would allow all Americans "the pursuit of happiness" and the presidential platform of Bernie Sanders? Is not Bernie's message the continuation of a great legacy in the Democratic Party—a legacy abandoned during the Democratic reaction of the 1990s and abandoned today by many of the party's institutions? FDR's warning—that returning to the gross income and wealth inequality of the 1920s would put us in danger of yielding "to the spirit of Fascism here at home"—seems to have been borne out in the outcome of the 2016 election, as does his observation that "people who are hungry and out of a job are the stuff of which dictatorships are made."

As reported by Kevin Hardy of the *Des Moines Register*, Bernie did invoke FDR during some of his speeches, including at a Boone, Iowa, event in August 2015. During his 1936 Madison Square Garden speech, FDR called out the forces arrayed against him as "the old enemies of peace—business and financial monopoly, speculation, reckless banking, class antagonism, sectionalism, war profiteering. . . . They are unanimous in their hate for me—and I welcome their hatred." Bernie's paraphrase of those words linked directly back to that FDR speech: "And let me echo that today: If the Koch brothers and the billionaire class hate my guts, I welcome their hatred. Because I am going to stand with working families."

Bernie as inheritor of the legacy of FDR is a topic that we revisited—most explicitly during the New York primary with our ad "Sons of New York," which drew the connection between the two. But it was a connection that we might have stressed more thematically throughout the campaign. Bernie Sanders represented a rediscovery of the values of the Democratic Party's modern roots and an articulation of the unfinished business of the New Deal. By contrast, the neoliberals are a recent aberration.

Hillary Clinton would often say that she was not running for either Bill Clinton or Barack Obama's third term. That has been debated quite a bit. But what was not sufficiently articulated by us was that in many ways Bernie was running for FDR's fifth term.

Bernie spent most of his time in December and January in the first four states, with Iowa getting a huge percentage of it. We leased a bus and wrapped it in a campaign design, and the Bernie Bus became the mobile command center as he crisscrossed the Hawkeye State. As the Iowa caucus neared, our internal polling and modeling continued to get better and better. But one of the issues that we had was the constant drumbeat of talking heads on the cable news channels who were almost exclusively public Hillary Clinton supporters. Mark Longabaugh and I ran into Mark Preston in Iowa after one of my interviews. Mark Preston is the executive editor for CNN Politics. We dealt with Preston many times during the campaign; he was also the point person for their debates, and we always felt he was a fair guy. Longabaugh asked him, "Hey, Mark, why is it that almost all of the political commentators on CNN are Clinton supporters and there's no Bernie people?" Preston replied, "That's a good point. I was thinking about calling Bill Press anyway." And Preston promptly lined up Bill Press (who had hosted the early pre-campaign meetings at his house) to appear regularly on CNN. At least there would be one Bernie person on the air.

I ran into Joel Benenson, the Clinton campaign's pollster, after one of my on-air appearances on CNN, within days of the Iowa caucus. He volunteered that we were going to lose by several points. In fact, the Clinton team was telling the media that they were up 5 percentage points. It sure didn't feel that way on the ground. Bernie's crowds were surging at events being held on very cold Iowa winter nights all over the state. It was hard to believe that all these people were just coming out to see Bernie so close to the caucus but were not going to come out for him on caucus night. But this was our first presidential contest. Maybe we were just wrong and Benenson was right.

About a week before the Iowa caucus, as it became a closer and closer race and it appeared Martin O'Malley was not going to reach the 15 percent threshold for getting delegates in most precincts, I reached out to Dave Hamrick, the O'Malley campaign manager. I wanted to propose a caucus night agreement whereby during the realignment we would set up ground rules: Each campaign would help the other maximize delegates, provided it didn't hurt the other. These types of arrangements were common in years past in the Iowa caucus—another aspect of the gamesmanship created by the realignment process. He said he'd think about it.

I didn't hear back from Dave, so I reached out again as the caucus drew near. I called from my cell in the hallway between the lobby of our hotel and the attached restaurant. It became clear during the conversation that we weren't the only ones reaching out to him; nor would I have thought otherwise. I laid out my case: Martin O'Malley was not going to win many precinct delegates on caucus night. And because the Iowa Democratic Party doesn't release raw vote totals, O'Malley's strength was going to be grossly underreported. Given that, his best hope was in New Hampshire. But if Hillary Clinton had a big win in Iowa, she might sew it up. It was in O'Malley's interest to have Bernie win (or at least to not have Hillary Clinton win big) in Iowa. Dave summed up my position: "So you are asking me to help you win today so that I have a chance to win tomorrow?" "Exactly," I said. "Let me discuss it with O'Malley and get back with you," he replied. In the end, Martin O'Malley decided to not make an agreement with either campaign.

The day of the Iowa caucus, when I walked into our campaign head-quarters, I stopped first to talk to Ken Strasma, the head of our modeling effort. He and his team were in a little side office. They were all sitting around a table with their laptops opened. "How's it look, Ken?" I asked him. His reply: "It's right down the middle." Not exactly what I wanted to hear.

We knew from our polling and modeling that the outcome in Iowa was all going to come down to turnout. If the turnout was small, it would favor the Clinton campaign—it would be comprised mostly of party regulars. If the turnout was larger, the additional people would be much, much more likely to be Bernie supporters.

In the weeks beforehand, Ben Tulchin had been providing horse-race numbers based on projected turnout. By caucus day, his projection was that if turnout was 160,000, we would lose by 2 points. If turnout was lower, we'd lose by more. On the other hand, if turnout reached 180,000, we would win by 2 points. And the more people who voted beyond 180,000, the higher our margin would be.

The cavernous campaign headquarters was buzzing with staff and volunteers. The huge Iowa volunteer contingent was supplemented with people who had driven in from all over the country, and even people who had shown up from foreign countries. All around the state, our GOTV operation was in high gear. But would it be enough?

In the afternoon, Tad and I heard the depressing entrance poll number that we were down 12 percent. Tad and I walked into the senior staff room to monitor the results. Everyone was gathered around a large-screen TV. Bernie was in the DoubleTree hotel by the Des Moines airport. Our caucus night celebration was booked for the Holiday Inn not far from there. We had booked a suite at the Holiday Inn where Bernie could wait while results were coming in.

Even though each of the precincts holds its caucus at the same time, the results don't come in all at once. Smaller caucuses or caucuses where there is no realignment come in sooner. Each precinct is supposed to have a chair appointed by the Iowa Democratic Party to run its caucus. However, that was not the case. A senior Clinton official who went to observe one of the Polk County caucuses later related to me that when people arrived, there was no one there to run it. So a couple of people who had caucused before stepped in to help.

Once the results of a precinct's caucus are determined, they are relayed by telephone to the state party's office. We had instructed our precinct captains to report the results of each caucus to us directly as they were reported. That way, we could see exactly which locations' results were being included in the television reporting and which locations were yet to come. We could also compare the results in terms of state delegate equivalents in each precinct against the outcome our models had predicted.

As the first returns were reported on TV, we were down considerably. It seemed that maybe the entrance polls had been right after all. But as our precinct captains started calling in to HQ directly, the modelers could see that a lot of the early results were coming from places we expected the Clinton campaign to do well in.

As the minutes ticked by, every update ate into Hillary Clinton's lead. We started having back-and-forth phone calls with Bernie, who understandably wanted information as quickly as possible. At one point in the evening, as results were entered, our model predicted that we would get more state delegate equivalents than Hillary (remember that they don't release the popular vote totals in the Iowa Democratic caucus).

At the same time, as on every election night, the reports of process problems started to roll in. There were reports of coin-toss issues (when a precinct is tied in Iowa, the result is determined by coin flip). Some reports had the Clinton campaign winning almost all of them. Others reported that we had won the vast majority. In some cases, the results that our precinct captains were calling in didn't match the information that the state party had. In a few cases, the reported numbers were nonsensical on their face. For instance, in one precinct only one person showed up. He was for Bernie, but the precinct result showed Clinton winning. Given how close the caucus was turning out to be (the closest in its history), every one of these issues mattered.

As the evening wore on and the race remained close, Tad and I headed to Bernie's suite at the Holiday Inn. The mood in the car as we drove out of the parking lot of the campaign headquarters was far different than it had been when we drove in just a few hours earlier. Instead of being a campaign-ending defeat, Iowa was shaping up to be the validation of the viability of Bernie's run for the White House. Those Iowa storm clouds weren't our bad omen.

As Tad and I entered the suite, Bernie greeted us with a huge smile. Jane and much of his family were watching the results in the living room area of the suite. Everyone wanted to know if we had more information about how it would turn out.

"Well," said Tad, "it's going to be close no matter how it turns out. And I think you have to go out there and declare this a victory, because it is a victory." Bernie and Tad went into a side room to work on remarks. I was on the phone with our folks camped out at Iowa Democratic Party headquarters. They were working to resolve the problems we had identified in several places. The party was helpful to a point. They could not reach some of their precinct chairs by phone, which seemed odd—there must have been times in the past when numbers had to be verified. Or maybe not.

Reports of problems poured in. The Iowa Democratic Party refused to release any paper records from the precincts and, as a matter of tradition, refused to release the statewide vote count (no doubt they knew, as most suspected, that Bernie had received the support of more Iowans than had Hillary Clinton). The party's refusal to be transparent elicited a scathing editorial from the *Des Moines Register*: "What happened Monday night at the Democratic caucuses was a debacle, period."

The editorial went on to call for an audit of the results, a release of any paper records, and a release of the popular vote count—all the items we were requesting. Even though the paper had endorsed Hillary Clinton, they were rightly standing for a fair and transparent review of the caucus so that the process could be improved and, importantly, preserved. They even went so far to call out Dr. Andy McGuire, the party's chair, for her refusal to act: "Her actions only confirm the suspicions."

Admittedly, the state party had a strong incentive to call the race that night rather than to hold off until everything could be resolved (as did

McGuire, a strong Clinton supporter). Later that night, over our objection, the Iowa Democratic Party put out a statement stating that Hillary Clinton had won the most delegates.

But even all the irregularities and the party's lack of transparency could not dampen the mood that night. As the evening played out, everyone knew who had "won" the Iowa caucus. Hillary Clinton gave a short six-minute speech in which she never declared victory. Robby Mook would later describe the night of the Iowa caucus as the worst night of their primary campaign. (In fairness, I'll tell you my opinion of our worst night when we get to it later.)

Bernie's event was like a pep rally. And it should have been. He had started 50 points down and fought to a photo finish. He showed that the Summer of Sanders was no fluke. People weren't just coming out to rallies. They were coming out to vote.

But we had a plane to catch. For the first time ever, we had a full-sized charter jet, which would transport Bernie and Jane, their family, a huge number of staff, and a large media contingent from the Hawkeye State to the Granite State.

The final turnout in Iowa was some 170,000 caucusgoers. According to our pollster, we would lose by 2 at 160,000 and win by 2 at 180,000. The number came in right down the middle, and so did the result. "Maybe this Tulchin guy really does know what he's doing," I quipped.

February 1 was not the only day we almost won Iowa, however. The number of national delegates won in many caucus states is not locked in until the precinct delegates who are elected on caucus day go to their county conventions and state delegates elected at county conventions go to the state convention. In Iowa, the national delegate numbers for the 2016 nominating contest weren't locked in until June.

We worked hard to turn people out for the subsequent conventions. At the Polk County convention in April, we almost flipped the state for Bernie. He won the first round of voting there, even though we had not won Polk County on caucus night. We just turned our delegates out, and the Clinton campaign did not. Then the Clinton campaign, not content to live with the results of their failure to turn out their delegates, threw a monkey wrench into the process. They decided to challenge the credentials of every delegate to the county convention—even their own!

Becker called me while this "process" was going on. "We won the first-round vote, but they are stealing it right now," he said. The problem was that there was no one to appeal to. The state party chair was certainly not going to be any help. Even after being criticized on the *Des Moines Register* editorial page, she never produced the appropriate audit of caucus night, or the paper records, or the popular vote count. What could we do? Call the DNC?

Verifying the credentials of hundreds of delegates took hours and hours and hours. As the time dragged on, some of our people had to leave. When the count was done again after the credentials challenge, the Clinton campaign won narrowly. While we were what can only be politely described as disappointed, we couldn't know that the shenanigans at the Polk County convention were just a preview of the goat-rope that the Nevada conventions would become.

12

THE GRANITE STATE REVOLUTION

GIVEN OUR STRONG SHOWING in Iowa, we wanted a rally for Bernie when he got to New Hampshire—at 4:00 a.m. Ever the miracle worker, Julia Barnes pulled it off.

Most of us on the plane from Iowa, including Bernie, got very little sleep. We were all running on fumes. Julia and her team had set up a rally in a parking lot across the street from the hotel where we were staying. Sure enough, there was a crowd of people holding Bernie signs. It was a very cold February New England night. Bernie climbed onto the back of a pickup truck. A noticeably tired Julia handed him the mic. Bernie gave a short speech and the crowd went crazy. It was a great visual that really captured the excitement that our people were feeling after Iowa. And it was a testament to the strength of our New Hampshire operation that they could pull it off with such little notice.

I spent relatively little time in New Hampshire prior to the last week before the primary. In part that was because there was a sense that we had a good understanding of New Hampshire generally because of its proximity to Vermont. In addition, the polling there had been considerably more positive for us than in any other early state. Bernie, on the other hand, spent a lot of time there, and with great results.

Given how well we were doing in New Hampshire, the campaign staff began to discuss whether it would be possible for Bernie to campaign in New Hampshire for a couple of days right after the Iowa caucus, then visit Nevada and/or South Carolina for two days before returning to finish out the weekend and the following Monday back in New Hampshire before primary day. We never got to try that, because suddenly the set-in-stone Democratic debate schedule was not so set-in-stone after all. Realizing that they had huge ground to make up in New Hampshire before the first vote was cast in Iowa, the Clinton campaign called for another debate in New Hampshire during the week between the Iowa caucus and the New Hampshire primary. The Clinton campaign was no doubt looking to repeat the events of 2008, when Hillary Clinton used the debate right before the New Hampshire primary to erase the lead that Barack Obama had built up there.

We weren't all that enthusiastic about the idea. First, we thought that Bernie might be able to do some extra campaigning outside of New Hampshire, and that it wouldn't be possible if debate prep had to take place. Second, debates are freewheeling environments, and we needed to win in New Hampshire. What benefit was there compared to the risk? Which leads to the third concern—the principle of the thing. When Bernie and Martin O'Malley had called for more debates the summer before the Clinton campaign, the DNC had stuck to the cramped debate schedule they had previously concocted. Why give Hillary Clinton a chance to make up ground when she had opposed a more expansive debate schedule earlier? (We didn't know at this time that in fact the DNC's debate schedule had been dictated by the Clinton campaign.)

We kicked it around internally. O'Malley quickly agreed, but he would ultimately not participate; he dropped out after the February 1 Iowa caucus. Then MSNBC delivered a blow. They agreed to host the debate before we'd even agreed and set it for Thursday, February 4. This was the only time during the entire campaign season that a network set a date and basically dared anyone not to show up. Later in the campaign, when we were trying to force a debate in New York (which we ended up getting) and get the promised debate in California (which the Clinton campaign backed out of), I used the example of New Hampshire to suggest to various networks that they just go ahead and schedule the debate and dare Clinton not to go. None of them had the guts to do it.

Once MSNBC publicly set the date before getting the agreement of all the campaigns, they no longer were merely reporting on the race. They had injected themselves as a participant—and squarely on the side of Hillary Clinton. Soon after the MSNBC announcement, we started hearing from our New Hampshire operation that there was a lot of negative buzz in Granite State political circles about our unwillingness to confirm our attendance. Hillary Clinton wanted to use the debate to try to fight back from a double-digit deficit in New Hampshire. If we didn't attend, she might get exactly what she wanted.

The question, then, was not whether we participated, but what we could get out of participating. As reported in the *Union Leader* on January 28, 2016, we would agree to the MSNBC blackmail (we didn't call it that at the time, but that's what it was) if the Clinton campaign would agree to add three additional debates to the calendar. One in March in Michigan, one in April in New York, and one in May in California. If Hillary Clinton wanted to debate, then so be it.

As reported in that same article, Clinton campaign spokesperson Brian Fallon responded to our offer this way: "We have always been willing to add additional debates beyond the six that had been scheduled and look forward to starting discussions on scheduling debates in April and May." Maybe he wasn't privy to the emails between his campaign and the DNC rigging the debate schedule in the first place.

The Clinton campaign dragged its feet on the locations for the later debates. They finally agreed to Michigan but were adamantly against New York. We held out on giving final approval for the February 4 debate. As late as February 2, 2016, *The Hill* was reporting that we still had not confirmed our attendance because the Clinton campaign would not agree to a New York debate. To this day, I do not understand why they fought so hard against debating in New York. It was completely favorable ground for them. Hillary Clinton had been elected twice statewide to the U.S.

Senate from New York. It was a closed primary, so no independents would be voting, and young people would be underrepresented.

As we neared the time for the debate in New Hampshire, it became clear that we would have to participate without the guarantee of a future debate in New York. They had given in on having the March debate in Michigan and seemingly the May debate in California. We would have to fight about New York later. On February 3, one day before the debate, Bernie confirmed on *Morning Joe* that he would attend.

And what of the DNC's strict rule against candidates participating in a debate other than the six announced in mid-2015? No problem. Chairwoman Wasserman Schultz "sanctioned" all four—the February 4 debate and the three additional we proposed. What had been impossible the summer before—expanding the number of debates—was suddenly done with a snap of the fingers.

As for the February 4 debate itself, it really did not break any new ground. Bernie was especially careful to avoid anything that looked like a personal attack. There would be no repeat of President Obama's "You're likable enough, Hillary" before the New Hampshire primary in 2008. The *New York Times* debate analysis by Nick Confessore, Maggie Haberman, and Alan Rappeport pointed out that Hillary Clinton tried to goad Bernie into attacking her on the issue of her financial support from big money interests. It would have been easy to land some points—the night before, at a CNN forum, Hillary Clinton had explained that the reason she took more than $600,000 in speaking fees from Goldman Sachs was because they offered it. But Bernie was too smart to fall for that one. He withheld the easy points to play for the win on the following Tuesday.

All the Sturm und Drang around scheduling the additional debate in New Hampshire netted the Clinton campaign zero benefit other than to keep us from sending Bernie to Nevada or South Carolina. On the other hand, we had secured three more debates in the following months. A pretty good trade.

Our campaign was housed in an aging Hampton Inn in Bow, New Hampshire. It was centrally located in the state, with easy access to most roads, so it did have that going for it. It was packed with headquarters staff who all had to share three small conference rooms. But one of the most memorable moments of the campaign happened there. Julian Mulvey, Tad and Mark's partner at DML (he's the "M"), was creating a series of five-minute videos for the campaign focusing on people of color. They were meant to tell the stories of real people in a more expansive way than is normally the case with thirty-second ads. We had given DML tremendous creative license, because we didn't want a run-of-the-mill product. Though much media attention was given to other ads they created, to me this series of five-minute ads represented their most powerful work.

While we were in New Hampshire, DML had just completed one of the ads. It featured Erica Garner, whose father, Eric Garner, had been choked to death by police on camera on the street in New York City. His crime was allegedly selling loose cigarettes. Mark Longabaugh started the video on his laptop as we all gathered around. I was sitting right next to Jane Sanders, and a large group of staff hovered behind us. The video focused on Erica Garner and her relationship with her young daughter, the death of her father, and her involvement in the Black Lives Matter protest movement. The video captured her real personal loss and her determination to fight back both to bring justice for her father's murder and also for her daughter's and her community's future.

As I watched the video and listened to her voice, her honesty overwhelmed me. Tears started streaming down my face. I looked over at Jane Sanders. Tears were streaming down her face. Symone Sanders was crying. And as I looked around at the rest of the staff, I understood what the expression "not a dry eye in the house" really meant. In the heat of the do-or-die New Hampshire primary, polls and debates and votes all became irrelevant for that all too brief moment.

While the polling in New Hampshire showed us winning, the margin was all over the map. The RealClearPolitics average of the polling for the week before the primary had Bernie up 13.3 points. But some of those polls had his lead only in single digits. The CNN/WMUR poll was the outlier, showing a 26-point lead. In 2008, Barack Obama had lost his single-digit lead over Hillary Clinton. If it could happen to him, it could happen to us. The importance of winning New Hampshire to the subsequent viability of the campaign cannot be overstated. Lose there and the race would continue, but we would have been fatally wounded. We all felt it, including Bernie.

On the Saturday before the primary, Bernie picked up the phone and called our pollster, Ben Tulchin, for the first time. "I'm a nervous guy. So what's the real story, Ben?" Ben reassured him. Our tracking had Bernie with a 21-point lead that had been maintained all week.

As Tulchin explained, the results of polling in New Hampshire were heavily driven by the assumptions the pollster made about who was going to vote in the New Hampshire primary—in particular, how many independents would participate in the Democratic primary. In the past, independent voters had comprised one-third to one-half of all Democratic primary voters in the Granite State. Bernie was winning that segment of the electorate by a 3-to-1 margin. If a pollster assumed only a third of voters would be independents, then one got a very different result than if one assumed, as Tulchin did and as the exit polling confirmed was the case, that independents would comprise 40 percent of the New Hampshire Democratic primary voters.

But that 40 percent number, despite turning out to be right, was an educated judgment, not a crystal ball. The wild card was the Trump candidacy. Despite his loss in Iowa to Senator Ted Cruz, Trump was running strong in New Hampshire. In the 2000 primary season, Republican John McCain had drawn many independents, sapping support for Bill Bradley in the Democratic primary, to the benefit of Vice President Al Gore. We were concerned that this phenomenon could repeat itself in 2016. In the end, Bernie's 22.7 percent margin of victory matched our tracking polls from the final week before the vote. Clinton's total was under 40 percent. We had won and won big. The result in Iowa was confirmed. We had the momentum.

A few words on the independent voters who are so important to the open primary process in New Hampshire and elsewhere, and the impact of excluding them from participating in the Democratic nominating contest in many states, including New York and Florida. Independent voters, according to a Gallup report on January 11, 2016, comprise 42 percent of all voters, while Democrats are 29 percent and Republicans are 26 percent. Democrats (and Republicans) need independent, or nonaligned, voters to win the White House. That is why success in a state like New Hampshire, which has a high percentage of independent voters participating in both parties' primaries, is an excellent indicator of strength in the general election. A failure to appeal to independents can spell real trouble in November. That is one reason why closed Democratic presidential primary contests (where only registered Democrats can participate) are bad. Candidates need to be tested in the primary season not only with core Democratic voters but also with independents in terms of general election viability.

In addition, Gallup's research puts the lie to the notion that independents are nonaligned. Most voters initially identifying as independent in fact lean toward one or the other party. Of the 42 percent of voters who identify as independent, 16 percent of that group lean toward the Democratic Party (putting Democrats plus Democratically aligned voters at 45 percent) and 16 percent lean toward the Republican Party (putting Republicans plus Republican-aligned voters at 42 percent), leaving only 10 percent who are truly nonaligned.

When Democrats close their primaries, they are excluding the Democratically aligned voters who comprise over 35 percent of its base of support. This hits young people particularly hard. As Gallup research has shown, while as a group they are far likelier to vote Democratic, they are also much more likely to be registered as independents (in the neighborhood of half). So closed primaries exclude over a third of base Democratic supporters and disproportionately push away young voters—the future of the party. That's a recipe over time for creating a Democratic Party that is older and much, much smaller.

And among young people, recent research suggests closed primaries may lock out a disproportionately higher percentage of young voters of color from the Democratic nominating process. According to the Pew Research Center data from 2014, 54 percent of millennials do not identify as either Democrats or Republicans. The number is highest among Latinos (59 percent), followed by whites (53 percent) and African Americans (43 percent).

The percentage of millennials overall who are independents but identify as Democratic-leaning is 27.5 percent. Only about 23 percent of white millennials fall into that category. But over 31 percent of African American and Hispanic millennials do. If you add in the number of millennial independents who are either Democratic-leaning or truly independent (that is, not Republican- or Democratic-leaning), the percentage of African American millennials who could be locked out of the Democratic primary process by a completely closed primary system would be almost 37 percent. The percentage of Latinos is almost 42 percent. That's no way to build a diverse party in the future.

The generational divide in terms of the percentage of voters who are Democratic-leaning independents is the widest among black voters. The percentage of African American millennials who identify as Democratic-leaning independents is twice that of those aged fifty-nine and above. It is hard to imagine any other context in which disenfranchising a disproportionate number of young people of color would be tolerated.

When looking at the impact of closed primaries across all age groups, Latino voters are particularly disadvantaged. The Pew research shows that Democratic-leaning independents make up a higher percentage of older Latino voters than in other racial groups. Over 20 percent of Latinos fifty-nine or older fall in that category and would be excluded under a closed primary.

How long will the millions and millions of voters who loyally vote for Democratic candidates in general election contests tolerate being barred from helping to choose the nominee of the party?

Finally, closing primaries to Democratically aligned voters means that members of the voting base who are otherwise identically situated are treated differently depending on where they live. Suppose you have a voter who consistently votes Democratic, gives money to Democratic candidates, and even volunteers for Democratic campaigns. If that voter lives in Virginia or Vermont, where there is no party registration, she can vote in the Democratic nominating process. If she lives in New York or Florida or Arizona, the fact that she doesn't have a little piece of cardboard in her wallet from the Democratic Party—and in that sense is the same as the voter in Virginia—means she is locked out of the process. So much for the principle of one person, one vote.

Closed primaries, then, produce weaker candidates and a weaker party; exclude base Democratic voters, especially younger ones; and disenfranchise people in selected states. So why do they exist? Well, they are good for allowing party bosses to more closely control who gets nominated and who runs the state party apparatus. It's not much more complicated than that. Opening the nominating process everywhere to nonaligned voters, who as a group constitute fully a third of the voters inclined to vote Democratic in a general election, is a priority for those of us who want the Democratic Party to be bigger, more successful, and more inclusive.

From a practical standpoint, reforming closed primaries may not be something the Democratic Party can do by fiat. The same is true of other, much-needed reforms, such as same-day registration and eliminating additional forms of voter disenfranchisement. These rules are put in place by state governments. Court challenges by the party to state-imposed closed primaries may yield positive results. But the Democratic Party does have complete control over how much representation each state has at the Democratic National Convention. The party can, for example, create incentives for states to do the right thing by awarding bonus delegates to the convention. By contrast, because caucuses are Democratic Party events, reforms to these contests can be mandated by the national party.

13

TRIPLE PARLAY CRAPS OUT IN VEGAS

FOLLOWING OUR BIG WIN in New Hampshire and come-from-behind tie in Iowa, our tracking polls showed Nevada closing to a dead heat. That was a tremendous improvement from our 33-point deficit in October and what was still a 15-point deficit in the third week of January. Tad's four-state knockout theory suddenly seemed not so crazy, even though we remained way behind in South Carolina. We acted immediately to take advantage of our newfound momentum.

We upped our TV buy there. And I authorized every single organizer from New Hampshire to go immediately to Nevada. But a number of critical factors conspired—both literally and figuratively—against us in the Silver State. The first was that our opponents also realized their deteriorating situation. They had talked for months about their racial firewall in Nevada and South Carolina. If we could breach it, they would be in real trouble. They also understood that, and started downplaying the importance of Nevada to their firewall, calling it an "80 percent white state," a move that created pushback from both then senator Harry Reid and the Nevada Democratic Party.

The entire Clinton family was dispatched to Nevada to fight for a comeback there. Campaign manager Robby Mook had run Nevada for the Clintons back in 2007–8, so he was familiar with the state.

They knew it inside and out in a way we did not, and they were going all-in.

Priorities USA, Clinton's super PAC, joined the fray. From the New Hampshire primary through the Michigan primary (a little over a month later), Priorities spent $4.2 million on direct mail and radio ads to support Hillary Clinton, as reported by *Time*'s Sam Frizell. The same article notes that Priorities intended to spend another $4.5 million on top of that in the March states that followed Michigan.

Our own organization in Nevada had had fits and starts from its very beginning. In the early fall, we hired Jim Farrell to be the state director. Jim was living in New Mexico and had worked with late senator Paul Wellstone when I was with Bernie in the House. We spoke by phone about the position, and he was extremely enthusiastic about it. He quickly moved to Nevada.

Jim began adding staff, but even early on we had problems—caused, in large part, by an internal power struggle in the state. Without laying the responsibility at anyone's feet, I would say that it created a toxicity in the organization that would have an impact until the caucus. As it came to a head in early November, Phil and I had conversations with Jim. We were going to be in Nevada in the next forty-eight hours for a rally in Las Vegas, so I suggested we put off trying to resolve the issue until we were on the ground and could meet in person.

Unfortunately, Jim decided to leave the campaign. On November 8, while we were in the air to Las Vegas, he packed up and left. Our arrival in Nevada was met with questions from the local media about our state director resigning when the Clinton campaign had such an early lead on us in terms of organizing. What we did not need was a negative narrative about our insurgent campaign coming apart in Nevada.

These stories practically write themselves. They have a timeline, identifiable personalities, and real or imagined drama. The truth is that the impact on a campaign the size of a presidential run (whether ours or anyone else's) of this or that person joining or leaving is almost always far less than is imagined.

Regardless, it was a political issue, if not a practical one, that had to be resolved quickly. Phil and I met with several staffers in the opulent lobby of the Mandalay Bay hotel. It was clear that there were two camps. Each had a candidate for Jim's replacement. Picking someone from one of the camps to succeed Jim Farrell would have created even more problems than we already had.

Phil and I sat privately after our meetings. We settled on Joan Kato as Jim Farrell's replacement. Joan had some Obama-related experience in Nevada. She was also extremely confident. In our interview that day, I asked her if she would accept the state director position if offered. She didn't skip a beat. "Yes," she said. We announced it to the staff. One of the other candidates for the position decided to leave Nevada. The other stayed on as field director. It turned out later that everyone would have been better off if he had been the one to leave.

Later in the campaign, he tried to lead a coup in Nevada against Joan Kato. He organized a letter from senior staff with a list of grievances against her. I don't like coups. They have no place on campaigns. If you have a problem or you believe the campaign has a problem, give me or someone else a call. That is everyone's responsibility on a campaign. But coups? Nope.

With the help of national field director Rich Pelletier and John Robinson, we fired the pretender to the throne. A deeper middle-level management structure would have allowed us to deal with some of the concerns in a more nuanced way. But we did not have the staffing or time. We had to push forward.

By the time we left Nevada, the *Las Vegas Sun* was reporting that after Jim's departure "campaign staffers were in disbelief. But by the start of the rally they already had a replacement, Joan Kato, and shooed off any notions that the campaign would suffer." We had turned a narrative of the campaign falling apart in Nevada to one of a smooth, professional operation that dealt quickly and decisively with bumps in the road. Immediate problem solved. Nevada, though, would continue to face challenges, internal and external.

Everywhere we went across the country, individuals were extremely kind to our campaign. And there was no place where that was more true than in Nevada. But that was not the case with the Nevada Democratic Party or some of the other insiders. The Nevada Democratic Party proved to be adversarial—a problem that worsened over time, until much-publicized confrontations between Bernie supporters and party officials occurred at both the Clark County Democratic convention and the state convention.

Joan Kato discovered, while traveling around the state, that Hillary Clinton's local campaign headquarters were in some cases co-located with the Democratic Party headquarters. This was clearly unacceptable. Our complaints to the party at first were ignored. Then the state party claimed that they had no control over local parties. Finally, after weeks of badgering, we got some movement in terms of separating offices.

Beyond that, the Nevada Democratic Party had real competency problems. For example, they had lost tens of thousands of records from the 2008 caucuses. This made it extremely difficult to contact voters who were previous caucusgoers.

In fairness, there were occasions when we unnecessarily rubbed them the wrong way. At the annual Nevada Democratic dinner, our people brought obnoxiously loud air horns and vuvuzelas. The noise was cacophonous. It made it difficult if not impossible to hear the speeches. Even when Bernie spoke, the revelers would break into "music," as he described it, every time he got to an applause line. As a result, the crowd could not hear him. I have since heard that such noisemakers are now prohibited. At the time, they were a sign of the growing frustration our people on the ground felt toward the conduct of the party establishment.

Speaking of the party establishment, Harry Reid publicly stayed neutral during the caucus process. He and Bernie had a long history together in the Senate, and Senator Reid had always been fair to Bernie. He also indisputably controlled the Democratic Party in Nevada. He was its patron, its protector, and its master. So having Senator Harry Reid be neutral was a big benefit to us.

Jon Ralston would later write, in *USA Today*, that Harry Reid had in fact intervened with both the biggest union in the state (also officially neutral) and casino owners to help ensure a Clinton victory. Describing Reid as a "man with one eye" and someone "Machiavelli would have bowed to," Ralston claimed that a major part of Reid's effort was to convince the casino owners and the casino workers' union to pump turnout at the caucus locations on the Strip.

Unique to Nevada, some caucus sites are located in the casinos. The well-intentioned purpose of these sites is to allow Nevada shift workers who wouldn't be able to make it home to participate in the caucus. However, establishing caucus locations that are essentially controlled by large employers has problems, and that system needs to be carefully scrutinized before the next cycle. I have heard more than one Obama supporter/worker complain that they were physically barred from entering caucus sites at pro-Clinton casinos in 2008.

That being said, the problem with Ralston's claim is that increasing the number of participants alone in these locations would not have benefited Clinton, because the number of county convention delegates allocated to each site was set prior to the caucus. The only way to ensure victory is to change the proportion of the people in the room who support each candidate. In other words, you would have to pack the room with Clinton supporters. Did that happen? Online video did circulate that shows people streaming into at least one casino caucus location without checking in, so it is certainly possible that there were shenanigans. But that is not Ralston's claim. In the end, it is difficult to know how accurate Ralston's narrative is.

Jon Ralston is a journalist/talking head held out as a local expert on state politics—your go-to insider. Most states have one. Unlike most, Ralston's view is, shall we say, more "truthy" than truthful. In fact, he was the source of all the false reporting about chairs being thrown at the May 14, 2016, Nevada state Democratic convention. Even though he had long left the event, he tweeted that chairs had been thrown by Bernie supporters. There was no evidence to back him up. No video. Nothing. In terms of fake news in the 2016 campaign season, Ralston was the king. (In 2014, he had been exposed by Watchdog.org after continually attacking the Nevada Republican attorney general candidate without disclosing that he was actively working to help elect the Democratic candidate.)

No evidence of chair-throwing could be produced because it never happened. A top Clinton representative who was there the entire time was greatly amused when I asked him about chair-throwing at the Nevada

Tad and I watch the Iowa caucus returns at the Des Moines Holiday Inn. Kenneth Pennington and Mark Longabaugh are in the background. *(Arun Chaudhary)*

Bernie delivers his Iowa victory speech. *(Arun Chaudhary)*

Bernie's 4am pickup truck address to New Hampshire supporters. *(Arun Chaudhary)*

Bernie and I deep in conversation in Nevada. *(Eric Elofson)*

Bernie at the Presidential Library of FDR whose unfinished work we fought to complete. *(Eric Elofson)*

Bernie supporters who our opponents and the media tried to erase. *(Hilary Hess)*

Black Men for Bernie campaigned across the country, including here in Pennsylvania. *(Fred Guerrier)*

Supporters at an event on Bernie's HBCU tour. *(Eric Elofson)*

Sorry, Gloria Steinem, they are not just here to meet boys. *(Arun Chaudhary)*

Bernie and a campaign worker share a moment. *(Hilary Hess)*

Bernie joyfully accepts the name bestowed upon him by Native American leaders in Washington State. The English translation of the name is "the one lighting the fires for change and unity." *(Eric Elofson)*

Let's hope this New York supporter isn't a Democratically aligned independent who could have voted in most states but whose vote was suppressed in the Empire State. *(Eric Elofson)*

How many of the 30,000 at Bernie's Washington Square rally were turned away at the polls by exclusionary Democratic primary rules or improper voter file purges? *(Arun Chaudhary)*

This is what panics the establishment and why they are trying to erase the existence of people of color who support Bernie. *(Arun Chaudhary)*

Bernie and Jane get a hero's welcome from Vermonters on March 1, 2016. *(Hilary Hess)*

National Nurses United members were always there to support Bernie. *(Fred Guerrier)*

This chapter is ended . . . for now. *(Arun Chaudhary)*

state convention when we were together at the Orlando Democratic plat-form committee meeting. "Was there a single chair thrown?" I asked him. Holding back laughter, he said, "No."

The national news media ran with Ralston's fake story—Alan Rappe-port of the *New York Times*, Erica Werner of the Associated Press, Rachel Maddow of MSNBC, NPR, and more. Later, in a May 18 determination, NPR's own ombudsman, Elizabeth Jensen, found NPR's story lead—which included reference to violence and chair-throwing—"misleading."

Never one to miss a chance to pile on, Debbie Wasserman Schultz went on CNN to attack Bernie. In an interview with Chris Cuomo, I subse-quently called her out for "throwing shade on the Sanders campaign from the very beginning"—a line that played all day long on CNN.

CounterPunch's Doug Johnson Hatlem reported that Jon Ralston later admitted to not having seen any chairs thrown (because he of course wasn't there at the time, and no chairs were thrown). Rather, he had been relying on a local reporter, Andrew Davey. In this Twitter exchange, Davey vouches for the false chair-throwing story:

Jon Ralston @RalstonReports

Convention ended w/security shutting it down, Bernie folks rushed stage, yelling obscenities, throwing chairs. Unity Now! On to Philly 2/2

> **Andrew Davey** @atdleft
> Replying to @RalstonReports
> Yep. We'll have a full report tomorrow. People had to be directed out of the room when the chair throwing began.

> **Jon Ralston** @RalstonReports
> You get video?

> **Andrew Davey** @atdleft
> I have plenty of stills, & I've seen some videos posted around social media.—at Paris Hotel & Casino Parking Garage

Davey, whose Twitter profile describes him as a "troublemaker" and "Managing Editor at Nevada Forward," proved that making trouble is a more important part of his résumé than journalist. He never produced any real proof.

What did happen was that a lot of our people showed up at the state convention expecting to be cheated. And with good cause. As Megan Messerly, then of the *Las Vegas Sun*, reported at the Clark County convention, only a few weeks before, party officials, at the express request of Hillary for America's head lawyer, Marc Elias, had unsuccessfully tried to depose their own credentials chair, Christine Kramar, at what was supposed to be a secret meeting. Our people got wind of it and showed up, which scuttled the plan. The next morning, party officials announced that the credentials chair had been suspended for the day.

When the credentials chair wouldn't leave the convention, the party called the police and threatened to have her arrested. Her crime: not being sufficiently reliable from the standpoint of the Clinton campaign. Elias's letter contained only vague allegations of bias as justification for Kramar's removal.

In hindsight, based on their challenge of the credentials of all delegates at the Polk County convention in Iowa, it is clear that manipulating the credentials process was a Clinton campaign strategy employed when they believed our delegates would outnumber theirs at party conventions. To pull that off, neutral credentials officials were not going to do. As in Polk County, our delegates at the Clark County convention outnumbered the Clinton delegates, even though more Clinton delegates were elected at the precinct level.

Matt Berg and Joan Kato were onsite and called me. They were discussing the incident with a representative of the party. I said to Matt Berg, "Please hand the phone over to him so I can talk to him myself." I could hear Matt telling him that I wanted to talk to him. Matt came back on the line, "He won't talk to you." So much for trying to work things out.

We took to social media to try to put some pressure on the party to handle the process fairly. As reported by the *Washington Post*'s John Wagner, "Weaver also complained about the messy process, saying on Twitter that the Democratic National Committee should take a hard look at whether Nevada deserves one of the first four slots on the nominating calendar."

I knew this was a pressure point for them. Because of Harry Reid's position, Nevada was third. It was prestigious to be in the first four. It was justified as a means to ensure that the nation's growing Latino population had a say early in the nominating contests. But that position didn't have to be filled by Nevada. Colorado or New Mexico were other possibilities. My point about Nevada's place in the calendar didn't get any results in terms of a fairer process that day, but it didn't go unnoticed.

I caught up to Bernie, who was preparing for a Wisconsin rally not long afterward. He wanted to see me right away. That didn't sound good.

I walked into a small room and greeted him. "Hello, Bernie, how are things?" I asked. "Well, not good, Jeff. I just got off the phone with Harry Reid," he said. His voice had a mischievous quality, indicating to me that there was more to come.

"Is that right?" I replied. I had a pretty good sense of what was coming.

"Yes, and guess what? Your name came up," he continued. I definitely knew what was coming now.

"Did you say that you thought that Nevada shouldn't be in third place?"

"As a matter of fact, I did," I replied.

"Don't you think you should have run something as important as that by me before you did it?" he said more seriously. Before I could answer, he continued, "Harry Reid is not a happy camper."

"Well, there wasn't a lot of time, Bernie. They were trying to rig the Clark County convention. We couldn't let them steal this election, and I needed a pressure point," I explained. "And it looks like I hit the right one if Harry Reid is calling you."

"Alright, I get it," he said. Then, almost as an afterthought because his attention was already returning to the upcoming rally, he added, "But next time you go after Nevada's place, let me know ahead of time."

"No problem, Bernie," I said, leaving him to review his remarks.

Bernie and the whole campaign had evolved since the early days. We were all ready to go on offense to protect our supporters. Harry Reid wasn't happy with me that day, but we were fine friends when we got to the Democratic National Convention in Philadelphia.

These contentious and controversial convention issues, however, were far in the future when we arrived in Nevada for our final push following Bernie's New Hampshire victory. With our polling now even, and with the cavalry in the form of dozens of New Hampshire field organizers on the way, we were in a very hopeful place.

Unfortunately, just as we were trying to ride the wave of momentum in Nevada and would have to effectively integrate all the new arrivals into a state organization that had its problems, I became quite ill. I spent days lying in my hotel bed fighting the fever, chills, and associated unpleasantness of the flu. I would sleep for two hours, then roll over to answer texts and emails before falling back to sleep. It was miserable.

I considered going home for a few days. But the thought of getting on a cross-country flight in my condition didn't make sense. I struggled through it in Las Vegas. Now I find Las Vegas to be a fun place, but I can tell you that it is a lonely place to be sick in bed.

As caucus day approached, we were still hopeful despite our polling having slipped by 6 points. The turnout was the wild card. You can be down single digits and make it up by having an enthusiastic base of support that comes out for you. One bright spot was Bernie's rapidly growing support in the Latino community. Among younger Latino voters in particular, that growth was explosive. From our first poll in October to late January tracking polls, Bernie's relative support among Latinos aged eighteen to fifty-four shifted a full 60 percentage points. In our January tracking poll, we had pulled ahead of Clinton with this group of voters even though we continued to trail with white voters. In Nevada, as everywhere else, we were winning overwhelmingly with millennials.

It was not surprising to us that support among Latino voters was growing. Bernie often spoke of his father's own immigrant story. And while every community's immigrant experience is different, it resonated that his father came to the United States, speaking almost no English and with almost no money, in search of a better life for himself and his future family. In addition, our campaign invested heavily in reaching out to the Latino community—as we did with the African American community, although it took longer for support to build with black voters. The effort was spearheaded by Erika Andiola, Cesar Vargas, and the rest of our Latino outreach team.

Tulchin's final tracking before the Nevada caucus, comprised of about 1,000 interviews, showed us up 9 points with Latino voters. The big driver of this win was a 14-point lead among Latinos aged eighteen to fifty-four.

On February 20, caucus day in Nevada, Bernie visited various caucus sites. As on every election day, we were scrambling for whatever intelligence was available. Tad and I were sitting in the backseat of a car when Tad called a friend at one of the media decision desks. A decision desk at a media organization is staffed by people who closely monitor voting patterns and election results on election day and make the judgment about when to call a race for this or that candidate. They look at all kinds of data, including turnout in various areas, and entrance and exit polls. It is their job to not make a mistake and embarrass their organization by calling a race wrong.

I remember driving down an interstate off-ramp in Las Vegas as Tad hung up his cell phone. He had been speaking with one of his decision desk contacts. It was early afternoon; the Nevada caucus had been going on for a couple of hours. As he hung up, Bernie asked, "So, what did they have to say?"

"Good news," said Tad. "Based on what they are seeing now, they think you are going to win."

The prediction was not confined to that one media organization. There was a growing expectation that Nevada could be as close as Iowa, or that Bernie could win outright. That expectations game would hurt us when the final results (a 5.3-point loss) came in, almost perfectly matching our late polling, which showed a 6-point deficit.

Both the Edison entrance and exit polls on caucus day confirmed another aspect of our polling. It showed us winning with Latinos by 8 to 9 points. Exit and entrance polls are media-funded interviews of actual voters at key voting locations. We put out a statement that we had won the Latino vote in Nevada, even though we lost the overall contest.

The Clinton campaign shot back. This reality went to the heart of their false narrative that Bernie had no support from voters of color. As reported by *Politico*'s Eliza Collins, the response of Clinton's traveling press secretary, Nick Merrill, to our claim was to tweet: "I don't typically like to swear on Twitter, but by all accounts so far this is complete and utter bull——t." The *New York Times*' Nate Cohn and FiveThirtyEight's Nate Silver challenged our claim as well. Cohn's piece cites the work of Latino Decisions—a firm that was retained by the Clinton campaign. If the Clinton campaign had any polling showing that it was winning Latino voters in Nevada, it never released them.

Here's ours (never before released):

NEVADA 2016 PRESIDENTIAL CAUCUS VOTE OVER TIME AMONG LATINOS

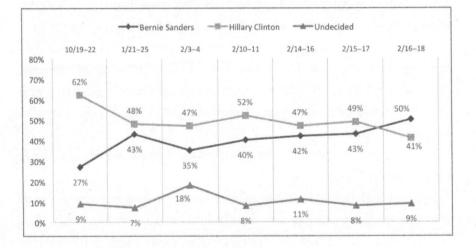

What was needed was an independent expert validator. Enter Antonio Gonzalez, president of the Southwest Voter Registration Education Project, a well-established Latino organization that, according to the *Los Angeles Times*, "has been working in Nevada ahead of the state's Democratic caucus." In a press release, Gonzalez took aim at the Clinton campaign's analysis to justify its claim it won Latino voters: "We note that some analysts have said that Secretary Clinton's victories in heavily Latino precincts proved that she won the Latino vote. However, the methodology of using heavily Latino or 'barrio' precincts to represent Latino voting behavior has been considered ineffective and discarded for more than 30 years due to non-barrio residential patterns common among Latino voters since the 1980's."

The press release, as quoted by CounterPunch's Doug Johnson Hatlem, continued: "The Clinton margin of victory is adequately explained by the large margin of victory Secretary Clinton won among African American voters. . . . There is no statistical basis to question the Latino vote breakdown between Secretary Clinton and Senator Sanders [in the Edison entrance and exit polling]." Our polling indeed showed that Secretary Clinton won overwhelmingly with African American voters in Nevada. In a phone interview with Hatlem, Gonzalez was more blunt in supporting the results of Edison's entrance and exit polling showing Bernie winning Latino voters in Nevada: "This whole dispute is baloney. I don't dispute the Edison numbers at all."

As the focus moved to South Carolina, the question of which candidate won the Latino vote was left hanging until it was irrefutably demonstrated on March 1 in Colorado. The media narrative was that our campaign had suffered a setback in Nevada. But if anyone back in the summer of 2015 had said that Bernie Sanders would come within 5.3 percent of Hillary Clinton in Nevada, he or she would have been a laughingstock. We were now competing in a new environment, with a 20-point win or greater in New Hampshire and rising expectations. And our first real setback was right around the corner.

With the loss in Nevada, we were now going to have to fight vote by vote, delegate by delegate, state by state. We went back to the week-by-week schedule that Mark Longabaugh had worked out, and we planned an approach that would provide us with wins every week.

We had some tough decisions to make. We would soon be leaving the phase of the campaign where it was one state at a time. Within a month, we would be competing in eleven contests on a single day, March 1, and less than two weeks after that we'd be competing in five states on March 15. Ohio, Florida, North Carolina, and Illinois had very expensive media markets. And there were important contests in between, including Michigan, which we viewed as critically important. Even with the millions now flowing into the campaign, we could not go full-bore everywhere.

The fourth of the first four states was coming up, but unlike the first three, it was being held only four days before March 1—the date on which ten states and one territory would all cast their votes. This would be followed by four more states before March 8, when Michigan would vote. A week later, big, expensive states would go to the polls. Until we got through South Carolina, the March 1 states, and the next four (Maine, Kansas, Nebraska, and Louisiana), we would not have the luxury of focusing on just one state in terms of Bernie's schedule.

Our benchmark polls in December of eight of the March 1 contests had been inauspicious. We were down by double digits in every single one. Four of those (Colorado, Massachusetts, Minnesota, and Oklahoma) were better (we didn't poll in Vermont, where we assumed we would be strong)—but, in the case of Massachusetts, not wildly better.

We had decided that these five represented our best chance of success on March 1, because we were doing better there, even if better was not great. Massachusetts was particularly troubling. We had run thousands of points of television in the Boston media market in the lead-up to New Hampshire. And we were still almost 20 points down. I met with Tad and Mark, both of whom had Massachusetts-specific campaign experience.

"What can we tell the people of Massachusetts that they haven't already heard?" I asked.

Tad weighed in. "Don't worry. We haven't advertised in the Springfield or Providence markets yet, and when we do you'll see dramatic movement."

That didn't seem right to me, but it turned out to be 100 percent correct.

The week before the New Hampshire primary, Mark Longabaugh and I laid out the states through March 15 on a whiteboard and worked out a preliminary paid media budget. We called Revolution Messaging and got fresh estimates on fund-raising. The all-in strategy of the first four states was not an option. It was not economically sustainable.

We assigned small buys for Kansas and Nebraska. We assigned nothing for Maine, because it was receiving a lot of Boston TV that we were running to reach southern New Hampshire, and we rightly believed we were strong there.

Michigan would be a priority because of its important place in our strategy. We would also make buys in Colorado, Minnesota, and Oklahoma. In Massachusetts, we would focus on the media markets outside of Boston. And in the South, outside of South Carolina and Florida, we would rely on a national cable news buy and African American radio. We just didn't have the resources to fight with equal intensity everywhere.

On March 15 we would invest in Missouri, Illinois, Ohio, and, to a lesser degree, North Carolina. Florida was another story. We expected Florida to be difficult. It had an older population and it was a closed primary. Also, there is a lot of early voting in Florida. Any meaningful paid media had to be spread over a longer time period to be effective. Finally, it's expensive. We decided to target advertising in central and upstate regions only.

When we had everything up on the whiteboard, Mark looked at it and then looked at me.

"We are going to be short in a bunch of places," he said.

"Well, I have to keep a reserve. We can't spend below $10 million, because I have to be sure we have money until the end," I replied.

"Okay, well, then, this will have to do," Mark said, resigning himself to the reality that we both understood. We couldn't do everything everywhere.

As it turned out, we ended up with more resources than we budgeted that day, but we also spent much more in Nevada than expected when we bumped our spending after New Hampshire.

Shortly before the South Carolina primary we did another round of polling. We were making progress in many states. In Colorado we were now down only 1 point among likely caucusgoers. In Minnesota we were down 9. In Massachusetts we were down 4 (quite an improvement), and in Oklahoma we were down 2. In the fall, Oklahoma Republican senator Jim Inhofe had told Bernie that he would do well there. Senator Inhofe and Bernie are polar opposites, especially when it comes to climate change. Inhofe is a climate-change denier. But they have a cordial relationship.

"You're going to do well in Oklahoma, Bernie," Inhofe said.

"Why do you say that?" Bernie asked.

"Because you've got to be really liberal to be a Democrat in Oklahoma," the Republican opined. That wasn't an entirely accurate assessment of the state of the race in his home state. Oklahoma allowed independents to vote as well.

But we certainly were doing better there. We also had a top campaign manager, Pete D'Alessandro, who had taken the helm there after Iowa. And we also had strong organizations in the other three. Colorado (led by Dulce Saenz) and Minnesota (led by Robert Dempsey) were both caucus states, so a strong ground game was especially important. And Massachusetts was led by Paul Feeney, who had been with the International Brotherhood of Electrical Workers (IBEW) before the campaign. The other important fact about these three was that the February polls were taken after our paid media campaigns had begun in each. As was the case throughout the campaign, the combination of a strong campaign on the ground and a robust paid media effort made for success.

In the four southern March 1 states that we polled in December (Arkansas, Texas, Tennessee, and Virginia), our February polls showed that, although we had made some progress, none of them were even close. We had people leading our ground efforts in each: (Kelvin Datcher (Alabama), Sarah Scanlon (Arkansas), state representative LaDawn Jones (Georgia), Matt Kuhn (Tennessee), Jacob Limon (Texas), and Peter Clerkin (Virginia). But our limited paid media was a serious problem.

Former NAACP head Ben Jealous, who had joined our effort by then, assisted in the placement of black radio ads. His strong support, including many effective public and television appearances, were critical throughout the primaries.

But our budget constraints hurt. A lot.

14

PALMETTO STATE SETBACK

SOUTH CAROLINA WAS THE THIRD STATE we organized. With the help of local political operative Lachlan McIntosh, Phil and I had traveled to South Carolina over the summer to begin interviewing staff. Lachlan was running a mayor's race in Charleston at the time, so he was not available to work on the campaign full time.

He did, however, line up a group of people for us to interview in his offices. Based on those meetings, we hired Chris Covert to be our South Carolina director in August. We also hired Lawrence Moore as political director. In September, we brought on Christale Spain, the former deputy executive director of the South Carolina Democratic Party. CBS News reported her hiring as a big coup for the campaign (that kind of coup I like), as she had strong ties to the South Carolina Democratic Party and to the African American community.

We knew from the beginning that South Carolina was going to be more difficult. As confirmed by our polling in October, Bernie was just not as well known there. The Clintons were. People forget that while Barack Obama ended up winning South Carolina in 2008 after his success in Iowa, Hillary Clinton led during the fall.

The Clinton campaign also had the advantage of having run a campaign in South Carolina (and in every other state in the country) before. They knew the political networks much better than we did. As was the case elsewhere, they also had many more operatives and surrogates who were tied into those networks. As NBC's Alex Seitz-Wald put it in a late November story, "It's not that Sanders can't make inroads into the African-American community in the primary, it's that he now has less than 100 days to make up for Hillary Clinton's two-and-half-decade head start."

With our close loss in Nevada, we were not heading into South Carolina with the kind of momentum that would be needed to actually win. Our goal was to not be entirely blown away there—to keep the delegate math competitive. More importantly, exceeding expectations in South Carolina (which were low) could help with the southern March 1 primaries. They were only four days after the South Carolina primary.

That being said, our campaign had been committed to competing in South Carolina. Bernie made more trips and spent more time there, according to Democracy in Action, than did Secretary Clinton in 2015–16. He held and attended events across the state, such as Congressman Jim Clyburn's annual fish fry, where he was mobbed by supporters. And we committed the resources beyond his appearance schedule. We had decided in the fall that it was the southern state where we would make a stand. We had a large staff and a paid canvass operation that employed dozens. As CNN's Elizabeth Landers reported on January 25, we had gone up on TV in South Carolina at the end of January. We had run ads there on African American radio featuring the voice of House of Cards star Reg E. Cathey since December.

By the time South Carolina voted, Bernie had not yet broken through with African American voters as he would later in the campaign. With his commitment to the Senate work schedule in the summer and fall, and the heavy focus on the two earliest states, there ended up just not being enough time to build relationships in a part of the country where he was not known, and in particular with African American voters.

This was compounded by the fact that as the election in South Carolina drew near, and voters were paying increasing attention, Bernie had to try to make appearances in a dozen states. In the week between the Nevada caucus and the South Carolina primary, he not only campaigned in the Palmetto State but also made appearances in Minnesota, Texas, Oklahoma, Michigan, Massachusetts, Ohio, Illinois, Missouri, and Virginia.

The Clinton campaign put on a full-court press in South Carolina, including deploying legions of surrogates. It made sense for Hillary, because she needed the big win that had so far eluded her, and after the Latino vote swung for Bernie in Nevada, she needed a proof point for her narrative that minority voters didn't like Bernie Sanders. In some appearances, she adopted a southern accent that I'm sure none of her New York constituents had ever heard.

She also stepped up an attack line that she would fall back on throughout the campaign—that she was loyal to President Obama and Bernie was not. Her proof points were that she had served as Obama's secretary of state and that Bernie had been critical of some of Obama's policies. The Clinton campaign even used Bernie's support of single-payer health care as evidence of animus against President Obama. Of course, she never raised all the acrimony of the 2007–8 campaign. The truth of the matter, as I would point out on occasion, was that if the Clintons had had their way, there never would have been a President Obama. Regardless, the Clinton campaign's argument proved to be an effective one with African American voters in the early states.

Our dedicated cadre of African American surrogates fought valiantly for Bernie in South Carolina. State representatives Terry Alexander, Justin Bamberg, Wendell Gilliard, and the late Joe Neal; Dr. Cornel West; state senator Nina Turner of Ohio; Ben Jealous; actors Danny Glover and Reg E. Cathey; state senator Vincent Fort of Georgia; and others all stood with him. We ran radio ads with Spike Lee later in the effort. Our local endorsers in particular risked a lot politically.

On the day of the South Carolina primary, I flew down to be with our staff. We knew we were going to lose, and I wanted to be there. Scott Goodstein of Revolution Messaging came along as well. Like everyone else, the staff on the ground also knew that we were not going to win, but they were hopeful that we would have a respectable showing.

At around 4:00 p.m. I talked with a reporter and asked about the exit polling. The reporter told me that we were at 23 percent. It was a devastating number.

I called Bernie. He took it in stride.

We ended up doing slightly better, but only slightly—26 percent.

Top Clinton aide Huma Abedin and I spoke in the late afternoon. I asked her where Secretary Clinton was going to be that night, so Bernie could call after the results were announced. She said that they were likely to be traveling. I told her I wanted to make sure that Secretary Clinton was able to receive the congratulatory call that night.

"If it's okay with you, let's just count the call we are having right now as the congratulatory call," she said, trying to come up with a resolution. "And if anyone asks, we will certainly say that Bernie called."

"That's fine with me," I said. I was confident that if Huma had said it, it would be the case.

Unlike Nevada, which was a setback in the eyes of the media, South Carolina was a real loss. A number of factors weighed against us. Our organization in South Carolina had had some difficulties during the fall. Our ambitious paid canvass operation had to be completely retooled from scratch at one point, which set us back. The Republican primary was held a week earlier than the Democratic contest. And the Republican contest was hotly contested. Many independent voters were pulled into that primary and were therefore ineligible to vote for Bernie. Young voters were not turning out in the percentages they had in earlier contests.

But the crux of the problem was that at this point in the campaign the African American community was still firmly behind Hillary Clinton. Even though the margin was much closer, Clinton was even ahead with younger black voters, something that would change once the campaign progressed. And among older black voters in South Carolina we had done very poorly. Bernie himself summed it up this way on CBS's *Face the Nation*: "No question, let me be very clear: we did really, really badly with older African American voters. I mean, we got decimated."

15

THROUGH THE SHOWDOWN
IN MOTOWN

MARCH 1 ENDED UP MUCH as we had anticipated. Hillary Clinton swept the South. Bernie's overwhelming victory in Vermont was deeply moving to the entire Sanders family. He won all the pledged delegates— the only state where one candidate captured them all. Thousands attended the accompanying rally at the Essex Junction fairgrounds, after which Bernie headed home. I went to our Burlington headquarters.

The other states we expected to win were going to be closer than Vermont had been for us or the southern states had been for Clinton, so the entire staff gathered to follow the results. I nervously paced for hours waiting for the results. If we were beaten everywhere outside Vermont, it would be hard to make the case that our campaign had a path forward.

In the end, we won three more contests that night and came within 2 points in Massachusetts. Our strategy paid off in terms of state wins. Significantly, the 19-point margin that Bernie won by in Colorado was so large that it would have been almost statistically impossible to have pulled it off without winning the Latino vote there. This clear win among Latino voters in Colorado—confirmation of our claim about Nevada—would be overshadowed by Clinton's wins with African Americans across the South.

In the next week, Bernie won four more contests, while losing only one. Between South Carolina and Michigan, each candidate had won eight contests. Clinton won Georgia, Alabama, Arkansas, Texas, Tennessee, Louisiana, Massachusetts, and American Samoa. Bernie had won Colorado, Minnesota, Oklahoma, Kansas, Nebraska, Maine, Vermont, and Democrats abroad. Hillary Clinton did have a large delegate lead after March 1. But we were intent on chipping away at that lead as the calendar moved forward. Hillary Clinton's lead looked far more impressive in news reports, because the media would include the hundreds of superdelegates that were pledged to—but not bound to—her.

Michigan had been a key target for our campaign since the early fall. It represented the first opportunity for Bernie to compete in and win a large, diverse primary state. Our benchmark polling in Michigan in mid-February had us down 9. Only single digits! That was the first state where our benchmark poll did not have us down double digits. Also important was the fact that we were doing much better with African American voters, particularly young African American voters, than we had in the South.

Michigan is one of the only states where we did focus groups. Through those discussions with voters, we learned that Bernie's rigged-economy message was extremely well received by working-class voters in the state. And his position on criminal justice reform was powerful with younger voters, particularly young voters of color. But the single most powerful issue with voters in Michigan overall was Bernie's opposition to the unfair free-trade agreements that had devastated America's industrial heartland. For people in Michigan, free trade was imposed with a high cost to workers, their families, and their communities.

It was an issue that cut across racial lines. Because of opportunities in the auto industry, a thriving black middle class had arisen in Detroit and surrounding communities. Articles like Jonathan Mahler's June 24, 2009, *New York Times Magazine* piece chronicle the vibrancy of that community and its decline as domestic auto production died. David Goldberg, an African American Studies professor at Wayne State University, is quoted as pointing out that "it wasn't that long ago that Detroit was the home of the nation's most affluent African-American population with the largest percentage of black homeowners and the highest comparative wages."

The impact of American trade policy, and NAFTA in particular—and its role in exporting American auto production—was an issue that we knew we had to focus on, especially as it was an issue where Bernie and Secretary Clinton had very different positions and records. In our paid media, we highlighted the rigged economy, the need for criminal justice reform, and trade.

The other issue that dominated the discussion in Michigan was the Flint water crisis. Due to neglect and malfeasance on the part of state leaders, the people of Flint, Michigan, were exposed to contaminated water—a fact that was kept from them. It had a devastating impact on the health of the community, especially on Flint's children. As early as mid-January 2016, Bernie had called for Michigan's governor to resign over the issue—a position that Hillary Clinton would not adopt until the March 6 debate. Bernie met with Flint families in a low-key meeting in mid-February. CNN's Elizabeth Landers observed that Bernie "struggled to describe the meeting when he took the stage last week at a rally in Dearborn, saying he cannot fathom a United States of America that allows children to be poisoned in 2016." ABC's MaryAlice Parks described him as "visibly and admittedly shaken by that meeting." And in fact he was. Although known for his large rallies, Bernie held small meetings—as he did with Flint families—in many different communities, often coming away unsettled. Early on, he met with a small group of Latinos who cried as they described how fearful they were that their families would be torn apart by broken immigration policies. In many of his speeches thereafter, he spoke of the "tears streaming out of" these young people's eyes. Flint, too, would find its way into his speeches across the country.

He followed up his meeting with Flint families with a community forum in the city in late February. "The event was a sharp contrast from the candidate's usual events, and Sanders began the community forum clarifying that this was not a rally. Instead, he spent most of the time listening to Flint residents," wrote Landers. It was indeed different from

Bernie's big rallies. But those of us who had worked with him knew well that this was exactly the kind of meeting that he had held in communities throughout Vermont for decades. I have little doubt that as president he would have held community forums from time to time.

The Clinton campaign sent top aides to meet with the mayor of Flint. This was heralded by some as a genuine sign of the secretary's interest and, in one *Huffington Post* piece, by Amanda Terkel, as evidence that Clinton "focuses on the pragmatic instead of the aspirational." I am confident that Secretary Clinton and her staff cared just as much as we did about the impact of Flint water contamination. How sending presidential campaign staff to meet with the mayor demonstrated her pragmatism, however, still escapes me.

We had two other big advantages in Michigan heading into the primary. The first was overwhelming support from the Arab American community. As reported by Michigan Radio, Maya Berry, executive director of the Arab American Institute and a Dearborn native, described why, in her view, Bernie did so well with the Arab American community: "The Sanders campaign did some 'very basic things' to draw Arab-American votes: reaching out to include the community in events, running a strong social media campaign in multiple languages, denouncing anti-Muslim and anti-immigrant rhetoric, and running Arabic-language ads."

The media made much about Muslims voting for a Jewish candidate, an observation that rightly struck many in that community as reinforcing stereotypes of Muslims as being anti-Semitic, as reported by the *Huffington Post*'s Kate Abbey-Lambertz and others. What the media missed was that Bernie's strong support among Arab Americans was another nail in the coffin of the false narrative that his political revolution was not multiracial.

Another important development was that the United Automobile Workers (UAW) elected to remain neutral in the election. This was important not only in Michigan but also nationally. Because the UAW, the National Association of Letter Carriers, IBEW, United Steelworkers, and other unions opted to stay out, and the National Nurses Union, the Postal Workers, the CWA, the Transit Workers, and others endorsed Bernie,

Clinton was denied an AFL-CIO endorsement—even though her campaign had hoped for the nod as early as August 2015. Reuters reported in July 2015 that the AFL-CIO was wary of an early endorsement of Clinton, because at that time she had not yet reversed her position to oppose the Trans-Pacific Partnership trade agreement: "President Richard Trumka said earlier this year that it was 'conceivable' that the AFL-CIO would not endorse any candidate in the 2016 race."

As John Nichols wrote in the *Nation*, by February 2016 AFL-CIO head Trumka announced definitively that no endorsement would be made. The work of union leader Larry Cohen and the many thousands of Bernie's grassroots labor supporters had paid off. Many locals, particularly of the IBEW, would go on to endorse Bernie. Even some locals of national unions that endorsed Clinton would back him, such as SEIU Local 1984, representing over 11,000 New Hampshire state employees.

Notwithstanding the fact that the UAW was officially neutral, there were many in its ranks and its hierarchy who were actively supportive of Bernie during the Michigan primary and played a critical role after the March 6 Michigan debate. Bernie campaigned in every corner of Michigan, because of its importance and because we had the luxury of a week's time before the next contests. Although he also made stops in Kansas, Nebraska, and Maine, this really was his first opportunity since before South Carolina to blanket a state with such intensity, sparking a *Grand Rapids News* story: "Bernie Sanders Goes Where Few Democrats Have Gone Before in Michigan."

As we headed to the finish line in Michigan, the public polling had Bernie way down. The RealClearPolitics polling average for the end of the race had Hillary Clinton up over 21 points. Nate Silver at FiveThirty-Eight predicted that Hillary Clinton had more than a 99 percent chance of winning Michigan. Still to come was the critical March 6 Michigan debate, one of the three we had secured in exchange for agreeing to Hillary Clinton's request for an additional debate in New Hampshire. Because Bernie was moving around Michigan so intensely, the amount of time for debate prep went way down. This was not really a problem; the national issues that would come up had been rehashed many times in previous debates. And Bernie was well versed on the issues that were more Michigan-focused, such as trade and Flint.

We began the debate with two pieces of good news. The first was that Bernie was announced the winner of the Maine caucus. The second, on which we held a pre-debate press conference, was the endorsement of Don Riegle, former U.S. senator from Michigan. In a speech announcing his endorsement, Riegle delivered broadside after broadside against both Hillary and Bill Clinton, as reported by Caitlin Dickson of Yahoo! News: "We have to do a necessary accounting of hurtful decisions of the Clinton administration between 1992 and 2000, key decisions made back then that badly damaged our country. The Clintons rammed NAFTA down the throats of the American people with false promises. This can't go on, unless you want to see a lot more communities look like Flint looks today." (If the Clinton campaign was following the rules of Honk-A-Mania that Bernie and I had established years ago, they were no doubt busily marking Senator Riegle down as "undecided.")

Then it was off to the debate. The tone turned out to be much sharper than previous ones. Both campaigns viewed Michigan as pivotal. For Clinton, it was a chance to land her own knockout blow against Bernie. We, on the other hand, were fighting for our lives to reestablish our momentum. The issues raised were as expected, until Hillary Clinton accused Bernie of having opposed the auto industry bailout during the Great Recession. Like Senator Riegle's attacks, hers was not nuanced. "I'll tell you something else that Senator Sanders was against," the *New York Times* transcript of the debate reads. "He was against the auto bailout." It was an attack that appeared to throw Bernie off a bit. He wasn't prepared for it because it wasn't true. He would later tell CBS's Kylie Atwood, "Sometimes somebody says something to you, and it is untrue, so it took me about 12 seconds or less than that, I figure, to try to understand what she was saying." But he quickly regained his footing. According to the *New York Times*, he responded as Clinton attempted to interrupt. "If you are talking about the Wall Street bailout, where some of your friends destroyed this economy . . ." In fact, she was.

Bernie had voted for a stand-alone auto bailout bill in December 2008. Republicans had killed that bill in the Senate when the UAW refused to cave to Republican demands that they cut their members' compensation, according to a December 2008 *Politico* story. What Bernie opposed was the release of the second half of the $700 billion Wall Street bailout package—which he had voted against when it was originally passed, and which the Bush administration was now promising to use a fraction of to help General Motors and Chrysler. (Ford never took any bailout funds.) At the debate, Bernie summed up his view on the Wall Street bailout in this way: "I believe that the recklessness, the greed, and the illegal behavior of Wall Street drove this country into the worst economic downturn in the history of the United—modern history of the United States of America. And I will be damned if it was the working people of this country who had to bail out the crooks on Wall Street." He then successfully pivoted to the issue of trade and Hillary Clinton's Wall Street connections. She was very vulnerable on both counts. We were pleased with the way the debate went. From our perspective, Bernie was strong on the Flint water crisis, trade, and Wall Street. Over the next few days, Clinton faced considerable backlash for her auto bailout claims.

On election day, David Axelrod, former Obama strategist and CNN commentator, called Clinton's auto bailout charge a "cheap shot" and "too cute by half." FactCheck.org called her claims "quite a stretch." Even Keith Hennessey, director of the White House National Economic Council staff for President Bush, wrote on his personal blog, "Secretary Clinton's attack misleads Michigan voters and others who supported the auto loans. She is playing semantic games in an attempt to create a policy difference where none exists."

Democratic senators who had voted the same way Bernie had, including moderate Democrat and Clinton endorser Evan Bayh, were quick to disagree with Hillary Clinton's attack, according to an article by David Sirota in the *International Business Times*:

> "My state, Indiana, is a big auto state, and I was always very
> strongly in favor of helping the auto companies, and I'm glad we

did," Bayh told Sirota. "So I would find it to be very unlikely that I cast something that at the time was perceived as an anti-auto vote. The United Autoworkers were always some of my strongest supporters; I had good relations with the auto companies themselves. So it couldn't have been primarily an up or down vote on the autos."

Pushback came from a lot of sources, but our looming concern was to get the word to voters. We were only a day and a half from the polls opening in Michigan, and if the false charge stuck, it could be devastating. Clinton aired an ad on the issue. We quickly aired radio ads the next day calling into question the honesty of the attack. Friends in the UAW circulated fact sheets to their email contacts.

The day of the Michigan primary, we moved to Florida. We were hopeful about Michigan, but the public polls had us way down and ours had us within single digits. My own prediction to the media traveling with us was that we would finish between 7 down and 2 up. We had a rally planned at the James L. Knight Center in Miami for that evening. It was scheduled to end before the final Michigan results came in. An enthusiastic crowd in Miami, which was holding its primary the following week, would be a much better visual than a disappointed crowd in Michigan if we were not successful there. Also, moving to Florida that day would give us time for prep on March 9 for that night's Univision debate. After Bernie's rally, we alerted staff and the media that all events were concluded for the day.

At 9:00 p.m., Decision Desk HQ, a website that provides real time election results, called the race for Hillary Clinton: "We project that Hillary Clinton will defeat Bernie Sanders in Michigan."

That's not a dig at them. They have a great track record. But it made the announcement even more inauspicious.

Bernie, Tad, Briggs, Bernie's son Levi, and I crammed into Bernie's small hotel room—the smallest in North America, it seemed—to watch the results come in. Tad started making calls to contacts in the media to see what information was available. He hung up his phone. "Well," he said, "everyone thinks it going to come down to Wayne County, and it will come in late." The time ticked by, minute by minute. Finally, around 11:30, the major networks called the race for Bernie. We cheered in the tiny hotel room.

There was a knock at the hotel door. A staffer was there to say that there was a media request for an interview with Bernie. "Well, I can't just talk to one media outlet without talking to everyone," Bernie said. "Let everyone know I'll come down and make a statement."

The job of setting up the poolside press conference fell to Joe Magee. Joe traveled with Bernie's party throughout the campaign and did a million different jobs, all of them well. But that night he didn't have the right tape as he tried to post Bernie placards on the poolside wall behind where Bernie would speak. The placards started falling, but he had managed to get a few to stick by the time Bernie came down. The pool area was poorly lit. Bernie looked like he was on the run giving an interview from an undisclosed location.

That same night, we lost the Mississippi primary by large margins, and Clinton actually increased her delegate lead. But because both campaigns had staked so much on Michigan, Bernie's victory there created all the buzz. The *Detroit Free Press* reported that turnout in Detroit was only 25 percent, and in Wayne County 31 percent, while it was closer to 40 percent statewide. For Hillary Clinton, the outcome of the Michigan primary was a foreshadowing of bad things to come in the general election. While she won black voters overall by large margins (but not younger black voters, according to all our internal polling), the turnout among black voters for her in the Michigan primary was not strong enough, and voters in small cities and towns and rural areas came out strongly against her.

In the general election, the *Detroit News* reported that "Trump also benefited from lower turnout in Wayne County and particularly Detroit, where Clinton received 47,840 fewer votes than Obama did in 2012. Clinton won Wayne County, but not by the margins Obama ran up in 2012 and 2008. She got 78,884 fewer votes than Obama, while Trump won 14,449 more votes in the state's largest county than Romney did." In the end, given the small margin by which Trump won in Michigan, all the warning signs were there but Brooklyn never tacked to address them.

What was also significant in Michigan was that Bernie did much better with African American voters than he had in the South. As Glenn Thrush pointed out the next day, Bernie's support among young voters broke through the final color barrier: "Sanders fought her to a draw among under-40 African-Americans."

This fact, that Bernie was winning with young people of all races, was ignored by most of the media. It ran counter to the Clinton campaign's self-serving message. And because the media did not do sufficiently expansive polling, they would never see it. But the young women and men behind #berniemademewhite got it right.

It wasn't until after the campaign was effectively over that the kind of polling and analysis would surface that would validate what young Bernie supporters of color (and our campaign staff) already knew. In June 2016, according to polling by GenForward, a survey of the Black Youth Project at the University of Chicago with the AP-NORC Center for Public Affairs Research, 54 percent of African Americans between the age of eighteen and thirty who voted in the presidential primaries supported Bernie Sanders—a full 14 points more than supported Hillary Clinton. Among Latinos age eighteen to thirty who participated in any primary, Bernie had the support of 60 percent, as compared with 20 percent for Clinton. Among Asian American millennials, it was Bernie, with 72 percent, and Hillary Clinton, with 13 percent. Among white millennials Bernie's support was 45 percent with 12 percent for Clinton (many more white millennials voted in the Republican primary than did millennials of any other race).

Taking millennials as a whole who voted in one or another primary during 2016, Bernie was far more popular with voters of color than with white voters. Jeff Guo, writing for the *Washington Post* in mid-July 2016, observed the following about GenForward's findings: "It challenges the stereotype that Sanders solely appeals to white liberal voters. Among millennials who are Democrats, Sanders commands majority support across ethnic groups."

Guo was right. If you look at just African American millennials who voted for Sanders or Clinton or O'Malley (and thereby exclude the small number of African American young adults who voted in the Republican primary or in a third-party contest), the report—based on almost 2,000 interviews—found that Bernie won the votes of well over 57 percent of young black voters. The same is true for other racial groups who participated in the Democratic primaries. Three-quarters of Latinos, over 80 percent of Asian Americans, and 79 percent of whites who voted in Democratic primaries went for Bernie.

Issac Bailey's piece for *Politico* on June 8, 2016, exemplifies the type of analysis that simply rested on inaccuracies. He wrote: "All the talk about Sanders representing the future of the Democratic Party because of his overwhelming popularity among young people leaves out an important caveat: He couldn't persuade minority voters to sign on." He then argues that black voters are more comfortable with incrementalist politics. For the record, I respectfully disagree with Bailey's claim that Dr. Martin Luther King, Jr.'s vision of a multiracial mass movement of poor and working people to secure civil and economic rights was incrementalist.

The GenForward research shows that whatever validity Bailey's piece may have had in terms of its analysis of politics in the African American community and its history, on this point—that the Political Revolution did not include a majority of young voters of color—he is empirically wrong. As are all the others who have denied the very existence, and in that sense the personhood, of the majority of millennials of color who supported Bernie's transformative vision for America. I don't have any particular bone to pick with Issac Bailey. It's just that his June 8 article is one of the most emphatic in terms of asserting this factually infirm premise. There were many others who perpetuated the myth for their own reasons.

The reason young people of color supported Bernie Sanders can also be found in the GenForward report. "Majorities of African Americans (60 percent), Asian Americans (69 percent), Latino/as (68 percent) and Whites (59 percent) picked Bernie Sanders as the candidate that best understands the problems of people like them." The corresponding percentages for Clinton were 35, 20, 23, and 11.

Bernie Sanders' strong favorability rating included young voters of all races—"73 percent of African Americans, 78 percent of Asian

Americans, 73 percent Latino/as, and 55 percent of Whites"—which led GenForward to the conclusion that so many have fought and continue to try to deny: "In many ways, our data suggests that Bernie Sanders appealed to Obama's coalition of young voters of color better than Hillary Clinton did." Contrast that with Bailey's assertion that "Clinton, for all of her supposed faults, has run a campaign so tactically effective she has been able to pull together a coalition similar to Obama's."

The findings of the GenForward study were confirmed by our own internal polling and, more importantly, what was happening on the street in 2015 and 2016, namely the Black Lives Matter movement. Started by young African Americans, Black Lives Matter's goals were supported by people of many races including Bernie Sanders. Their efforts to highlight and stop the killing of African Americans at the hands of or in the custody of authorities was so successful that in all our polling, no message was received more positively by young voters of all races than Bernie's call for criminal justice and police reform.

In his many meetings with Black Lives Matter activists, and in mine, from one end of the country to the other, participants could not have been more clear that the last thing they were interested in was incrementalism. The Black Lives Matter movement's uncompromising demand for bold, swift action does not represent "the ultimate expression of privilege"—a charge that Bailey (quoting Jonathan Chait) levels at other elements of the progressive movement whom he argues are too uncompromising.

The question is, if Bernie Sanders was winning the young African American vote, how come his overall vote totals among African Americans in so many states were low? Here's at least part of the answer: As Perry Bacon, Jr., then at NBC, reported at the end of May 2016, Bernie Sanders was winning the vote of African Americans under thirty based on Democratic primary exit polls in twenty-five states. While African Americans as a whole represented 25 percent of voters in the exit polls, African Americans under thirty were only 3 percent. Put another way, only 12 percent of black voters in the Democratic primaries were under thirty. That compares with an overall percentage of Democratic primary voters under thirty, who, according to CBS News in mid-May 2016, comprised 17 percent of Democratic primary voters. If my math is still good, that translates to a turnout percentage of 18.66 percent among voters under the age of thirty drawn from the 75 percent of Democratic voters who were not African American.

The low turnout among young black voters meant that Bernie's performance in the black community was going to be lower than among those communities with higher young voter turnout. According to Bacon, "Sanders' weak performances among African-Americans may have been because of their age, which made them more likely to back Clinton, like other older voters, not their race." That is certainly an important part of the explanation. Another is a phenomenon we witnessed consistently in our polling throughout the primaries. Among voters who had favorable opinions of both Hillary Clinton and Bernie Sanders—a number that grew substantially as the campaign progressed—Clinton was winning by over 30 points.

That Hillary Clinton was popular in the African American community as a whole from the beginning of the campaign is well documented. Even as Bernie became better known and more popular with black voters, we still had to overcome that challenge. The same was true of older voters, particularly women over fifty-five, who, from the start of the race, overwhelmingly viewed Hillary Clinton positively.

Compare that with the portions of the Democratic electorate that had less favorable views of Hillary Clinton—young voters and independents aligned with Democrats. They came out overwhelmingly for Bernie. In that sense, Bernie's commitment to run a positive campaign benefited Clinton. Democratic voters seemed unwilling to move away from her (for a lot of reasons) as long as they had a favorable view of her, even as Bernie's favorability with those same voters soared during the course of the campaign.

More recent polling shows that Bernie Sanders' high favorability rating with voters—voters of color in particular—is enduring and not limited to the young. *The Hill*, reporting in April 2017 on a Harvard-Harris poll, wrote that Bernie Sanders "is the country's most popular active politician." That article points out that he is popular among all racial groups—and most popular with African Americans (73 percent favorable), followed by Latinos (68 percent), Asian Americans (62 percent), and whites (52 percent). The reality is that the increasing number of young people of color coming of age in the country and within the Democratic Party bodes well for the future of the multiracial movement for transformative political and economic change that Bernie dubbed the Political Revolution.

16

TERRIBLE TUESDAY

AFTER BERNIE'S COME-FROM-BEHIND VICTORY in Michigan, we approached the race with renewed optimism. We had viewed Michigan as the gateway to Missouri, Illinois, and Ohio, which were coming up the next week. Having earned a share of the African American vote, we had finally broken through the last piece of Clinton's racial firewall.

As it turns out, her real firewall had been and would continue to be older voters. The single dominant determinant of who someone supported in the Democratic primaries was age, not race. In addition, after March 15 the remaining states were in the West, the Plains, the Midwest, and the Northeast—all areas where Bernie had demonstrated success.

But March 15 was still going to be a challenge. There were five big states at play, and a strategy of planting Bernie in a single state where he could go from town to town, rally to rally, was not going to be possible. Our job on March 15 was twofold: work to limit any further increase in Secretary Clinton's delegate advantage and to win in at least two states (three would be a home run!) so that we could maintain the momentum that we had coming out of Michigan. But our own internal polling showed another unexpected challenge.

We had polled all the March 15 states in mid-February. As had been the case almost everywhere else up to this point in the calendar, we found ourselves down by double digits, with Missouri having the best result and Florida the worst. We were also doing slightly better in North Carolina than in Ohio, which came as a surprise to us. When we did a new round of polling in the middle of the first week of March, our position was basically the same, except in Ohio, where our support had cratered. It made no sense. What would explain a precipitous loss of support in Ohio that would not also have affected Illinois and Missouri? It was a big concern.

We followed up with another round of polling right after the Michigan primary. We had made up a lot of ground in Illinois (where we were now only 12 points down) and Missouri (where our deficit had fallen into single digits). Ohio was better, but we were still down over 20 points, and below our original benchmark poll in February. Choices had to be made in terms of resources, the most valuable and scarce of which was Bernie's time. Should we scale back in Ohio and Florida and focus on our most promising two (or three) states? Winning Florida we knew was basically out of the question. With its high level of early voting, its older electorate, its closed primary, and its expensive media markets, the Sunshine State was always going to be a tall order. We had a few dedicated staffers there, and as we had concluded at our whiteboard session in New Hampshire, we were only going to be able to advertise in certain markets.

We talked with Bernie on March 9 about the schedule and laid the options on the table, carefully reviewing his time and the allocation of other resources. Bernie always wanted to compete everywhere. There were people hurting in every state, and he did not want to abandon them. As he frequently said, the national Democratic Party had basically ceded a large number of states to the Republicans—and the people of those states to often harsh Republican policies.

As a practical matter, we were already in Florida for the Democratic debate. We had done a rally in Miami the night of the Michigan primary. He would spend the day after the debate doing events in Florida and the rest of his time in the other four states. Because North Carolina was looking better than Ohio, Bernie wanted additional events there. Okay, no problem. We would cut events elsewhere so he could spend more time in North Carolina. But that was not what Bernie meant.

"Add them and leave the others in place," he said. "I'll just work really hard this week." With the Michigan winds at our backs, Bernie wanted to do it all. And he did. It was this boundless energy, borne of an incredible will, that allowed him to campaign day after day, from morning to night, with very few breaks throughout the race. But before we could get him on the road, we had the Miami debate on the evening of the ninth.

The afternoon before the debate, our team gathered for prep at our hotel. It seemed that the only space smaller than the room of Bernie's from which we'd watched the Michigan primary returns was the conference room we used for this debate prep. Most of us crowded around a little table, but some people sat along the wall or stood because the room was so tiny.

With Univision as host, the March 9 debate would give immigration greater prominence that it had in prior debates. That's one of the benefits of having a diverse set of media hosts for debates. Different hosts will accentuate different issues.

We were confident that Hillary Clinton would attack Bernie again for having voted against the proposed Comprehensive Immigration Reform Act. That 2007 bill would have created a guest worker program that the Southern Poverty Law Center characterized as close to slavery. The bill had been opposed by other liberal senators, including Iowa's Tom Harkin, and by Latino civil rights groups such as the League of United Latin American Citizens (LULAC), which bills itself as the nation's largest and oldest volunteer-based civil rights organization. Hillary Clinton, who voted for the bill, often called it Ted Kennedy's immigration bill, but it was really George W. Bush's.

Were there good people who voted differently than Bernie on the issue? Yes, there were. And Bernie would be the last one to suggest that Hillary Clinton and others who supported it were proponents of modern slavery. We certainly never did. The Clinton campaign's attack was a cheap shot, really, given Bernie's fight on behalf of immigrants in Immokalee,

Florida; his support for the 2013 immigration reform bill, in which guest workers programs played a lesser role; his longtime support of the Dream Act; and his own bold immigration reform plan. In the fall of 2015, none other than the editorial board of the *New York Times*—no fans of his, to be sure—had written a rare editorial praising Bernie for his immigration plan and challenging Hillary Clinton "to match his boldness." Not to mention the fact—which we did—that Hillary Clinton had advocated for the deportation of unaccompanied minors who showed up on the U.S. border in an effort to escape violence in Central America.

In short, we expected immigration and every other issue to be debated, in an environment where the sharper elbows shown by all at the March 6 Michigan debate would also be in evidence. And we weren't disappointed. The Miami debate covered a range of issues, from immigration, to Wall Street reform, to Hillary Clinton's debunked but continuing attack over the auto bailout, to Cuba. There was also a heated exchange over Hillary Clinton's Wall Street speeches and her refusal to release the transcripts. It had been an issue for a while, but in the more combative debate environment we had entered, it gained new prominence. According to a CNN story that ran on April 20, 2016, "Clinton gave 92 speeches between 2013 and 2015. Her standard fee is $225,000, and she collected $21.6 million dollars in just under two years. Clinton made 8 speeches to big banks, netting $1.8 million." Three of those speeches had been made to Goldman Sachs, and others to foreign banks.

In addition to the fees, a memo referenced in the CNN story from her speaking agency noted that Clinton also required a private jet, a presidential suite, and, importantly, $1,000 so that she could hire a stenographer to make a record of the speech. That meant that Clinton herself had transcripts of every speech. Her reply to the request to release the transcripts was that she would do so if all the Republicans would release transcripts of any speeches they had given. Bernie quickly offered to release his, as there were none.

As the campaign progressed, Bernie would raise the speeches issue at rallies. It became almost a shtick. NPR's Tamara Keith quoted him thus:

"If you're going to give a speech for $225,000 it's gotta be really, don't you think an extraordinarily brilliant speech," Sanders said to roars of laughter and cheers from a crowd in Appleton, Wisconsin. "I mean why else would they pay that kind of money? And it must be a speech which will open up the eyes of the world, transform our country. Must be a speech written in Shakespearean prose. So I think, if it is such a fantastic speech, the Secretary should make it available to all of us."

As part of his presentation, he would tell the crowd, "I'm now going to release to you the transcripts of all my paid speeches." He would then pick up an invisible pile of paper in both hands with great effort and heave it toward the crowd. The press corps who followed him regularly was so amused by it that they would mimic his tossing of the huge pile of invisible transcripts from the press riser.

The issue of the transcripts was an important one. Hillary Clinton had the transcripts and wouldn't release then. The Clinton campaign had clearly reviewed every one of them and determined that whatever was in them was bad enough that they would rather take the criticism for not releasing them than take the criticism for what was in them. That made us want them even more.

According to CNN, during the debate, "when asked whether he believed that she was saying one thing in public and another thing to Wall Street firms privately, Sanders said, 'That is exactly what releasing the transcripts will tell us.'" And they did. Hillary Clinton never released the transcripts, but they became public as part of the WikiLeaks dump of John Podesta's email in October 2016. In one speech, she explicitly said, "You need both a public and a private position." Remarks like that and others that demonstrated her friendliness with Wall Street, her continued support for free-trade agreements, her admission that she had lost touch with middle-class Americans—all back her campaign's political calculus that the contents of the speeches would be much more damaging than the negative press over withholding them.

In fairness to the Clinton campaign, the Miami debate was the one where Hillary Clinton was asked the most unfair question of the campaign. As widely reported, moderator Jorge Ramos asked Hillary Clinton, "Would you drop out of the race if you were indicted?" It was a ridiculous and gratuitous question that didn't warrant a response. A few uncomfortable minutes passed during which, understandably, she tried to dodge the question, and he—unbelievably—asked it again. Rightfully, she replied, "I'm not even answering that question."

But my sympathy for Secretary Clinton that night was tempered when we caught her cheating. During one of the breaks, she huddled with her staff, and one of our enterprising staffers photographed them coming out of their meeting. As the subheadline of Rachel Dicker's *U.S. News* story pointed out, "phoning a friend is a no-no" during the debates. We had photographic evidence that during a critical debate following a surprise loss in Michigan, the front-runner for the Democratic nomination was cheating. Fox's Ed Henry tweeted the photo. The mainstream media's response? Radio silence.

We did not know it at the time, but the Clinton campaign also cheated during the Michigan debate, and would again during a March 13 CNN town hall meeting in Ohio. In those instances, the Clinton campaign was given questions ahead of time by CNN commentator Donna Brazile. The heads-up at the Michigan debate was substantively not that significant. It warned that there would be a question about the Flint water crisis. That was pretty obvious to everyone without a heads-up—the debate was held in Flint, and the water crisis had dominated the news.

The second instance was more problematic. The Clinton campaign was sent the exact wording of a question that would be asked on the death penalty. Hillary Clinton has the same kind of "nuanced" and "ever-evolving" position on the death penalty that she has on gun control. So being able to prep for it was a big advantage for her. (It would not have been for our campaign. Bernie is against the death penalty. Period.) The death penalty had not been a widely debated issue in the campaign. The question would not have been anticipated. And her position is out of sync with Democratic primary voters, particularly voters of color. At the

CNN town hall, Clinton gave what I thought was a very smooth response when asked the question by audience member Ricky Jackson, who himself had been on death row. In a Cleveland.com interview, however, Jackson gave her answer to his question less credit than I did, calling it "somewhat 'canned.' "

Regardless of the actual benefit to the Clinton campaign, getting the questions in advance was cheating. No ifs, ands, or buts. And it was wrong for Donna Brazile to do what she did. As detailed later in this book, Donna, after taking the reins of the DNC, did work hard to undo the damage that Debbie Wasserman Schultz had done to the party and to mitigate the Clinton campaign's expropriation of the party's resources.

Following the debate, Bernie embarked on a schedule of a least three events a day across five states through March 15. Our advance department was straining but it held. Clinton easily won in Florida as everyone knew would happen. North Carolina ended up being our best southern state—we lost by only 13.5 points. That was a far cry from the drubbing we took almost everywhere else south of the Mason-Dixon line. We had moved up 10 points in Ohio since our last tracking poll, but that still left us down 13 points. Our chance to win even one state seemed to be slipping away.

In Illinois, Hillary Clinton's home state, the race proved tight. Bernie won some 37 percent of voters of color, according to the CNN exit poll, including winning the Latino vote outright, thanks in part to the support of Cook County commissioner Jesús "Chuy" García and other Latino leaders. Chicago mayor Rahm Emanuel had become an important focus of the 2016 Democratic primary because of his suppression of video showing his police department's unjustified killing of African American teen Laquan McDonald. Back in December 2015, Bernie had issued a statement calling for a federal investigation and for people to be held accountable. His statement was reported by Lynn Sweet in the *Chicago Sun-Times*: "I join with those calling for a federal investigation into the practices of the Chicago Police Department. Furthermore, any official who helped suppress the videotape of Laquan McDonald's murder should be held accountable. And any elected official with knowledge that the tape was being suppressed or improperly withheld should resign. No one should be shielded by power or position." Everyone knew who the "any elected official" was.

Bernie had been personally aware of racial discrimination in Chicago from his early days as an activist with the Congress of Racial Equality (CORE) when he attended the University of Chicago. His arrest for protesting racial discrimination in the public school system was memorialized in a photo found in the *Chicago Tribune* archives and video footage discovered by the documentary film company Kartemquin Films. *IndieWire* reported that the video had been made by principals of the company who were fellow students at the University of Chicago.

The video, which is understandably somewhat grainy, appeared before the very clear *Chicago Tribune* photo. When Kartemquin Films posted the video online asking if anyone could confirm that it was Bernie Sanders being arrested, Tad sent it to Bernie. I remember Bernie saying to Tad, "Well, I was certainly there and I was certainly arrested that day. I'm 99 percent sure that it's me, but if you want me to say 100 percent that that's me, I can't from the video."

His reluctance stemmed from controversy over another photo from that era that the campaign was using. It shows what appears to be Bernie in profile standing with a group of students who were holding a sit-in. *Time* had run a story back in November 2015 questioning whether it was Bernie or another student who looked like him named Bruce Rappaport— also a leader in the movement. The widow of that other student (who also had been at the University of Chicago) and some other former students (all of whom supported Bernie) believed it was Rappaport.

The *Washington Post*'s Jonathan Capehart made it his mission to cast doubt on Bernie's civil rights bona fides, going after the photo in a February 11 opinion piece. The photographer, Danny Lyon, according to *Time*'s Sam Frizell, was so offended by Capehart's piece that he dug up the contact sheet showing the disputed picture in a series of photos all taken one after the other of the same person. Some of the photos show the person head-on. It is clearly Bernie.

After Lyon came forward, Frizell wrote a follow-up piece that showed the contact sheets and corrected the story from November. (It's notable because it is so rare for a reporter to make that kind of effort to clear up a previous story when new facts come to light.) Capehart responded quickly with another piece on February 13 to defend himself and to make sure the seeds of doubt he had planted were properly watered.

Unlike Frizell, Capehart engaged in a meandering he said, she said exercise in which even he had to admit that Lyon, a well-known civil rights–era photographer, had called his original piece "outrageous" and that Lyon had in fact publicly vouched for the disputed photo subject's being Bernie earlier in the month, *before* Capehart wrote his attack piece. Capehart confined his mea culpa to the dubious admission that Lyon's statement was "unbeknownst to me." He neglected to address whether it should have been familiar to a national columnist blundering into a hotly contested presidential primary.

The situation was resolved when the *Chicago Tribune* ran a photo that showed Bernie, in the same outfit he was wearing in the video, being arrested. When we showed Bernie the *Tribune* photo he quickly said, "Oh, that's definitely me. I remember that watch." In the video, he's also wearing the watch.

Bernie's fight against racial discrimination against the Chicago school system, and in the University of Chicago's own student housing practices, was the foundational motivation for his entire political career. Rahm Emanuel's knowledge of or actual hand in the suppression of the Laquan McDonald murder tapes was to Bernie an extension of the racism he had fought as a young man. One of his most forceful allies in the Chicago effort was Troy LaRaviere, a principal in the Chicago school system, who during his tenure had brought his elementary school to a ranking of #1 in *Chicago* magazine. LaRaviere's extremely moving and inspirational personal story was featured in one of the five-minute longform videos that DML made for the campaign, and he appeared in our television advertising. Voices like his greatly aided the campaign's efforts to reach out to all Chicagoans.

In a sad postscript, after the campaign ended in Illinois, Rahm Emanuel tried to have LaRaviere fired, despite his professional success. This is the type of hardball retribution many chose not to risk in the 2016 campaign by coming out for Bernie Sanders. In the end, LaRaviere's own accomplishments and vigorous advocacy for the students of Chicago won out. He was elected president of the Chicago Principals and Administrators Association in an election where pro-Emanuel forces intervened in an attempt to defeat him.

On primary day, March 15, the result in Illinois had us down only 40,000 votes out of over 2 million cast. That meant a split in delegates, which would have happened if we have been 40,000 votes up. But it denied us the all-important momentum of having won the state outright.

In Missouri, the result was even closer, and for much of the night it remained our last hope for a win. Like neighboring Iowa, Missouri was razor-close, with Hillary Clinton winning by a couple thousand votes, or 0.2 percent.

It was not the night we had hoped for. We engaged in the same self-reflection that every campaign does when it has narrow losses. Should we have pulled events in other states to spend more time in the more promising state? Should we have gone on TV earlier? These are the types of questions to which there are no right answers. One thing was sure, though. The drumbeat of the delegate math in the media narrative, which had started after the March 1 primaries, was going to get louder and louder even as the primary map was opening up for us in significant ways.

17

ROLLING THE BALL (MOSTLY) DOWNHILL

HAVING PUSHED THE BALL UPHILL for much of the campaign, we were now at a point where we hoped to see it roll downhill over the course of the next eight contests so that we would enter the pivotal New York primary with a lot of momentum. If we were successful, we might have a chance to win in Hillary Clinton's adopted home state on April 19. March 15 through the New York primary was dominated by caucuses. Only two states were holding primaries, and only one of those was a closed primary. There was a possibility we could run the table. Arizona, with its closed primary and pattern of early voting, would be the most challenging; and it was in the first group of three states to vote on March 22, along with Utah and Idaho. Four days later, Alaska, Hawaii, and Washington would have their turn, followed by Wisconsin, on April 5, and Wyoming, on the ninth. Our internal benchmark polling showed us ahead in four of the contests. In three others, we were within the margin of error. This was a new position for us to be in.

But after the breakneck pace at which we had all been running, we needed a little bit of downtime both to recharge our batteries and to reassess our best path forward. We flew to Sedona, Arizona, and stayed at the Las Posadas Inn, a series of two-story buildings housing suites set among the red rocks. It was exactly the kind of place you go to escape the rat race. When it became known that we were going to be "down" for a couple of days, rumors began to swirl in the media that we were planning to withdraw. Nothing could have been further from the truth.

My line to the media was that we were just having a team meeting in the locker room at halftime. It evoked images of a team catching a second wind after a tough first half and then coming back out and turning things around in the second half. Plus, who doesn't like a good sports metaphor?

The truth was the metaphor wasn't really forced. We did have a lot of planning to do. Since our huge victory in New Hampshire only a little over a month earlier, the path to victory had become much narrower. We wanted to stay on it, and key was not only winning states—which we clearly had to do—but winning them convincingly, to create momentum and eat into that now rather large lead the Clinton campaign had in pledged delegates.

We met in the Mission-style living room of Bernie's suite. Sitting on the brown leather couches, Tad handed out a state-by-state list of the contests, with the delegate results of those that had passed and percentage targets in the remaining states. The targets were ambitious, to say the least.

Bernie sat on the edge of his couch, leaning forward. "So how we gonna win this thing?" he asked the room. It was an open-ended question typical of the kind he used to begin meetings.

"Look, I'm not going to say it's going to be easy," Tad started. "We are going to have to start winning, and winning big. We have got to win in Wisconsin, and then New York will be a pivotal showdown. If we can beat her in her home state it is really going to shake people's confidence in her, and then we will see a lot of those superdelegates start to take a second look at the race. And if we do that, then we can succeed in Pennsylvania and push for a sweep in early June, including in large states like California and New Jersey."

That was the theory of the case in a nutshell. We then turned to scheduling, media buys, and other more nitty-gritty logistical details. It was not long before Bernie was back on the road crisscrossing the country, talking to voters.

Arizona was to prove the first hurdle in the second half that we could not clear. Our internal polling showed the state within reach, and it was home to our first congressional endorser, Rep. Raul Grijalva, who himself had traveled the country for Bernie and whom we featured in our paid advertising. On election night, the networks called Arizona for Secretary Clinton. When they did, the vote count that they were reporting, and the percentage of the overall vote that represented, was totally out of sync with what our models were showing should be the case.

While campaigning in western states, Bernie started making some appearances in California to lay the groundwork for the June 6 contest there. We were at a Bernie rally in San Diego that night as the Arizona returns were coming in. One of my closest friends from high school, Earl Greenia, showed up with his daughter to see Bernie, and in hope that I would be there. Earl had had much more conservative politics than I did when we were younger (probably still does), but he had been at Bernie's 1988 congressional victory party (which turned into a congressional narrow-loss party) and admitted he had voted for Bernie that day.

I brought Earl into the backstage area and we stood at the back dock of the convention center. It was a surreal experience in many ways. Earl and I had been close friends in northern Vermont. Now, not only was I talking to him at a Bernie rally in California, but he had a daughter who was a big Bernie fan. Talking to an old friend from simpler times was a very memorable moment in those stressful days. I got Earl's daughter in to meet Bernie after the rally, and he signed her "Future to Believe In" placard.

Even though I was catching up with Earl, I still had to attend to business. What concerned me was not that Secretary Clinton was winning in Arizona (although I can't say I was pleased with that), but that the turnout was so far off from our assessment. We had been right in every state previously (and would be in every state going forward). In particular, the "day of" vote totals, as opposed to the early vote totals, were drastically lower than we had anticipated. It was the only time in the campaign that I called a network to question their reporting on returns.

I talked with a top CNN political reporter I knew. "Something is wrong here," I said. "This turnout is way low based on everything we had been expecting."

The reporter said, "Let me check into it and get back with you." I think that the reporter took my concern seriously because we did not make a habit of questioning election night reporting and estimates. I got a call back not long after.

"They've rechecked with the AP and they say it's right," the reporter said. It turns out it was correct. Some two-thirds of the Democratic primary vote had been cast earlier than election day. According to an MS-NBC analysis, only 7 percent of the early vote represented voters under thirty; 41 percent of the early ballots were from voters over sixty-five. That was a real problem for our campaign. In order for the Arizona electorate to match the 17 percent national average under-thirty turnout in the Democratic primary process, some 37 percent of voters casting ballots on election day would have to be under thirty. That didn't happen anywhere, and given the disproportionate number of young people who are not registered with any party, it certainly wasn't going to happen in Arizona's closed primary.

That being said, Bernie generally did better with "day of" voters than with those voting early. But the election day balloting was completely botched by the Republicans, who control the process in Arizona.

As was widely reported, the authorities in the largest county, Maricopa (which the *Washington Post*'s Amber Phillips points out is home to 60 percent of the population), cut the number of polling sites from 200 in 2012 to only 60—one for every 21,000 voters, reported the *Arizona Republic*. Many observed that the shortage of voting locations was particularly acute in minority communities. This created massive lines that resulted in some voters not casting their ballots until after midnight—five hours after the official closing time, and hours after Hillary Clinton had already been declared the winner by the national networks.

We knew that there were problems all day in Arizona. Long lines were being reported, and story after story poured in from our supporters who tried to vote before work but had to leave. They then returned at lunchtime to vote, but their lunch hour ran out. Returning a third time after work, they were forced to leave the line because of children waiting at home. People were effectively disenfranchised by the outrageous lines.

Additionally, voters were being barred because of so-called computer glitches that changed their registration from Democratic to nonaligned, as reported by *Salon*'s Lisa O'Neill and others. That meant that they couldn't vote in the closed Democratic primary, even though they had registered as Democrats. O'Neill told the story of one voter who had been a registered Democrat since 1988: Arriving to vote, he learned that his party ID had changed mysteriously. One aspect of this "glitch" was that people who had switched their party ID from nonaligned to Democrat before the deadline found that the change had not been made and that they were barred from voting. Let's sit and ponder for a second the question of who those voters would have overwhelmingly supported.

As the polls closed and voters were still standing in long lines, our campaign used social media and our field volunteers to encourage voters to stay in line even after the race was called for Hillary Clinton. She might win, they explained, but for purposes of delegate allocation, the margin mattered.

All the mess that was the administration of the primary in Arizona destroyed whatever opportunity there was to have a close result there, let alone an outright win. The Maricopa County recorder in charge of the disaster blamed the long lines on the large number of independent voters who waited only to be told that they were ineligible to vote in the closed primary. We know that many such voters were registered Democrats who were victims of those pesky computers and their glitches.

It's also not surprising that many independent voters arrived at the polls believing that they could vote in the Democratic primary. In Arizona's primaries for state and local office, independent voters can vote in the primary of their choice. Only the presidential primary is closed to them. The day after the debacle, the state's Republican governor called for the presidential primaries to be opened to independents, according to AJ Vicens at *Mother Jones*. Time will tell whether his call was serious or just political cover in the face of voter outrage.

In the wake of the problems in Arizona, the Democratic Party, the

Clinton campaign, and our campaign jointly filed suit to prevent this massive de facto disenfranchisement of voters from happening again. This was not the first time we had sued a state to protect voters. Our campaign and state organizations had previously successfully blocked the Republican secretary of state in Ohio from disenfranchising young voters in that state.

Without getting too deep at this juncture into the debate over caucuses versus primaries and open primaries versus closed primaries, the troubles in Arizona highlight one important issue. Some of the critics of caucuses and open primaries point to the potential for Republican meddling (largely through imagined mass strategic crossover voting—something that really does not occur) as a reason to support closed primaries. In truth, there was no Democratic nominating contest in 2016 the integrity of which was more compromised by Republican malfeasance than the closed Democratic primary in Arizona. (Primaries in general put the integrity of the Democratic nominating process in the hands of state officials—in recent years, largely Republicans. One other reality of primaries is that all the voter suppression and disenfranchisement measures enacted by Republicans in state after state to keep people from voting against them in the general election are imposed on the Democratic nominating process.)

Even with the problems in Arizona, Bernie ended the day knocking down the Clinton campaign's delegate lead by twenty-five. He won Idaho with 78 percent of the vote and Utah with 77 percent. The overwhelming totals in the other two states were important indicators that we could in fact rack up victories by large margins.

Four days later, we went three for three with overwhelming margins. Bernie got 79.6 percent of the vote in Alaska, 69.8 percent in Hawaii, and 72.7 percent in Washington. He had wanted to visit Alaska and Hawaii, but travel time and expense made it impossible. Jane ended up visiting both on his behalf, so those victories belong to her. Significantly, Hawaii is the least white state in the nation. It is and always has been a majority-minority state. And as *AlterNet*'s Sarah Lazare pointed out, in a story with a headline that called out media "whitewash[ing]" of Bernie's support, over 30 percent of Alaska's population is comprised of people of color.

In terms of delegates that day, Washington represented a huge step forward because of its large number of pledged delegates (101 total). Clinton's lead was cut that day by another 66 delegates. In just two days' contests, including Arizona, where we lost by 15 percent, her delegate lead had dropped by 91. The ball was indeed rolling down the hill, and it was picking up speed as we moved to Wisconsin.

The schedule once again allowed Bernie to campaign heavily in a single state. After a few days in Burlington, he was back on the road in the Badger State. He held over a dozen rallies and town hall meetings and numerous smaller meetings with leaders of various communities, and appeared at the Wisconsin Democratic Party's annual dinner. He only left the state for two days—to do stops in Pittsburgh and New York City, where, on April 1, he met with the editorial board of the *New York Daily News* (more on that to come).

Because of Bernie's ability to spend a lot of time with voters in Wisconsin, where we invested in a full ground operation and paid media, the state handed Bernie his sixth win in a row, on April 5, with a margin of over 13 points. Bernie got the results that night in Laramie, Wyoming, where he was holding a rally in advance of its April 9 caucus. He had had to cancel an earlier planned event near the end of March because of a snowstorm, so this was his only appearance in Wyoming.

Bernie would end up winning the Wyoming caucus by over 11 points. Because of the delegate allocation formula there, he and Hillary Clinton both received the same number of pledged delegates. It would be our seventh win in a row. We had been concerned about the outcome at one point, because there seemed to be a huge influx of absentee votes (yes, some caucuses allow absentee voting) after the declared deadline for their submission, and they didn't come from our campaign. To make matters worse, they were counted in the house of the state party chair, without any paid Bernie staffers being allowed to observe the counting. We won in the end, even if the delegates were split. The caucus was a few days in the future when Bernie took off from Laramie to head back East for the pivotal contests in New York, on April 19, and in five other northeastern states a week later, on the twenty-sixth.

18

THE ESTABLISHMENT STRIKES BACK IN THE EMPIRE STATE

ONE OF THE GREAT BEAUTIES of the country that we experienced traveling from one end to the other is how different one place can be from another. And that's certainly true of how politics is done as well. What's off-limits in one state is more than fair game in another. New York is one of those places with a reputation for a more rough-and-tumble sort of politics, as CNN's Jeff Zeleny described the coming contest in an April 6 story.

Tad told Bernie before we arrived in New York, "This isn't going to be like Iowa or New Hampshire. Voters in New York are much more used to bare-knuckle politics. The Clintons know that. They've played politics here a long time, so you should be ready for them to really come after us in a way that would have backfired in other states."

New York had become a critically important state for both campaigns. There were 247 delegates at stake, so a win in New York could help us further close the delegate gap. But New York had a closed Democratic primary, and New Yorkers had elected Hillary Clinton to the U.S. Senate twice. She was a favorite for both those reasons, although that also meant that expectations were very high for her.

A few critical events happened before Bernie even arrived in New York, on April 7, after spending the day before in Philadelphia—including that we won the debate over whether there would be a debate in New York before the primary. Of the three additional debates we had secured before the New Hampshire primary, the campaigns had relatively quickly agreed that the first would be in Michigan and the third in California. The location of the second debate—to be held in April—had long been a point of disagreement. We wanted it to take place in New York prior to the primary there. The Clinton campaign wanted it held in Pennsylvania in the week after the New York primary.

In late March we stepped up the pressure for a New York debate. I sent a letter to my counterpart, Robby Mook. On the Sunday news shows, Bernie called for a New York debate. I did the same on cable news. The Clinton campaign spent a couple of days trying to keep the debate from happening. Campaign strategist Joel Benenson went on TV to make the case that they would not debate unless Bernie changed his "tone," as reported by CNN and many others.

It looked more and more like the Clinton campaign was trying to dodge a New York debate. And that suited us just fine. We had a great two-day back-and-forth, which they also obviously understood they were losing. They wisely just gave in. I was disappointed when they did. My arguments with Clinton folks on cable media about the New York debate were some of the easiest of the entire race because their position was so indefensible, including in the eyes of the media, who wanted either to host the debate or cover it. We were hoping the Clinton campaign would dig in their heels and keep the discussion going for another week. But all good things must come to an end.

Another critical event, or series of events, was that we were coming off seven straight wins, our longest streak so far. All those wins had been by double digits—we were coming into New York with a head of steam. Bernie's string of wins had caused Hillary Clinton's lead in New York to shrink. Our polling showed her 21 points ahead in the third week of March. At the beginning of April her lead slipped to 17 points, and within a few days it was down to 14. Bernie's win in Wisconsin was sure to shrink it even more. And in fact it did. Our polling over April 6 and 7 found that Hillary Clinton's lead was down to just 10. We had overcome 10-point deficits in a number of states, so we were feeling positive.

Whittling Clinton's lead to only 10 points was impressive from our standpoint because of New York's closed primary. Since only registered Democrats could vote, Bernie would not be able to rely on the support of Democratically aligned independents, among whom he had won by 3-to-1 margins in most states. To make matters worse, the rules in New York required voters who wanted to switch their party registration to do so six months before the primary. New York's closed primary and its draconian registration-change deadline meant that over 3 million voters were excluded from participating in the Democratic primary.

The Clinton folks also knew what we knew about Bernie's momentum, and their response was to go on the attack. With Bernie in Wyoming on the night of the Wisconsin primary, I was on set at CNN in Washington with Jake Tapper and Dana Bash. They cut to Jeff Zeleny, who reported that he had just talked with Clinton campaign officials and that they were going to employ a new strategy against Bernie. They would "disqualify him," "defeat him," and "worry about unifying the party later." In other words, they would do whatever it took to win, no matter how much damage they did to the party.

Zeleny reported further on this later that night on Anderson Cooper's show. He said that one of the issues on which the Clinton campaign was going to step up its attacks was guns. The Clinton campaign was taking off the gloves. This is the part where the *New York Daily News* reenters the story, as do the columnists at the *Washington Post*.

Before I explain how the Clinton campaign, with the complicity of the *New York Daily News* and pro-Clinton columnists at the *Post*, masterfully executed a plan to knock Bernie out in the New York primary, I'd like to issue a caveat: It is not my intention to demonstrate that there was some grand conspiracy where Hillary Clinton, Jeff Bezos, and *Daily News* publisher Mort Zuckerman got on a conference and plotted a "kill Bernie" strategy—although if anyone was on that call I'd love to hear about it. What is clear, however, is that the Clinton campaign used sympathetic columnists at the *Post* and editorial writers at the *Daily News* who, knowingly or not, functioned in this effort as campaign proxies for Hillary Clinton.

Just a bit of background on the owners of the two papers at issue. I think many people are somewhat familiar with *Washington Post* (and Amazon) owner Jeff Bezos. What many do not know is that he has donated to such right-wing entities as Reason.com, and he fought raising taxes on the rich in his home state of Washington. Of Bezos, in an article that unflatteringly compared the local charitable giving of Amazon with that of other Seattle-based businesses, such as Microsoft and Boeing, the *Seattle Times* wrote: "[Early Amazon investor Nick] Hanauer and others who know Bezos describe him as a libertarian. In 2010, Bezos contributed $100,000 to help defeat Initiative 1098, which sought to impose a state income tax on Washington's wealthiest residents. 'There's almost nothing I could have predicted with more precision than that Jeff would hate the idea,' said Hanauer, an advocate for I-1098. 'He's a libertarian, and I am not.'"

The media watchdog Fairness & Accuracy in Reporting found that in the days immediately preceding the Michigan primary, the *Washington Post* put out sixteen negative stories about Bernie Sanders in sixteen hours. That wasn't the first time the *Post* had gone after Bernie. Back on January 27, shortly before the Iowa caucus, the *Washington Post* published an editorial, the crux of which was the following sentence: "But Mr. Sanders is not a brave truth-teller. He is a politician selling his own brand of fiction to a slice of the country that eagerly wants to buy it." Ruth Marcus (formerly on the *Post* editorial board herself), in a column the next day defending the *Post*'s anti-Sanders rant, was quite honest about the editorial board's feelings toward Bernie: "To put it mildly, the editorial board doesn't ♥ Sanders either."

For those not moved by the editorial board's hit-you-over-the-head approach, *Post* columnist Dana Milbank had penned a softer piece, imploring all those who, like him, thought Bernie was the cat's pajamas to vote for Clinton because Bernie was unelectable: "I adore Bernie Sanders. I agree with his message of fairness and I share his outrage over inequality and corporate abuses. I think his righteous populism has captured the moment perfectly. I respect the uplifting campaign he has run. I admire his authenticity. And I am convinced Democrats would be insane to nominate him."

To show how personally painful it was for him to suggest that all good progressives vote for Hillary Clinton, Milbank wrote, "Hillary Clinton, by contrast, is a dreary candidate. She has, again, failed to connect with voters. Her policy positions are cautious and uninspiring. Her reflexive secrecy causes a whiff of scandal to follow her everywhere. She seems calculating and phony. And yet if Democrats hope to hold the presidency in November, they'll need to hold their noses and nominate Clinton." I give Milbank an A+ for his electability appeal to voters but an F for political soothsaying. He was not alone in the latter category within media or establishment political circles.

Milbank's piece is representative of the consistently pro-corporate, pro-establishment, and, as a consequence, anti-Bernie spin that pervaded the *Washington Post* editorial and opinion sections. In fairness to the *Post*, its political reporters, including Karen Tumulty, Dan Balz, John Wagner, Dave Weigel, and Phil Rucker, have made the DC paper the premier print source for political news. Compare that to the *New York Times*, which had a more evenhanded editorial policy. Its dismissiveness, cynicism, and at times hostility toward Bernie were much more likely to find their way into the actual news reporting.

The *Daily News'* Mort Zuckerman is a billionaire real estate magnate who has been involved in politics for a long time. Many will remember his many appearances on NBC's political roundtable program *The McLaughlin Group*. Zuckerman was never shy in his defense of the monied. He was extremely critical of Obama for what he considered inflammatory rhetoric against the rich. In an October 15, 2001, *Wall Street Journal* article, John Freeman wrote: "As Mr. Zuckerman ponders the Occupy Wall Street movement, he concludes that 'the door to it was opened by the Obama administration, going after the "millionaires and billionaires" as if everybody is a millionaire and a billionaire and they didn't earn it. . . . To fan that flame of populist anger I think is very divisive and very dangerous for this country.'"

Back in 2010, when Zuckerman was considering a U.S. Senate run against Kirsten Gillibrand, the late Wayne Barrett wrote, in the *Village Voice*: "Fox asked him what he thought of Obama's attacks on Wall Street 'salaries and bonuses' and Mort rallied to the cause: 'I don't think it's right to demonize these people. You just don't diminish them and beat them over the heads and shoulders for political reasons. And that's what it's about.'"

Whatever one's view of the billionaire class, I think it is fair to conclude that Bernie is not exactly Bezos's or Zuckerman's cup of tea.

The first volley from the Clinton campaign through Zuckerman's *Daily News* was launched on March 27, when the paper printed a Clinton campaign–authored op-ed on the issue of guns that took a swipe at Bernie. On the day after the Wisconsin primary, as the campaign moved to New York, the *Daily News* decided to chime in, based on answers he gave during the April 1 editorial board meeting—a transcript of which they released on their website the afternoon of April 4. The blaring tabloid headline: "Bernie's Sandy Hook Shame." The story inside the paper in fact distorted what he had told the editorial board.

The lead:

> Presidential populist Bernie Sanders came under blistering fire Tuesday for opposing efforts by families of Sandy Hook shooting victims to sue gun manufacturers.
>
> Sanders, in an exclusive interview with the *Daily News* last week, said, "No, I don't," when asked if victims of a crime with a gun should be able to sue the manufacturer.

In truth, Bernie never said in the interview that the Sandy Hook families should not be able to sue. Okay, based purely on the one quote pulled out of context, the quote seems to confirm the inflammatory conclusion of the previous sentence. But waaaay down in the editorial, even the *New York Daily News* had to confess that there was more to it.

"But I do believe that gun manufacturers and gun dealers should be able to be sued when they should know that guns are going into the hands of wrong people," Sanders said.

"So if somebody walks in and says, 'I'd like 10,000 rounds of ammunition,' you know, well, you might be suspicious about that. So I think there are grounds for those suits, but not if you sell me a legal product."

Oh, so Bernie's position is more nuanced than the conclusion. Even these quotes are just a fraction of what he said in the interview. Here's the full exchange:

DAILY NEWS: There's a case currently waiting to be ruled on in Connecticut. The victims of the Sandy Hook massacre are looking to have the right to sue for damages the manufacturers of the weapons. Do you think that that is something that should be expanded?

SANDERS: Do I think the victims of a crime with a gun should be able to sue the manufacturer, is that your question?

DAILY NEWS: Correct.

SANDERS: No, I don't.

DAILY NEWS: Let me ask you. I know we're short on time. Two quick questions. Your website talks about . . .

SANDERS: No, let me just . . . I'm sorry. In the same sense that if you're a gun dealer and you sell me a gun and I go out and I kill him [gestures to someone in room]. . . . Do I think that that gun dealer should be sued for selling me a legal product that he misused? [Shakes head no.] But I do believe that gun manufacturers and gun dealers should be able to be sued when they should know that guns are going into the hands of wrong people. So if somebody walks in and says, "I'd like 10,000 rounds of ammunition," you know, well, you might be suspicious about that. *So I think there are grounds for those suits,* but not if you sell me a legal product. But you're really saying . . .

DAILY NEWS: Do you think that the discussion and debate about what defines a legal product, what should be a legal product, hence AR-15s, these automatic military-style weapons . . . which is the grounds of this suit at the moment is that this should have never been in the hands of the public.

SANDERS: Well, you're looking at a guy . . . let's talk about guns for one second. Let's set the record straight because of . . . unnamed candidates who have misrepresented my views. You're looking at a guy who has a D, what was it, D minus voting record from the NRA? Not exactly a lobbyist for the NRA, not exactly supporting them.

But it's interesting that you raised that question. If you'll remember this, if you were in Vermont in 1988 [gestures to Vermonter in the room], three people were running for the United States Congress. We have one seat, Vermont. Two of them supported assault weapons. One candidate, Bernie Sanders, said, in 1988, *"No, I do not support the sale and distribution of assault weapons in this country."* I lost that election by three points. Came in second. And that may have been the reason, that I was opposed by all of the gun people, okay? *So to answer your question, I do not believe, I didn't believe then and I don't believe now that those guns should be sold in America. They're designed for killing people.*

DAILY NEWS: So do you think then, with that in mind, that the merits of the current case are baseless?

SANDERS: *It's not baseless.* I wouldn't use that word. But it's a backdoor way. If you're questioning me, will I vote to ban assault weapons in the United States, yeah, I will.

[Emphasis added.]

Whoa! So what Bernie actually told the *New York Daily News* is that he does not support suing gun sellers when the guns are used for criminal purposes and the sellers are not culpable in some other way. He specifically lays out one instance in which a transaction should result in liability because the seller knows or should know that the gun or ammunition will be used improperly. "So I think there are grounds for those suits." Huh?

How is that opposing the suit of the Sandy Hook family? Although he appropriately doesn't weigh in on the specific claims in a specific pending lawsuit, Bernie is crystal clear that, when gun manufacturers or dealers act in a way that contributes to the likelihood of criminal activity or ignores suspicious conduct, they should be subject to suit. When the *New York Daily News* directly asked him if he believed that the Sandy Hook suit was baseless, Bernie was pretty direct. "It's not baseless." Exactly!!

More to the point, he stated without qualification that he had consistently supported in every public statement, including those going back as far as 1988—and still supported—a complete ban on the sale of semi-automatic assault weapons. He voted that way in Congress 100 percent of the time. His support of banning assault weapons was one of the primary motivators for his voting yes on the 1994 Crime Bill (along with the Violence Against Women Act provision), which he otherwise condemned on the floor of the U.S. House of Representatives.

The *New York Daily News* completely ignored Bernie's policy release in mid-January calling for changes to the gun liability law so that it was substantially narrowed to reflect his view on the matter—that in cases where gun manufacturers and rogue dealers are culpable, they should be held accountable. But that did not fit into the political agenda of the *New York Daily News.*

One of Clinton's frontmen in her attacks on Bernie was Connecticut governor Dannel Malloy. After the horrendous Sandy Hook shootings, he helped pass a number of important gun safety measures in Connecticut. But Malloy (and others, including Connecticut senator Chris Murphy, who criticized Bernie) has nothing to say about the fact that Connecticut is home to several firearms companies, that assault weapons are manufactured in their state, and that Malloy's administration made state money available to the gun industry for expansion.

Gun sales in Connecticut make up a tiny fraction of these companies' sales, so the new laws put in place in Connecticut (including a ban on large magazines and semiautomatic assault rifles, which Bernie consistently voted for on a national basis in Congress) don't have a significant impact on their profits. As long as their product is being shipped to other states, Malloy appears indifferent. Indeed, he actively aided them with state money.

Eight days before the Sandy Hook shootings, as reported by the *Hartford Courant* on March 13, 2013, the Malloy administration offered the parent company of Bushmaster—the company that made the assault weapon used in the shootings—a $1 million loan (most of which could be forgiven) to entice it to move its headquarters to Connecticut. That deal was withdrawn in the aftermath of the tragedy. But Malloy's administration continued to offer financial support to gun makers. As recently as March 2017, the *Hartford Courant* reported Malloy speaking approvingly of a $10 million state loan ($2 million of which could be forgiven) to Colt Industries for headquarters expansion in Connecticut.

Why did Malloy never push for a ban on the manufacture of civilian versions of military-style assault weapons in the state of Connecticut? It is true that the companies could move that production elsewhere, but at a cost of millions of dollars to ship machinery out of state, build or lease new facilities, and train new workers. And isn't that what the concern over the liability bill is all about? Hitting the manufacturers of semiautomatic assault weapons where it hurts—in the wallet.

During a political trip to New Hampshire in August 2015 that was covered by the *Union Leader*, Malloy is reported to have said: "With respect to Bernie's position on [the Brady Bill]. It is anathema to my own. I don't understand it. I think [it's] political expediency." I certainly would never accuse Governor Malloy of "political expediency" because he talked about gun control out of one side of his mouth while providing state dollars to the gun industry out of the other. There's another technical term in politics that's more fitting: hypocrisy.

After the release of the transcript of Bernie's *New York Daily News* editorial interview on April 4—the day of the Wisconsin primary—the Clinton campaign launched phase 2 of their announced "disqualify him" attack. As Bernie was winning Wisconsin and Clinton's campaign spilled the beans to CNN's Jeff Zeleny about their strategy to attack Bernie, two—yes, two—*Washington Post* writers, Chris Cillizza and Jonathan Capehart (the same "that's not really Bernie fighting racial discrimination in those photos" columnist), published columns parroting the very attacks the Clinton campaign would make.

Cillizza played the role of articulating the main part of the Clinton attack around bank reform. "Time and again, when pressed to get beyond his rhetoric on the evils of corporate America and Wall Street, Sanders struggled. Often mightily," he wrote. He made sure to remind readers that none other than Hillary Clinton herself had seen this coming: "For Sanders's critics—including Hillary Clinton—the *Daily News* interview is the 'aha!' moment that they have been insisting will come for Sanders, a time when his pie-in-the-sky proposals are closely examined and found wanting."

In an email to supporters attacking Bernie—sent out the evening of the fifth, according to CNN's Dylan Byers—the Clinton campaign wrote, "We've said for a long time that this primary is about who's really going to be able to get things done. And from reading this interview, you get the impression Senator Sanders hasn't thought very much about that." It's like Chris Cillizza was reading their minds.

Capehart included the same banking reform attack as Cillizza—that was, after all, the central Clinton messaging point, so it had to be in more than one column. Repetition in politics is important so voters don't miss the main proof point. But his piece offered more of an overview of Bernie's inability to answer questions on a wide variety of topics—the Israeli/Palestinian crisis, combatting ISIS. For comic relief, Capeheart resurrected Bernie's reference to the now-discontinued use of subway tokens in New York. Good to remind anyone who missed it that, despite Bernie's accent, Hillary Clinton was the real New Yorker, not Green Mountain Bernie.

Once the story line was put out there by the Clinton campaign and the *Washington Post* columnists, others in the media started repeating it: Dylan Byers and many others listed in his story: the *Atlantic*, *Vanity Fair*, and Bloomberg's Mark Halperin. That's a grand slam in politics. Create a story, get it validated in the media, and then have it bleed into all the other outlets. Priceless!

The pile-on as Bernie came into New York with a string of victories and a head of steam could not have been better choreographed. Juan Gonzalez, a twenty-nine-year veteran reporter, now retired from the *New York Daily News*, was present at the editorial interview. When asked by *Democracy Now*'s Amy Goodman about the charges in the media that Bernie had bungled it, he strongly disagreed: "I certainly didn't get that impression, tell you the truth. The editorial board is notorious, especially our editorial page editor, Arthur Browne, for his laserlike one question after another, and he bombarded, as several others of us also asked questions. I, overall, thought that Bernie Sanders handled the exchange very well." He did acknowledge that he felt Bernie stumbled "a little bit" on the question of breaking up the banks.

Dean Baker, an economist with the Center for Economic and Policy Research, described the criticism of Bernie this way: "Some of the complaints are just silly. When asked how he would break up the big banks Sanders said he would leave that up to the banks. That's exactly the right answer." And the fact that Sanders didn't know the specific statute—who cares? How many people know the specific statute for someone who puts a bullet in someone's head? That's murder, and if a candidate for office doesn't know the exact title and specifics of her state murder statute, it hardly seems like a big issue.

Mike Konczal, an expert on financial reform at the Roosevelt Institute, wrote, "Yes, these are answers I'd expect for how Sanders approaches financial reform." He continued, "Sanders has a clear path on how he wants to break up the banks, which he described"; "If anything, Sanders is too wonky."

Peter Eavis, a business reporter at the *New York Times*, took issue with the Clinton/Cillizza/Capehart/*Daily News* line that Bernie didn't understand his banking plan. "Bernie Sanders probably knows more about breaking up banks than his critics give him credit for," Eavis wrote. "In the interview . . . Mr. Sanders does appear to get tangled up in some details and lacks clarity. Breaking up the banks would involve arcane and complex regulatory moves that can trip up any banking policy wonk, let alone a presidential candidate. But, taken as a whole, Mr. Sanders's answers seem to make sense. Crucially, his answers mostly track with a reasonably straightforward breakup plan that he introduced to Congress last year."

The *Huffington Post*'s Ryan Grim went even further in debunking the media narrative: "In fact, in several instances, it's the *Daily News* editors who are bungling the facts in an interview designed to show that Sanders doesn't understand the fine points of policy. In questions about breaking up big banks, the powers of the Treasury Department and drone strikes, the editors were simply wrong on details."

Grim's conclusion: "This wasn't an interview about policy details. It was about who the media has decided is presidential and who isn't, who is serious and who isn't. The *Daily News* and much of the rest of the media don't think Sanders is qualified to be president, and that's the motivation for an interview meant to expose what the media have already decided is true." In other words, some members of the media had bought the Clinton narrative, and others were affirmatively pushing it, and all the pushback from economists and financial experts was going to get little traction, because it was in conflict with what they believed or were trying to get others to believe.

Our strategy in New York was to repeat what we had successfully done in other contests where Bernie had the time to blanket a single state with events. The *Washington Post*'s Phil Rucker accurately captured our strategy: "To capitalize on his fresh momentum, Sanders plans an aggressive push in New York, modeled after his come-from-behind victory a few weeks ago in Michigan. He intends to barnstorm the state as if he were running for governor."

On the way to New York we hit another media-driven bump in the road. At his rally in Philadelphia the day before, Bernie moved to counter what Jeff Zeleny had reported was the Clinton campaign's strategy of disqualifying and defeating him and what the *Washington Post* had announced in a headline: "Clinton Questions Whether Sanders Is Qualified to Be President." Responding to the emerging Clinton narrative, Bernie told the crowd, "She has been saying lately that she thinks that I am not qualified to be president. Well, let me, let me just say in response to Secretary Clinton: I don't believe that she is qualified, if . . . ," and he proceeded to list the reasons—having a super PAC, coziness with Wall Street, trade positions, voting for the Iraq War, and more—why she should be disqualified from being president. But the phrase he used was "not qualified."

The Clinton folks struck back immediately. Their first line of attack was that Hillary Clinton herself had never used the words "not qualified" or "unqualified" with respect to Bernie. That was technically true. In a *Morning Joe* interview, pressed on the point, Clinton said: "I think the [New York Daily News] interview raised a lot of really serious questions"; "I think he hadn't done his homework, and he'd been talking for more than a year about doing things that he obviously hadn't really studied or understood, and that does raise a lot of questions"; and "I think that what he has been saying about the core issue in his whole campaign doesn't seem to be rooted in an understanding of either the law or the practical ways you get something done. And I will leave it to voters to decide who of us can do the job that the country needs, who can do all aspects of the job, both on the economic domestic issues and on national security and foreign policy."

It was these comments that led to the *Washington Post* headline about Clinton's questioning Bernie's qualifications. In attacking Bernie for what it called his "false attack" on Clinton for calling him "not qualified," the *Washington Post*'s Glenn Kessler threw its own headline writers under the bus. "Many Washington-based reporters have experienced the frustration of having an accurate article denied by an agency spokesman because of a headline that went a little far off the mark." In truth, the

Post's headline dovetailed with the lead of the story: "Former secretary of state Hillary Clinton on Wednesday questioned whether her rival in the Democratic presidential primary, Sen. Bernie Sanders (Vt.), is qualified to be president."

Kessler's attack piece then engaged in an incredible feat of political contortion. It was acceptable for the *Post's* reporters to thus characterize Clinton's remarks, but Bernie could not draw the same conclusion: "Those kinds of answers certainly give license to reporters to offer an interpretation that Clinton is raising questions about her rival's qualifications. Clinton, after all, is a former secretary of state and is adept at signaling messages without actually saying the words out loud. But it's not the same as 'quote unquote' saying Sanders is unqualified."

I certainly was not aware, until this flap, that columnists (or reporters writing opinion columns) carried such sharp razors that they could engage in this type of hairsplitting. But the establishment was petrified that Bernie was going to win in New York and upend the Democratic primary. Any perceived mischaracterization, no matter how tiny or how immaterial to the substance of what Bernie was saying, was going to draw a blistering counterattack not just from the Clinton campaign but from its media allies. The proof is that the media gave Clinton a pass when she made the same kind of mischaracterization: In response to Bernie, she tweeted the following: "I've been called a lot of things over the years, but 'unqualified' has not been one of them.—Hillary."

Wait a minute. Bernie never said Hillary Clinton was "unqualified." He said she was "not qualified" by virtue of the positions she had taken during her political career, thereby suggesting she was disqualified. In Glenn Kessler's subsequent article criticizing Clinton for misstating what Bernie said, he wrote " ". That's right: He wrote nothing because there was no Glenn Kessler article holding Clinton to the same standard Bernie was being subjected to.

In fairness, perhaps Hillary Clinton mistakenly believed that Bernie had called her "unqualified" because she was relying on media headlines such as this one from *The Hill*, on April 7: "Sanders Defends Calling Clinton Unqualified for White House." Or maybe she read articles like Ben Geier's piece in *Fortune*: "In a speech on Wednesday evening, Sanders said that Clinton was 'unqualified' to be president. He again alluded to payments she received for speeches she delivered to big banks and the fact that she is supported by a Super PAC, arguing that these items made her unqualified to be president." If so, she was doing exactly what Kessler had excoriated Bernie for.

One reporter who did understand what Bernie was saying at the Philadelphia rally sent me an email: "I have a theory Which is that he mean to say she's DISqualified, not UNqualified. Am I right? Is he planning to say anything about this today."

Yes, Nancy Cordes was right.

But the Clinton campaign quickly pivoted to turn Bernie's attack on Clinton's positions and fund-raising that "disqualified" her, and twisted it to argue that Bernie was attacking her résumé or credentials, which of course he did not do because that was impossible to do. By moving to the "unqualified" frame, rather than the "disqualified" frame, the Clinton campaign could highlight her extensive résumé, while the media echo chamber repeated over and over again the Clinton/Cillizza/Capehart/ *NYDN* charge that Bernie's *Daily News* editorial interview demonstrated he was unqualified.

Yet, both Bernie and I had to defend on TV how Bernie could claim she's "unqualified," which he never did, when she had been a U.S. senator and secretary of state. We were then left in the position of having to acknowledge Hillary Clinton's admittedly impressive résumé and credentials. To voters in New York, who had elected Hillary Clinton to the U.S. Senate twice, the idea that Bernie believed Clinton "unqualified" must have seemed bizarre indeed.

In the end, our internal polling showed the impact of the one-two punch we got from the Clinton campaign and the media. We had whittled Clinton's lead down to 10 points, according to our April 6–7 tracking poll right after Wisconsin. Over the next few days, her lead quickly grew to 12 points, to 14 points, and, finally, in our April 9–11 tracking poll, to a whopping 22 points. That was more than double the deficit of only a few days before. We were in free fall!

———

While the Clinton campaign waged its campaign in the press, Bernie held rally after rally in the New York City area. Across the boroughs, tens of thousands of enthusiastic New Yorkers came to hear him. The energy of the crowds has received a lot of coverage elsewhere. It stood in stark contrast to the cynicism that dripped from the pages of the tabloids.

Bernie left the city to crisscross upstate New York. As part of his tour, he highlighted his opposition to fracking—a position that Hillary Clinton had refused to take since Iowa and would refuse ever to adopt. Bernie's upstate tour ended as he returned to the city for the Brooklyn debate with Secretary Clinton. All of his campaigning was paying off. The nosedive in the polls leveled out, and we began to see some recovery as the newness of the "disqualify him" effort began to wear off. But we were still in a big hole—bigger than when we had arrived in the Empire State on the seventh.

The debate CNN hosted on the fourteenth became increasingly important as our numbers in New York suffered. Both candidates came in "hot" and ready to spar. In terms of tone, what turned out to be the final such contest of the primary season was also the testiest. In substance, however, it covered mostly well-trodden ground, making it unlikely to move the needle substantially. There was an exchange over what appeared to be Hillary Clinton's newfound support for a $15 federal minimum wage. She had campaigned on a $12 floor throughout most of the campaign. But she had found religion at a press conference with New York governor Andrew Cuomo on April 4 to celebrate New York's new $15 minimum. Those not already bothered by her flip-flop on the Trans-Pacific Partnership or the Keystone XL pipeline were unlikely to find her support for an extra $3 in the minimum wage that troubling.

In another development, Bernie agreed to release his 2014 tax returns. As promised, they were boring. I went on the *Anderson Cooper 360°* show that night to discuss them. Cooper came on the mic before the show and expressed to me his surprise at just how boring they were. It was a short interview.

With the debate in the rearview mirror, Bernie headed to Rome at the invitation of the Vatican to participate in an international conference on economic and social justice. Pope Francis had publicly sparred with candidate Donald Trump over Trump's anti-immigrant rhetoric. Now Bernie was being invited by the Vatican. The contrast was hard to miss. On the campaign trail, Bernie had repeatedly expressed his admiration for the pope's call for a greater focus on the Social Gospel. There never was much question that Bernie would accept the invitation even in the midst of a hard-fought campaign.

He returned from Rome for a few final events in New York and some media interviews. On election day, he had already moved on to Pennsylvania, which was voting a week later.

Our election night war room was in a conference room in our Manhattan hotel. As always, we were looking for any information about how the voting was going. We started getting reports of big problems in Brooklyn, where over 100,000 voters were improperly dumped from the rolls. Just as in Arizona, we heard all day about people whose party registration was incorrect and who were therefore denied access to the ballot box.

As the afternoon grew late, a pile of pizza arrived. I got a call from a media contact with an update on the late exit polls, which showed us losing by only 4 points. "Congratulations!" my contact said. Losing by 4 points would have been widely perceived as a victory for us—or at least not a victory for the Clinton campaign. Politics is a game of expectations, after all. But we were going to lose by much more than 4 points. The fact that the media was seeing the race so close in the exit polling was raising their expectations only a short bit before those expectations were about to be severely disappointed. Their disappointment came through in their election night commentary. You can't put even seasoned journalists on a roller coaster like that without it affecting them.

As the increasingly grease-soaked pizza boxes sat next to me on the wooden conference table, the actual results starting coming in. In the end, we would be down 16. In other words, we gained back 6 of the 12 points we'd lost earlier in the pummeling we took from the *New York Daily News*, the *Washington Post* columnists, and the media echo chamber. Upstate, Bernie beat Hillary Clinton (remember, only registered Democrats could participate). But her margins in New York City and the surrounding counties more than made up for her loss there. As in so many places, Bernie won the geography primary.

The loss in New York was a severe blow to our chances. The primary season had been a series of ups and downs so far, with successes followed by setbacks. This last drop had been a severe one. We all knew that climbing the next hill would be more of a challenge than we had faced in the past. In addition, April would see our fund-raising start to come down out of the stratosphere.

In March we had raised an unbelievable $44 million. In April that number was below $26 million—an extraordinary amount of money and still well above our monthly campaign average of around $17 million. But it was almost $20 million lower than the month before. That presented two problems. The first was the political expectations game. If we had raised $20 million in March, the $26 million April total would have been hailed as a sign of momentum. But we were victims of our own success and the incredible generosity of Bernie's donors. The second problem is that the road ahead included several very expensive states, including California. The current spending levels could not be maintained. Although our April fund-raising totals were not released until May, we began internally to plan for the major adjustments that were inevitably coming without a major turnaround. John Robinson and I met frequently to track our spending and to begin planning where to scale back. It was depressing work, done as far from the spotlight as possible.

While we were scrambling to adjust to a financially tighter reality, the Clinton campaign had cleverly devised a way to rake in the dough— abuse of the joint fund-raising committees established with the DNC and state parties.

19

THE NOT-SO-JOINT JOINT
FUND-RAISING AGREEMENTS

ONE OF THE MOST EGREGIOUS EXAMPLES of the DNC's lop-sided support for the Clinton campaign was the abuse of the joint fund-raising agreement signed by them and a number of state parties. It allowed Hillary for America (HFA) to launder millions in donations that were above the limit they could accept under federal election law and robbed cash-starved state parties of tens of millions of dollars.

The purpose of a joint fund-raising agreement is to allow big donors to write a single check to the parties to the agreement. What is raised is then divided up among the parties, according to the terms of the agreement and in accordance with federal election law. The DNC's joint fund-raising agreements provided that the first $2,700 (the maximum amount an individual can give to a federal candidate per election) would go to the candidate. The next $33,400 would go to the DNC, and then the partici-pating thirty-two state parties would get up to $10,000 each. The goal is to get a donor to write one big check of over $350,000. There is no purpose to the joint fund-raising committees doing small-dollar fund-raising. That's because in that scenario, all the money raised would go to only one of the parties—in this case, the Clinton campaign, because under the agreement the Clinton campaign sets the first $2,700 of each contribution.

One interesting feature of the DNC's joint fund-raising agreements was that there was no deadline for the dispersal of the money raised by the committee to the various participants. The committee could keep the funds and use them to do additional fund-raising. Okay, fair enough. Turning money into more money in the fund-raising world seems like a good move.

However, the joint fund-raising committee's goal was to take those larger-than-$2,700 checks (which the Clinton campaign could not accept under federal election law) and convert them into smaller donations that all went to HFA. They accomplished this by using joint fund-raising dollars to do direct-mail and online solicitations.

It is empirically true that both direct-mail and online fund-raising almost always bring in contributions well below the federal limit, regardless of who sends the solicitation. Bernie's average contribution of $27 (raised almost entirely online) is a prime example of this reality. Online donations to HFA or the DNC would also have been relatively low—certainly low enough that HFA would have captured almost all the money raised in that way. In this way, HFA and the DNC could take $350,000 donations (of which HFA could accept only $2,700) and turn it into multiple $25 or $35 contributions from the online or direct mail program—all of which could flow into HFA's coffers under federal election law.

And they were successful at it. The $2,700 limit that the Clinton campaign had to observe is a small fraction of the amount that could be raised in a single check. It's only seven-tenths of 1 percent of $350,000. Even if the average donation to the joint fund-raising committee was only $20,000 instead of the over-$350,000 limit, the Clinton campaign share would only be 13.5 percent of the funds raised.

But *Politico*'s Kenneth Vogel, in a story that ran May 2, 2016, noted that the disbursement of the $61 million raised by the Clinton/DNC joint fund-raising committee was "$15.4 million to Clinton's campaign and $5.7 million to the DNC." That's 25 percent for the Clinton campaign. It gets worse. As Vogel reported, the joint fund-raising committee put out over $11 million that "has gone toward expenses that appear to have directly benefited Clinton's campaign, including $2.8 million for 'salary and overhead' [to the Clinton campaign itself] and $8.6 million for web advertising that mostly looks indistinguishable from Clinton campaign ads and that has helped Clinton build a network of small donors." With those figures added in, the Clinton campaign was getting almost 44 percent of the money. That would only make sense under the distribution formula if the average contribution to the joint fund-raising committee was in the $6,000 range.

As anyone who has built an online donor list can tell you, it is an enormously expensive proposition. The much-talked-about Bernie 2016 email list cost millions of dollars to create. And unlike in our campaign, where money spent for online ads always yielded more than they cost, it takes multiple solicitations for almost any other candidate to recoup the investment. Not the Clinton campaign. They got it for free. Not only did the Clinton campaign benefit by converting above-the-limit contributions they couldn't accept to small-dollar contributions they could accept. They also got a free email list that our campaign had to spend millions to create with money given to us $27 at a time.

They protested loudly when we called this arrangement out for what it was—a device for laundering big donations. Our attorney Brad Deutsch laid this all out in an April 18, 2016, letter to Chairwoman Wasserman Schultz. Needless to say, the DNC jumped in to defend the operation of the agreements, because they were in on the scheme.

And what of the state Democratic parties who were participants in the joint fund-raising committee? The donors to these big-ticket events were told that the bulk of the money was going to help down-ballot candidates. As reported by *Politico*, George Clooney, who hosted one of the Clinton/ DNC events in April with an over $350,000 ticket price, "admitted that was 'an obscene amount of money.' But he justified it by saying 'the overwhelming amount of the money that we're raising is not going to Hillary to run for president, it's going to the down-ticket.' "

Unfortunately, for state parties and down-ballot candidates that was just not true. The Clinton campaign snookered Clooney and the other guests, as well as the participating state Democratic parties. They weren't the only ones. Among others snookered were pro-Clinton writers, including one who penned the following for the *Washington Post* at the end of March: "Sanders makes it sound like Clinton is raising such obscene amounts of money for her campaign. In actuality, she's raising money for herself, the Democratic Party and state Democratic parties around the country." Oops!

An analysis by *Politico* on May 2, 2016, revealed that less than 1 percent of the funds raised by the joint fund-raising committee was left with state parties. That's because money that was deposited with state parties was almost immediately withdrawn from their accounts by the DNC. According to a CNN story that ran on the same day, some $3.8 million had been transferred to the states, but 88 percent of it had been almost immediately taken by the DNC—leaving the thirty-two state parties collectively with only about $450,000 out of $61 million.

More than one state party chair has told me since that they would never have participated had they known how this joint fund-raising agreement would operate. Usually some variation of "they lied to us" is in their description of the sales pitch they were given to participate. This is in part why so many state parties are resource-starved. Even when money was donated specifically for their benefit, it was grabbed away by the DNC bureaucracy and the Clinton campaign.

Some of the money snatched by the DNC from state parties would eventually find its way back to state-level operations but only in those states targeted by the Clinton campaign as presidential battleground states. That meant a lot of money spent in Florida and Ohio. But if you were in a red state like Alabama, South Carolina, Montana, or Texas, you got virtually nothing. I specifically asked a top Texas party official how much money they kept from the joint fund-raising. "I don't think we got anything," he told me.

The parties in heavily red states will never be able to become competitive if this practice continues. It was a point that Bernie raised on the trail often—the complete abandonment by the national Democratic Party of over half the states. It is a shortsighted policy that had disastrous effects in November 2016. Because the Democrats are locked out of so many states, Trump's flipping of a few states in the "blue wall" doomed the Clinton campaign.

On top of that, down-ballot candidates were left high and dry. The Clinton campaign ultimately had so much financial control over the DNC that after Donna Brazile became acting chair and was desperately scrambling to find money for down-ballot candidates, she told me that "the Clinton campaign has complete control of every dollar that comes into this [DNC] building." And according to Brazile, HFA had little interest in letting the national party spend money on down-ballot candidates. Our meeting took place in her DNC office. She gave me a tour of the building. We ran into New Hampshire state party chair Ray Buckley in the hallway. He was surprised that I had never had a tour before. I said to Ray, "In the past, the only thing they've wanted to show me here is the door." Donna Brazile was holding a DNC staff get-together following our meeting. The libations for the get-together were from the liquor Debbie Wasserman Schultz left in her office when she departed.

This reality of what was happening with the Clinton/DNC joint fund-raising agreement was in stark contrast to the attacks leveled by Hillary Clinton herself against Bernie. Gabe Debenedetti's April 13, 2016, *Politico* story reports that Clinton had started attacking Bernie for his ties to the Democratic Party "after decades as an independent, even appearing to specifically jab his lack of down-ballot fundraising while campaigning in Wisconsin before its primary." According to Debenedetti, former Goldwater Girl Clinton said, "I am also a Democrat and have been a proud Democrat all my adult life . . . I know how important it is to elect state legislators, to elect Democratic governors, to elect a Democratic Senate and House of Representatives." Important, maybe, but not enough to let the DNC spend any money to help them. Of course, none of this—the looting of state parties and the use of the joint fund-raising committee as a vehicle for HFA to avoid FEC contribution limits—could have taken place without the active support of the Democratic Party's then chair.

In late May 2017, Hillary Clinton blamed the financial condition of the DNC and its poor data as a factor contributing to her loss. CNN's

MJ Lee quoted her as saying, "I'm now the nominee of the Democratic Party. I inherit nothing from the Democratic Party. It was bankrupt, it was on the verge of insolvency, its data was mediocre to poor, non-existent, wrong. I had to inject money into it—the DNC—to keep it going."

The irony, of course, is that the operation of the Clinton/DNC joint fund-raising agreement was one of the key reasons the DNC lacked money. By taking all those big-dollar contributions (which would have gone to the national and state Democratic parties) and turning them into small-dollar contributions (which all went to HFA), the Clinton campaign itself bore responsibility for the money problems at the DNC.

Immediately after Clinton's attempt to blame the DNC, a former senior DNC data staffer responded forcefully on Twitter only to pull down his tweets not long afterward. While most of the coverage of his tweets focused on his defense of the DNC's data operation, he also tweeted about Hillary Clinton's role in starving the Democratic Party of resources:

Andrew Therriault @therriaultphd tweeted · May 2, 2016:
Also, that's pretty precious when she couldn't have raised all that without the DNC's higher limits as a laundering vehicle.

Bernie for his part raised millions that actually went to down-ballot Democratic candidates in the last election cycle. Combined with the amount raised after the Democratic national convention by Our Revolution, the progressive nonprofit inspired by Bernie's historic run, over $5 million went to down-ballot Democratic candidates at the federal, state, and local level. Compare that to the measly $450,000 that *Politico* reports was left with state parties from the Clinton/DNC joint fund-raising arrangement.

As for the joint fund-raising agreement we signed with the DNC, they completely left it inoperative. Our agreement with them was that they would organize events of large donor Democrats, which Bernie would attend. Despite plenty of prodding by Mark Longabaugh, the DNC never organized a single event.

20

WILD RIDE ON THE ACELA

Coming out of our defeat in New York, there were five contests—four of them closed primaries—the following week. Only in Rhode Island did our internal polling have us ahead. After New York, we had to start pushing the ball back up the hill, but we all knew that April 26 was going to be tough without momentum from New York.

Pennsylvania was the big prize, on April 26, with the greatest number of delegates. Our internal polling in the Keystone State had us dead-even with Hillary Clinton until the New York primary, when her big win translated into a widening margin in her favor.

One group among whom the margin for Hillary Clinton was going the other way in Pennsylvania was younger African American voters. As was widely reported at the time, Bill Clinton condescendingly responded to two attendees at an April 7 rally who were opposed to the harsh incarceration policies that he and Hillary Clinton had championed in the 1990s. In a speech in 1996, Hillary Clinton had called some young African Americans "superpredators."

Bill Clinton has been called the first black president. But at times he's not been very nice when he's talking about or with black people outside a carefully scripted appearance. Most famously, he dismissively took a swipe at Senator Obama (and the Rev. Jesse Jackson) in 2008—all part of the dog-whistle campaign, documented by Geoffrey Dunn at the *Huffington Post*, and others, that the Clintons ran against Obama.

Bill Clinton's attack on Black Lives Matter and his defense of Hillary Clinton's use of "superpredator" fell flat—very flat. It was made worse by his comment afterward that he "almost wanted to apologize." In the days immediately following this performance, our polling numbers showed Hillary Clinton's support among black voters falling rapidly and Bernie's support rising, African Americans aged eighteen to fifty-four supporting Bernie by some 12 points over Clinton. As was the case with all voting groups, that support was stronger with younger voters than with older voters. Our lead with younger African Americans pulled Bernie's overall support among all black voters in the Keystone State to within 10 points of Clinton.

In our campaign, there was universal support for a more visible and vocal role for Bill Clinton throughout the campaign, even before his Pennsylvania gaffe. He can be counted on to vigorously defend policy choices made during his administration that ended up hurting a lot of people, even when it is clear that they were rooted in political calculation and, in hindsight, politically unnecessary. Hillary Clinton shared Bill Clinton's Achilles' heel in this regard at times—most notably when she attempted to defend DOMA in the fall of 2015.

Activists continued to show up at Clinton campaign rallies in Pennsylvania, including one presided over by Chelsea Clinton on April 13, as reported by *Salon's* Sophia Tesfaye. Hillary Clinton led a rally on April 20, and CBS News reported, "The protesters chanted, 'Don't vote for Hillary! She's killing black people!' as they were led out of the Fillmore Theater."

Hillary Clinton did recover somewhat from the initial drop in her support among younger black voters in Pennsylvania immediately before and after the New York primary, and she regained a small single-digit lead over Bernie. By election day in Pennsylvania, that lead had evaporated. Bernie won African American voters in the eighteen-to-fifty-four age range in the Keystone State handily, even as he lost the overall race by 12 points—exactly where our internal polling showed the race to be.

He continued his pattern of intense campaigning throughout the

April 26 primary states. His barnstorming after the New York loss bore results. Our lead in Rhode Island expanded, with the result being a double-digit win in our only victory that day. In Connecticut's closed primary, Hillary Clinton won by only 5 points, even with the support of Governor Malloy and others.

In both places, the statewide leaders had lined up with Hillary Clinton. Rhode Island U.S. senator Sheldon Whitehouse, who, like Bernie, had been elected in 2006, was a particularly active critic of Bernie early on. In a WPRI interview, he declared Clinton the most electable while declaring, "I adore Bernie, and I love seeing him succeed after all the effort that he's put in over many, many years." Coincidentally or not, Whitehouse made his "Bernie is adorable but not electable" remarks to Rhode Island television exactly one day before Dana Milbank wrote his "Bernie is adorable but not electable" column in the *Washington Post*.

Whitehouse was not so kind behind the scenes, however. In a February 4 email to Clinton staff, he suggested that the Clinton campaign tie Bernie to Karl Rove as part of their New Hampshire strategy, because Rove's group had run some ads in the early states tying Hillary Clinton to Wall Street, per *USA Today*'s Nicole Gaudiano. According to Jimmy LaSalvia, writing in *Salon*, Rove hoped to curry favor with Republican donors.

Whitehouse's theory of the case got even more zany in an April 4, 2017, appearance on *Morning Joe*. He claimed that Wall Street money backed Bernie to defeat Clinton. It's not debatable that financial interests poured tens of millions into Clinton-world over the years in the form of campaign donations, speaking fees, foundation donations, and donations to her super PAC. Kyle Clauss's *Boston* magazine article debunking Whitehouse's flight of fancy is appropriately subtitled, "With all due respect, Senator, what are you talking about?" Twitter used the word "delusional" to describe Whitehouse.

It's one thing to point out that Karl (not my cousin, not my in-law) Rove tried to raise hell and some money by jabbing at Hillary Clinton in the early states. It's another to claim that Wall Street backed Bernie over Clinton, particularly when later, in the same *Morning Joe* interview, Whitehouse acknowledged that Wall Street probably preferred Clinton to Trump.

Huh? All I can say is I'm glad, for the sake of Senate Democrats, that Rhode Island is a solidly blue state. One can only imagine how short-lived Whitehouse's political career would be in a competitive state. Thankfully, his constituents don't share his bizarre political notions. Bernie won there by almost 12 points. Unfortunately, that was our only win of the day, with both Delaware and Maryland going strongly for Clinton.

From my perspective, this was the worst day of the campaign. The required belt-tightening meant we were going to have to substantially downsize after the twenty-sixth. As a practice, we had moved staff to states later in the calendar when a primary or caucus contest was over. With the calendar coming near the end, the decision was made to let go of all the staff working in the March 26 states, along with many at our already understaffed headquarters. That amounted to about 225 people out of our remaining staff of 550. We were by this time already at less than our staffing high of about 1,200 staff and paid canvassers on February 1. Even so, having to let so many dedicated people go at one time weighed heavily on me.

News of the layoffs was inadvertently given prematurely to the *New York Times*. By the time I had arranged an all-staff call, everyone already knew what was coming. The call was relatively short. I really did not know what I could say to so many who had worked so hard. If we had had the financial resources, we would have moved staff forward, even though there were only a few states left and most of them were fully staffed.

After the call, I looked over to John Robinson, who shared an office with me. "I'm going out for a bit," I said. I went back to my hotel room and for the first and only time during the campaign I cried in sadness.

> *When you have eliminated the impossible, whatever remains, however improbable, must be the truth.*
>
> —SHERLOCK HOLMES

Even with a big win in Pennsylvania and an upset elsewhere (Connecticut being the most likely on the twenty-sixth), the pledged delegate math, while difficult before New York, had become almost impossible without a complete collapse of the Clinton campaign. That was true even though after the twenty-sixth the campaign would once again move to states where we were doing better. There are only fifty states, the District of Columbia, and six territories, and we were running out of pledged-delegate runway.

Superdelegates constituted another source of support. These are people who by virtue of their present or former elected office or party position are entitled to cast a vote at the national conventions. They can support whomever they choose and can switch their support at any time before the actual voting.

And there were a lot of them. They numbered over 700 and represented some 15 percent of the total delegates. Someone who sewed up the support of the superdelegates would start the primary process with 30 percent of the delegates they needed to win the nomination before a single vote by rank-and-file Democrats and Democratically aligned independents. In fact, the total number of superdelegates was greater than the number of pledged delegates chosen by voters in twenty-four states and the District of Columbia combined. Put another way, the number of superdelegates exceeded the total number of pledged delegates from New York, Texas, and Florida (with a combined population of over 68 million people).

As early as mid-March we began to discuss superdelegates internally. Mathematically speaking, neither candidate was going to win enough pledged delegates to secure the nomination. That meant whoever won would owe their victory to the superdelegates. We were not enamored of the system. But we did not create superdelegates or write the rules. Bernie was running with the rules he was given. We were not going to ignore their potential to swing the race in our favor.

We understood that getting them to switch in any large numbers, particularly after the shutout on March 15, would require a forceful show of momentum on our part in the contests afterward to create doubts about the inevitability of Clinton's nomination. If we could do that we would then have to convince them of what almost every public poll was showing (and what the November election verified): that Hillary Clinton had real problems as a general election candidate. Since relatively early in the primary contest, Bernie was consistently outperforming her in head-to-head polls against the Republicans, especially against Trump.

PolitiFact confirmed in two separate articles that Bernie was consistently stronger against Trump than Clinton in the public polling. On March 8 it found that Bernie outperformed Clinton against Trump in six of the seven public polls it reviewed. PolitiFact's follow-up review, published on May 29, showed even more dramatic results. In eight public polls since its March 8 story, Bernie was outperforming Clinton against Trump by an average of more than 6 points.

In both its analyses, PolitiFact qualified its findings with a narrative about how Bernie had not been subjected to grueling Republican attacks; therefore, his standing in the polls might be overstated. This argument ignored the steady stream of attacks Bernie had withstood from the Clinton campaign, its surrogates, allies like Correct the Record, and the media—including characterizations, in some cases, and outright charges, in others, that Bernie was too old (CTR), too radical (CTR), a socialist (every media outlet repeatedly and often multiple times in the same story), unqualified (HFA, *Washington Post, New York Daily News*), a snake oil salesman (*Washington Post*), a misogynist (Hillary Clinton herself), an NRA stooge (HFA, *Daily News*) and unelectable (every establishment voice, including those adoring ones).

However, they ignored the flip side of that argument. Hillary Clinton was perhaps the best-known presidential candidate in a long time, and substantial numbers of voters had concerns about her. In all our polling, independent voters, in particular, had real questions about her credibility and trustworthiness. Granted, she had been subjected to an incredible amount of negative attacks by Republicans for years. And many of them stuck. Being so well known made it extremely difficult, if not impossible, for her to change voters' impressions in the short span of a hotly contested presidential election. To us, that was a real warning sign of problems to come. Somehow those who thought Bernie would be turned to mincemeat during a general election campaign implicitly believed that firmly held concerns about Hillary Clinton, especially among young and independent voters, were going to miraculously improve.

One Clinton adviser was asked, after the general election, how it was that the least popular presidential candidate in history had won in November. The adviser replied, "Well, we ran the second least popular candidate in history." Again, I'm not validating the electorate's impressions of Hillary Clinton. But they existed. And the establishment ignored them.

Although a narrative about Bernie's race for the nomination necessarily centers on the back-and-forth with Hillary Clinton, the candidacy of Donald Trump was an ever-looming reality that shaped the substance and coverage of the race. From the "be careful what you wish for" files, as early as April 2015 Clinton campaign emails revealed that they wanted to elevate candidates whom they viewed are marginal and right-wing. The goal of elevating them was for them to push more mainstream Republican candidates—read Jeb Bush—to take similarly extreme positions that would be harmful in the general election. Donald Trump is specifically named as one of those candidates (Dr. Ben Carson and Senator Ted Cruz being the others). The belief that Donald Trump was so unacceptable as to make him unelectable not only underpinned this pied piper strategy but drove the general election strategy that running as the not-Trump candidate would propel the Clinton campaign to victory.

Reporting by *Politico*'s Gabe Debenedetti and others had Clinton aides rejoicing over Donald Trump's triumph in the Republican nominating contest. Even after watching him, in B-grade horror movie fashion, dismember all the other members of the Republican clown car during the primaries, the Clinton camp believed that they had the magic formula for beating the crude, xenophobic, pompous real estate magnate. That proved wrong. While the Clinton campaign made mistakes, it fell victim to Trump's dominance of "earned media," as had his Republican opponents before.

Setting aside the Clinton campaign's hunger for an extremist Republican opponent and their glee at having secured one, the evidence is clear that the rise of Trump and his eventual success was a direct result of the media's unceasing coverage of everything Trump. In a March 15, 2016, story the *New York Times* documents that Trump had only spent about 35 percent of the amount that either our campaign or the Clinton campaign had spent on television advertising up to that point. An analysis by MediQuant in the same article shows why that is just a small part of the story. Their analysis found that the value of the free media coverage that Trump had received to that point was nearly $2 billion. Hillary Clinton, on the other hand, had received less than $750 million worth of free media coverage. Bernie, who some have said was a victim of the media's "Bernie Blackout," received only $321 million worth.

An updated analysis by MediQuant, reported by Reuters right after the general election, found that the total value of free media coverage that Trump received through the whole campaign equated to $5 billion—more than twice what Hillary Clinton received. This fact alone explains much of Trump's success in securing the nomination and his victory in November 2016. His candidacy was propped up and propelled by the media, particularly cable news, in the interest of the high ratings that his antics produced. It's not much more complicated than that. The business imperative of cable news allowed Trump to capture an unprecedented amount of television coverage. That gift took a reality TV star to 1600 Pennsylvania Avenue.

Trump uniquely benefited from consistent start-to-finish coverage of his rallies. Who knew, after all, what outrageous or offensive thing he was going to say next? On election nights, it is standard practice for the various candidates to confer with the media for the purpose of staggering their statements for maximum coverage. The Trump campaign always got precedence. Time and time again we were informed that if Trump came on while Bernie was speaking they were going to cut to Trump. There were even election nights on which the results of both the Republican and the Democratic contests were crawling along the bottom of the screen, while the main visual was the empty podium from which Trump would later give his remarks.

The media's coverage of Trump's empty podium is a metaphor for the wall-to-wall coverage he received. This was raised quite vocally at Harvard University's Institute of Politics quadrennial post–general election conference in the fall of 2016. After each presidential election, the IOP invites all the campaign managers and other top campaign officials from the past season, along with leading journalists and political strategists. On the Democratic side, there were representatives of our campaign, Clinton's, and O'Malley's. There were many more Republican managers and staffers because of the large pool of Republican candidates in the primaries. And they were bitter.

At one of the dinners during the conference, there was a media panel on an elevated dais that included Jeff Zucker, president of CNN. The rest of us were all seated at round tables. I was with Mark Longabaugh and some of the fellows from the IOP. To my right were Republican staffers for Trump's primary opponents.

Zucker, who while an NBC executive green-lighted Trump's *The Apprentice*, admitted that he had frequent phone conversations with Trump during the election season. He was loudly and bitterly called out by some in the audience. The boos and catcalls were not from our campaign. Nor from the Clinton campaign. It was angry Republicans who berated Zucker for CNN's nonstop Trump coverage.

Politco's Gold and Debenedetti offered this account of the scene at the Harvard dinner:

> "I don't remember getting invited to call in, though," Sarah Isgur Flores, Carly Fiorina's deputy campaign manager said, kicking off a parade of comments.
>
> More irritated voices across the room quickly chimed in: "We didn't get that call." "We'd be invited for eight seconds." "At 2 o'clock in the afternoon we'd be invited on," another said sarcastically.
>
> "All of the Republican candidates were invited to come on," Zucker said. "Cable news in general, CNN in particular, should not be held responsible for the fact that Donald Trump said yes to those interviews."

"It's not the interviews," Rubio senior advisor Todd Harris said as another audience member shouted, "You showed empty podiums!"

"You showed hours upon hours of unfiltered unscripted coverage of Trump, this was not about interviews," he added.

Some members of the audience applauded, and the tension in the room built up as salads were left untouched and more wine was poured.

I certainly had another glass of wine while this was going on.

But we should be clear that CNN was not alone in monetizing Trump. CBS CEO Les Moonves, speaking to the *Hollywood Reporter* about presidential campaign ad spending in February 2016, famously said, "It may not be good for America, but it's damn good for CBS."

More to the point, Moonves credited Donald Trump with keeping the money flowing in: "Man, who would have expected the ride we're all having right now? . . . The money's rolling in and this is fun"; "I've never seen anything like this, and this going to be a very good year for us. Sorry. It's a terrible thing to say. But, bring it on, Donald. Keep going."

That attitude continues to this day. Cable news and much of the rest of the media continues its Trump obsession. Every tweet, every outrageous act or statement, every leaked bit of White House intrigue fills the twenty-four-hour news cycle. Even as Trump belittles and demeans the media as an institution and retweets video of himself violently assaulting CNN, they just cannot look away. The money is too good. "Bring it on, Donald. Keep going."

21

FROM THE OHIO RIVER VALLEY TO THE GOLDEN GATE BRIDGE

WITH NEW YORK AND THE April 26 states in the rearview mirror, our last best hope for demonstrating strength to the superdelegates was to rack up a series of wins on June 7, as difficult as that would be. Six states were holding contests that day, including New Jersey and California, which had the biggest delegate total of any state. But we had to get back on our feet first. Indiana was the next state on the calendar, followed by West Virginia, Oregon, and Kentucky, and then Puerto Rico. If we were going to have a big showing on June 7 we had to win most, if not all, of these.

Indiana was a state we had polled well in earlier, but after the New York and April 26 losses Hillary Clinton had pulled ahead. The public polling was also bad for us. FiveThirtyEight gave Bernie only a 10 percent chance of winning. The RealClearPolitics polling average had Clinton up by nearly 7 points.

Four key factors played into Bernie's upset victory in the Hoosier State. The first was our strong local campaign, which had been on the ground since after Oklahoma on March 1. The second was Bernie's ability to campaign intensely there. The third was the help of labor in Indiana—spearheaded by United Steelworkers Local 1999 president Chuck Jones. Importantly, the Steelworkers represented workers at a Carrier plant targeted for closure. These workers understood in a very personal way the impact of the free-trade agreements that Bernie had opposed for his entire political career. The fourth was Bernie's continued growing support among African American voters. By the night of his 5-point upset in Indiana, Clinton's lead among all African Americans in Indiana was only 10 points. Given the age divide in Bernie's support, that margin meant that he was winning the votes of African American voters under forty by a huge margin—and likely the broader eighteen-to-fifty-four age bracket.

The win in Indiana showed Bernie might be down but never out. It also presaged Clinton's general election problems in the industrial Midwest. Bernie also used his win as an opportunity to lay out the case for why superdelegates should move to him.

NBC's Carrie Dann reported, "In remarks to reporters in New Albany, Indiana, Sanders argued that he is the better candidate to compete in a general election against Donald Trump, whose win in Indiana Tuesday night set him on course to become the likely GOP nominee. 'I sense a great deal of momentum,' Bernie said. 'While the path is narrow—and I do not deny that for a moment—I think we can pull off one of the great political upsets in the history of the United States.' A week later he enjoyed a 15-point win in West Virginia, where he prevailed in every county.

Oregon and Kentucky were the next week. Both were closed primaries, and Oregon's voting is all done by mail. As many expected, Bernie won Oregon, although by a smaller margin than our earlier polling had shown. The narrowness of our path forward was starting to have an impact on voters. But Oregon was a milestone for the campaign. It was Bernie's first win in a closed primary state.

Kentucky proved in many ways the more interesting contest that day. Despite its closed primary, our campaign had an active ground operation in place, and Bernie spent considerable time campaigning in person. Due to resource constraints, we put up only a relatively modest television buy.

The Clinton campaign decided to go all-in, as reported by CNN's Dan Merica, with television, radio, a dozen surrogates, and eleven appearances by the candidate herself. During the primary, I got an email from Tad and Mark's firm that Clinton was outspending us on television. To match them, we'd need another $150,000 or so. Bernie, who always preferred grassroots campaigning over television ads, decided that we would use Kentucky to show that a campaign could win without spending a lot on television. We would let the Clinton campaign have the television advantage. We almost pulled it off.

Clinton won in the Bluegrass State by two-tenths of 1 percent. In hindsight, that extra television money would have put us over the top (as would have also been the case if we had come in with more momentum). Kentucky confirmed what we had seen in other states: a grassroots campaign, Bernie's personal presence, *and* a robust paid media campaign was the formula for winning. Take out any of those pieces and our chances of victory went down substantially. Still, Bernie's tie in Kentucky, even though we were outspent on television, validated what Oregon showed. Bernie could do well in closed primaries—even when he was outspent on television.

The last contest before California voted was in Puerto Rico. Puerto Rico was experiencing incredible financial problems, and wealthy creditors were squeezing the island hard for repayments at the expense of vital services like education. Bernie had spoken strongly against the type of austerity regime Puerto Rico was being forced into—not unlike what the European Union was doing to countries like Spain and Greece.

Bernie went to Puerto Rico to campaign. It was an expensive detour; by this time, he was trying to spend a lot of time in California. In the end, Clinton won, as she had in 2008. But her margin over Bernie (22 points) was far smaller than her margin in her previous presidential run (36.5 points).

June 7 represented the last hope to create the momentum that could convince superdelegates to take another look at Bernie Sanders. Six states were voting that day: Montana, South Dakota, North Dakota, New Mexico, New Jersey, and the largest state, California, which alone had 475 pledged delegates (still only about two-thirds the value of the superdelegates).

With resources a major issue now, we made the difficult choice to forgo television ads in the expensive media markets of New Jersey, even though it was the second-largest prize of the day. We also were "dark" in Montana and the Dakotas. We did put some ads up for New Mexico's closed primary. California was a challenge. Many voters in California vote early; in the case of those voters, television advertising is a waste. We also didn't have the tens of millions that would be needed to blanket the state anyway. We focused our advertising in Southern California, where the percentage of voters casting early ballots was lower. It also allowed us to reach more of California's considerable Latino population, with whom our organizers were working intensely.

This relatively small buy would be backed by nonstop Bernie appearances in California, from one end of the state to the other. Our scaled-down staff worked to pull off the overwhelming schedule of rallies. We were also trying to contend with California's balloting system. The primary in California was technically open, but independent voters had to explicitly request a "Democratic" ballot to receive one that included the presidential primary. Otherwise they would receive one that had only the down-ballot primaries. Because of the size of the state, it was extremely expensive to get word to independent voters. The result was a lot of confused and frustrated Californians and suppressed participation of independents in the Democratic presidential primary.

There was grumbling from the other side about Bernie's continued campaigning in California when the pledged delegate math was so stacked against him. Just on the basis of pride points, the Clinton campaign didn't want to lose in the nation's largest state. Although I've never discussed it with people in the Clinton campaign, I am sure they were not happy to be investing money in a state so close to the end of the process that they believed they would win hands down in the general election. But there were many voices in the Democratic Party who welcomed our contesting the primary there.

Bernie's decision to fight in California was a potential boon to down-ballot Democrats. Under California's primary system for down-ballot candidates, all contenders, regardless of party, appear in a single "jungle" primary, and the top two finishers go on to the general election. A huge turnout among Democrats to vote in the Bernie-Clinton race made it more likely that two Democrats would emerge victorious in congressional primaries and other down-ballot races. In those instances, the Democratic Party was guaranteed a general election win. This was perceived to be more true in 2016 than before, because on the Republican side Donald Trump had already locked up the nomination in Indiana, so there was less incentive for Republicans to come out to vote. In addition, a contested primary in California activated the volunteer base, whether they were for Bernie or Clinton. We got a lot of private praise from organs of the party who were focused on winning down-ballot races, even if a contested primary in California was not popular in the Clinton camp.

The issue of debates raised its head again during the California primary, but in an unusual way. The first development was that the Clinton campaign reneged on their previous commitment to participate in a May debate in the state. This is one of the three they had promised in exchange for getting their extra New Hampshire debate. During the debate over debating in California, Fox offered to host. We would have done it on any network, so when Fox stepped up, we agreed to it. I get why the Clinton campaign didn't want to debate this late in the process, but they had publicly committed to it at the highest levels of their campaign. A promise made was not a promise kept in this case.

While the debate with Hillary Clinton was falling through, it looked as if there might be an even more noteworthy event—a Sanders vs. Trump debate. On his May 25 show, Jimmy Kimmel asked Trump if he would agree to debate Bernie Sanders. According to CBS News, Trump responded, "How much is he going to pay me?" Kimmel said, "You would do it for a price? What would the price be?"

Trump continued, "If he paid a nice sum toward a charity, I would love to do that." "What if the network put up the money?" Kimmel asked. "That could happen also," Trump replied.

We responded in a tweet from Bernie: "Game on. I look forward to debating Donald Trump in California before the June 7 primary."

Although his staff tried to spin that he had been kidding, the next day

Trump said that the number he had in mind was in the $10 million to $15 million range. Every network was immediately interested in hosting the debate—including at least one that offered to put up millions and millions for charity to satisfy Donald Trump's demand. I said at the time that it might have been the most-watched presidential contest debate ever. And it might have been.

I went on TV to prod Donald Trump to go through with the debate, telling NBC's Andrea Mitchell, Bloomberg's Halperin and Heilemann, and CNN's Wolf Blitzer that I hoped Trump wouldn't "chicken out." "What we'll have to see, Wolf, is does Donald Trump have the courage to get on the stage with Bernie Sanders. That remains to be seen." In the end, Donald Trump did chicken out. Even though there were millions on the table for charity, he didn't quite have the "fortitude," as I said on Bloomberg, to match his bravado.

In many of those interviews, the host tried to get me to engage on the issue of Hillary Clinton's emails. A State Department inspector general report had been issued on the topic. As was the case throughout the campaign, I didn't bite, and neither did Bernie or any of the staff.

As June 7 drew near, the polling in California got supertight, with the RealClearPolitics poll average showing Clinton with only a 2-point lead. That is, until the Associated Press decided to become a newsmaker instead of a news reporter.

The night before the June 7 primaries in six states, the AP ran a story, based on its count of superdelegates, explaining that Hillary Clinton had enough combined pledged and superdelegates to lock up the nomination regardless of how the six contests came out. It would have been bad enough if the AP in the normal course of its delegate counting had come to this determination and put it out the day before this critical primary day. Their reporting was to have a serious impact on voter turnout and sentiment the next day. But the greater issue about the AP's conduct is far more distasteful. It wasn't reporting news. It was creating it.

The AP engaged in an active campaign of harassing and cajoling super-delegates to get the result it wanted. Below is an email I received from

Nick Carter of our staff with a synopsis of what he heard from more than one superdelegate about the AP's efforts. This is a summary of a conversation Nick had with the friend of a superdelegate who was badgered, as well as a text exchange between that superdelegate and the Associated Press.

Nick's synopsis:

> Weird stuff seems to have transpired in last 24 hours. . . . the AP started aggressively calling uncommitted supers as early as 6:00 am. I know of at least 2 supers who got called several times by multiple AP reporters. They didn't seem to just want an answer on who they're supporting, but in at least one situation the AP was described as actively trying to persuade supers to take a stand and wasn't satisfied with the answer "uncommitted."

Nick's summary of the conversation with the superdelegate's friend and the text exchange:

> The superdelegate's friend says that she was called six times today by the AP beginning at 6 am. She was also texted several times by at least two different reporters. One left a voicemail. Below is from a text conversation between an AP reporter and an uncommitted super.
> The Clinton campaign later emailed and later called and told her what the AP was doing, apologized and said not to talk to them. The Clinton campaign told the superdelegate that it was happening to many others and not to talk to them.
> The superdelegate's friend writes that the superdelegate reached out to the Clinton campaign after AP made it sound like the campaign had given her contact info and declared her preferences on her behalf.

The superdelegate refused to speak to them, so the texts continued.

TEXT MESSAGE EXCHANGE BETWEEN
SUPERDELEGATE AND AP:

AP reporter: I didn't receive your cell number randomly so am hoping we can chat . . .

AP reporter: Could you just verify yes re your support-not seeking to publicize just have you in broader tally—that's why I was given your number.

> **Superdelegate:** I plan on staying uncommitted until the Convention in Philadelphia.

> **Superdelegate:** I know that not what you want to hear but that is my intention.

AP reporter: Oh it was suggested to me otherwise . . . so you're not backing Clinton? That's why I was given your number

> **Superdelegate:** I am not publicly stating either way at this time.

AP reporter: I guess in terms of my request I don't see it as public in terms of putting your name out there—included as part of broader tally that show sentiment of superdels if national convention were today, how would you vote?

AP reporter: Call me to chat?

BREAK IN MESSAGES

AP reporter: [. . .] necessarily being publicized or have names attached to votes . . .

AP reporter (1:25 pm): The tally shows how superdels would vote if convention were held today . . .

AP reporter (2:49 pm): The tally shows how superdels respond who are clearly for Clinton but not seeking publicity at this time, agree to be included as part of tally that reflects sentiment of superdels if national convention were held today. . . . Not to much to ask? I know your preference bc I was given your number. . . . Can you verify yes? And then I'll leave you alone . . .

AP reporter (5:27 pm): Last try—we basically are looking for 1 more—want to be a part of that big moment? No names . . .

END OF FIRST EXCHANGE

A SECOND REPORTER TEXTS HER:

AP reporter 2: Ms #### I am Stephen Ohlemacher at the Associated Press. I believe you texted with a colleague of mine. We are very close to making history today so I am eager to talk with you. Thank you!

In fact, the second reporter who texted the superdelegate bragged on Twitter about how he had badgered superdelegates:

Stephen Ohlemacher @stephenatap tweeted · June 6, 2016:
Dear superdels, I promise to stop calling you 6X a day AP count: Clinton has delegates to win Democratic nomination.

Note that the Clinton campaign told the superdelegate not to answer the AP at the same time the AP is strongly suggesting that the Clinton campaign has given the AP the superdelegate's contact information and indicated that the superdelegate is pro-Clinton. A senior Clinton staffer confirmed to me after the primaries that they were not happy about the story coming out the night before the California primary; they feared there would be a voter backlash. That didn't stop the AP from trying to deceive the superdelegate that the Clinton campaign wanted the super-delegate to cooperate.

The conduct of AP reporters in browbeating and deceiving super-delegates dealt a severe blow to the credibility of an important media institution and to the media as a whole. It is hard to defend the media in other instances from charges that it manufactures news when there are examples like this one. This type of conduct spreads disrepute over an entire profession. Reporters and editors who are not willing to police their fellows when this type of thing happens share the blame for the loss of faith that Americans have in the fourth estate.

As the day ended, a few of us huddled around some laptops in a sparsely furnished room in our Los Angeles headquarters. We lost badly in New Jersey, won in both Montana and North Dakota, and came up only about 1,100 votes short in South Dakota (oh, for just a few paid media dollars!). In New Mexico's closed primary, we lost by only 3 points.

As the California results came in, Ben Tulchin, who has loads of ex-perience in politics in the Golden State, gave us his interpretation of how things were going. (It took weeks for the California numbers to be final-ized. Still not sure why it takes so long there.) We were doing very well up north and along the Nevada border. We also ended up winning Santa Barbara, Santa Cruz, and San Luis Obispo. But it was not enough. Hillary Clinton's margin ended up being 7 points.

For us, that June 7 primary had been do-or-die. Without winning Califor-nia, there was no prospect of even starting a conversation with super-delegates. Any chance of winning the nomination—however slight it was by that point—was over on the seventh, even though the voters of the District of Columbia would not have the final word for another week.

From the beginning of the race, Bernie had said he would support the

Democratic nominee. Hillary Clinton was not yet technically the nominee; the convention had not occurred. But now that really was just a technicality. She had more pledged delegates, and the loss in California meant that any appeal to superdelegates would be futile.

Bernie's race had always been about advancing progressive change in the country. An endorsement of Hillary Clinton was only a matter of time, but he had to figure out the most effective way to do it while protecting the interests of the over 13 million people who voted for him and the tens of millions more who supported him by the end of the campaign. He wanted to continue to advance their issues, at the same time ensuring that he was not a spoiler. Above all, he did not want the country to elect Donald Trump. Bernie took his pledge to support the Democratic nominee seriously, and he intended to keep it. It came down to a question of when and how, not if.

In the days leading up to the California vote, Robby Mook and I had talked cordially. Our talks were mostly not substantive, but the lines of communication were open. Bernie decided that he should meet with Hillary Clinton and discuss a list of items he supported before there would be any talk of scheduling an endorsement. I sent Robby Bernie's list.

The list was a combination of process and policy initiatives. Bernie wanted reform of the Democratic nominating process and of the party itself. He wanted the removal of Debbie Wasserman Schultz as head of the DNC. (Only later, when the hacked DNC emails were released, was a fuller picture of the DNC's role exposed.) He also asked for adoption of his college plan, the centerpiece of which was free tuition at public colleges and universities. He knew that Hillary Clinton would not agree to adopt his position on single-payer health care, but he did put forward a bold proposal to double access to primary care through community health centers, triple funding for the education of health care providers who agreed to serve in underserved communities, expand Medicare to people in their mid-fifties, and commit to including a public option in the Affordable Care Act (ACA) exchanges. This last provision would create a voluntary public health insurance plan that would compete in the exchanges with the private plans. The public option and the Medicare expansion had been components of the ACA, but they were stripped late in the legislative process by allies of the private insurers who did not want the American people to see how much more cost-effectively the government could provide health insurance—and they still don't.

Robby and I arranged for Bernie and Hillary to meet on the night of June 14. That was the day of the Democratic primary in the District of Columbia. Bernie had pledged to take his campaign through every primary and caucus on the calendar. On this point he was also determined to keep his word. And he did. DC's primary was the last one.

We agreed to meet at the Capital Hilton in DC. The Clinton campaign agreed to make the meeting room arrangements. The attendees would be Bernie, Jane, and me from our side and Hillary Clinton, John Podesta, and Robby Mook. We agreed to arrive separately, knowing that the media would be everywhere.

Our contingent arrived first. As we pulled up, the media was in full force outside the hotel. We were escorted past them into the hotel and up the elevators and were shown into the suite where the meeting was to take place. While waiting for Secretary Clinton and her advisers, we briefly discussed Bernie's asks. I think each of us understood that we were in a position we had hoped never to be in. We had fought so hard to win, and at times it had seemed possible. But at the end of the day, Hillary Clinton had just gotten more votes.

Bernie is not a "sitter." As we waited, we all milled about the suite. I was nearest to the door when Secretary Clinton and her team arrived. I extended my hand and said, "Nice to see you, Secretary Clinton."

"How are you, Jeff?" she replied. It felt almost as if I should hand her my sword. Not that I carried one, but it would have been appropriate for the moment if I had.

Greetings were exchanged all around. Hillary Clinton and John Podesta sat on a small couch, Robby Mook in a chair beside them. Bernie, Jane, and I sat in chairs across from them separated by a small coffee table.

Secretary Clinton was obviously not feeling well. She coughed throughout the meeting, consuming a lot of cough drops. The Trump campaign subsequently tried to create a narrative that she has a severe health problem. That night I had a lot of sympathy for her. The campaign had been grueling for everyone, and I also had personally pushed on while being quite sick at times. I viewed it as a sign of strength, not weakness, on her part.

Bernie congratulated Hillary Clinton on the race, and she returned the compliment. Of course, they had known each other for over twenty years. And while there were certainly policy disagreements between them—in some cases deep policy disagreements—Bernie had always respected her. On the campaign trail, he had often expressed the fact that he personally liked her. I can't say that was the most popular applause line with his supporters, but it did reflect his true feelings.

When we then turned to the list, my belief was that it would be relatively easy for them to agree to the process items Bernie had proposed and less easy for them to move on policy. Over the course of the campaign, candidates become boxed into the policy proposals they advocate for and are forced to defend in debates and in the media. The process issues were the first to be discussed.

One of the first subjects was Debbie Wasserman Schultz. Bernie and his supporters deeply resented the entirely biased role she had played in the campaign. It had started with the number and schedule of debates. Then she had tried to impose a political death sentence on the campaign in December 2015 over some low-level staffers getting access to ultimately inconsequential data because of the DNC's defective systems. She had unnecessarily injected herself into a dispute over the Nevada party convention and had overseen the joint fund-raising program that starved state parties and allowed the Clinton campaign to dodge campaign finance limits. In short, she had been throwing shade on our campaign from the beginning.

I knew that there was no love between the Clinton campaign and the chairwoman. Nor was there any in the White House. Or among large numbers of the DNC's top leaders. When Bernie was on his way to meet President Obama on June 9, Senator Harry Reid had made a point of calling Bernie during the car ride to remind him to ask the president to dump Wasserman Schultz.

Every time I had raised the issue of Wasserman Schultz with the Clinton campaign, they had blamed her continued tenure on the White House. Whenever I raised the issue with the president's people, they blamed the Clinton campaign. From my calls with them, I knew that the Clinton people were exasperated with Wasserman Schultz. But I could never tell whether it was because she had put her fingers on the scale in such an incompetent way. Regardless, it just always seemed the case that no one wanted to expend the political capital necessary to push her out, especially as her term would be ending soon anyway.

At our meeting at the Hilton, Hillary Clinton balked at forcing her out. My suspicion was that the Clinton campaign did not want to do anything that would impugn the legitimacy of her victory. Forcing out Debbie Wasserman Schultz would be an acknowledgment that the DNC chairwoman had stacked the deck in Clinton's favor. That was not our point, however. Debbie Wasserman Schultz, as chair of the Democratic Party during a vigorously contested primary, was supposed to be neutral. She clearly was not. This action item would resolve itself at the Democratic National Convention, when the chairwoman was pushed out after DNC emails were released proving how the organization had worked against our campaign.

Bernie also expressed concern about Debbie Wasserman Schultz's appointment of Connecticut governor Malloy and former congressman Barney Frank as chairs on the Democratic Platform Committee and the Democratic Rules Committee. We expected that Clinton partisans would be appointed to both those positions. But Malloy and Frank both had viciously attacked Bernie personally. Our campaign felt very strongly that these committees, which would meet before the Democratic National Convention, should be run in an evenhanded way.

In this case, Hillary Clinton refused to agree; these were her supporters, and she could not abandon them. I understood her loyalty, but this had seemed one of the easiest items going in. Not a good sign for finding common ground.

The discussion turned to policy. I feared we were going to hit more brick walls, and at first it seemed that it might go that way. Bernie raised the issue of free tuition at public colleges and universities. He talked about how transformative it would be in terms of opening college for many middle-income and working-class families. On the trail, this had been one of the most popular planks in his platform. People understood that what once had been an attainable path to a better life for their children—a college education—was increasingly a pipe dream that could never be realized. Even if it could be realized, it came with years of crushing debt payments.

Hillary Clinton reiterated her view that she did not want to send rich kids to college on the public dime. This had been her critique of Bernie's plan during the campaign. (Inconsistent, we thought, with the fact that American public high schools and grade schools are open to all.) At this point, I felt that we all might be spinning our wheels. Then John Podesta leaned in and asked if Bernie would be willing to consider some kind of cap on income. Bernie said it depended on what the cap was. Podesta threw out a hypothetical $100,000 or $150,000. Finally, a breakthrough. We agreed that this needed further discussion to see if an agreement could be reached.

Bernie turned to his health care agenda items. This time there was no hesitation. On point after point, Hillary Clinton agreed. She agreed with adding a public option to the Affordable Care Act and to opening up Medicare to those between the age of fifty-five and sixty-four. Both had been part of the ACA originally but had been stripped to accommodate conservative Democratic senators. The loss of these two provisions created many of the current problems with the ACA (but not all of them, to be sure). She agreed to tripling the National Health Service Corps, and doubling funding for community health centers.

She also agreed that we needed to review the nominating process and the focus of the DNC. Both items would find their way into a commission that would come out of the pre-convention rules committee.

As the meeting wound down, it was suggested that Robby Mook and I stay behind to work out next steps for getting agreement on the specifics of the policy proposals. There was not a lot of talk about the timing of an endorsement. The Clinton campaign clearly wanted it sooner rather than later, but they did not push for a date.

Once everyone else had left the room, Robby Mook and I talked for another two hours about the process that we would use to work through these policy items. We set up telephone meetings for the coming days. Jennifer Palmieri came in, and we were entertained with Robby Mook's impersonations of both Bernie and Bill Clinton. His Bill Clinton was much, much better.

That night we were soundly defeated in the District of Columbia primary. But there was a sense of relief that we had agreed on a path forward. Major policy differences were being worked out, and we had agreed to review an improved process for nominating and party reform. It was a good sign for the future. Hillary Clinton and Bernie Sanders would be able to find common ground on some issues and constructively work together as president and senator in a way that was true to the principles of each.

PART FOUR

THE CONVENTION

22

UNITY AROUND A PROGRESSIVE AGENDA

FOLLOWING THE MEETING WITH HILLARY CLINTON, we were faced with two immediate tasks. The first was to find a meeting of the minds on the details of the policy positions around education, health care, and reform of the nominating process and the DNC. The second was handling all the logistics of prepping for the convention. That meant negotiating things like speaking times and setting up our operation at the convention. It also meant ensuring that all our elected delegates had the resources and information they would need to get to and participate in what for many would be their first Democratic convention. It was certainly mine. All of this was made more difficult by the reduction of our staff, now drastically pared down to a couple of dozen people.

Policy discussions got off to a slow start. By our first call with the Clinton folks, they had retreated substantially from the suggestion Podesta had put out at the meeting. They wanted to cap the benefit at incomes of only $65,000—for Bernie, a nonstarter. He had already agreed that we would accept something less than a universal program, but an income level of $65,000 left out far too many middle-class families.

Their position was that moving the cap to $150,000 would cost too much money. They wanted only to support campaign proposals they could fund once elected. My suggestion was to tax the rich a little bit more than the modest increases the Clinton campaign had been advocating during the primaries. Charlie Baker later told me that after the first call, Clinton policy guru Jake Sullivan's office was packed with policy people debating back and forth.

We then began about a two-week series of calls with the Clinton campaign to try to push them to accept a number that would make the college plan meaningful to the broadest swath of Americans possible. Slowly but surely, the number the Clinton campaign would accept began to go up, though in tiny increments. I spoke with Bernie, who wanted to ensure we got as close to universal as possible. His position was that we would split the difference of John Podesta's suggestion between $100,000–$150,000 cap at $125,000, but that was as low as he would go.

In our second-to-last phone call on the topic, Robby Mook said that they just could not go any higher; the policy people were against it. I suggested again that they go back and tweak their tax plan—taxing the wealthy a bit more to make room for the $125,000 cap. It seemed so simple, and the dragged-out negotiations were delaying Bernie's endorsement of Secretary Clinton. I said, "You have to make a decision. It's called a political campaign, not a policy campaign, for a reason." If they wanted the votes of Bernie supporters, they needed to be willing to make a commitment to a strong college plan.

The timing of an endorsement became an internal topic of consideration. One key point that Bernie expressed publicly was that he was not the dictator of his supporters. Ultimately the Clinton campaign wanted his endorsement because they wanted the votes of the 43 percent of Democratic primary voters who had pulled the lever for Bernie. Those voters were as committed as Bernie was to the fundamental changes he advocated on the trail. Racing out and endorsing Hillary Clinton within days of the last primary contest, without any sign of good faith from the Clinton camp around the issues that had animated Bernie's campaign, would have done more harm than good. The Clinton folks got this point, but they didn't necessarily like that it was true.

In addition, Bernie wanted to cement in as many policy gains from the Clinton side as possible. In that sense he was being practical in terms of advancing the progressive issues he has championed for a lifetime. He had leverage—leverage created by the millions of people who supported him—and he intended to use it on their behalf.

We had many internal meetings about the timing of an endorsement. Tad was much more in the camp of endorsing quickly. At one meeting at Bernie's house—which has been grossly mischaracterized elsewhere—he made the case that endorsing before having secured commitments from the Clinton camp would engender goodwill from them that might result in greater policy gains down the road. Bernie, Jane, and I were not convinced. Given how hard it was to negotiate the income cap on the college plan, Tad's point of view didn't line up with the reality we were experiencing on the ground.

Perhaps an earlier endorsement would have tipped the balance on the free college cap sooner. But we would have lost all the leverage we had on other issues we were pursuing in connection with the upcoming platform and rules committee meetings—issues like the $15 minimum wage, ending superdelegates, trade, and criminal justice reform, to name just a few.

While discussions were taking place, some voices on the periphery of Clinton-world (I called them the "political peanut gallery") started grousing publicly about why it was taking so long for an endorsement to be announced. Within the campaigns themselves, everyone understood that an endorsement was coming but that there were things to be worked out first. No one in the Clinton inner circle criticized the timing publicly. Maybe they were really upset and just trying to play nice. Or maybe they understood that the process we were undertaking was necessary to make Bernie's endorsement meaningful. There's no way to know, but those closest to Clinton kept their powder dry. In truth, during this period, you could tell who really was a Clinton insider and who was not. All the bellyachers were not. Whenever someone on television attacked Bernie over the endorsement timing, I would look to John Robinson and say, "Well, there's another name we know won't be in the cabinet."

Our final conversation about the college plan happened the day after the "it's called a political campaign" call. Team Clinton agreed to support a $125,000 income cap. That figure would cover some 80 percent of all U.S. households. If the plan were enacted, the doors of higher education would be thrown open for millions.

Per our agreement, HFA released their updated college plan on July 6. It married our agreed-upon free tuition proposal with the college plan that the Clinton camp had rolled out during the primaries. The addition of our provision, free tuition at public colleges and universities for families making up to $125,000, to Clinton's previous plan made the new plan in many ways the best of both. Bernie was quoted as saying as much in a CNN story that ran that day: "This proposal combines some of the strongest ideas which she brought forth during the campaign with some of the principals [*sic*] that I brought forth." And how did they pay for raising the cap? The Clinton policy people did the right thing. An unnamed Clinton aide in that same CNN story said that the additional cost of adding the Sanders provisions would be paid for by "closing additional high-income tax loopholes—focusing on loopholes available especially to Wall Street money managers, like hedge funds and private equity firms."

The outcome was a very positive sign that once Hillary Clinton became president there would be opportunities to make progress. But that required that Hillary Clinton be elected—a goal that Bernie Sanders threw himself into in the fall.

One pre-convention task was finalizing our slates of pledged delegates. Democratic pledged convention delegates—earned in actual elections—come in three varieties. The first group are elected at the congressional district–level conventions. In those elections our campaign played no role. People ran for delegate, and they were either elected by their Bernie-supporting peers or they were not.

The second group are at-large delegates—chosen differently from state to state but for all practical purposes picked by the campaigns. One of the major purposes of at-large delegates is to allow the campaigns to achieve diversity in their state delegations, as mandated by the Democratic rules. For instance, if there is an imbalance in the number of men or women chosen at the congressional district level, that can be remedied with at-large delegates of the underrepresented gender.

The same is true of racial diversity and in other categories for which there are representational targets. There was some confusion about this in several states among people who wanted to be considered for at-large delegate spots who felt they were unfairly excluded. In most cases, it was because our campaign took very seriously the need to meet the diversity guidelines in the Democratic rules. There were a few instances of people who applied for our at-large spots who were actually public Clinton supporters. I guess getting to go to the convention was enough incentive for them to suddenly like Bernie. We culled them.

The third group of pledged delegates are party leader and elected officials (PLEOs). This category is often confused with unpledged superdelegates. PLEOs are pledged delegates, and the number of PLEO slots won in each state is based on the elections in those states. But the slots do have to be filled by the campaigns with party leaders (for instance, county party chairs) or elected officials who are not superdelegates. In the rules, preference is given to certain categories of elected officials, but of course they have to support the candidate to whom they are pledged. Because most electeds were lined up behind Hillary Clinton, our PLEOs often held lower offices—they tended to be state representatives or local government officials.

Many of our pledged delegates were having difficulty coming up with the money to get to the convention and to pay the wildly expensive hotel rates that were being charged in Philadelphia. That is just a reality when working-class people, students, and others without a lot of money become involved in the political process. Many of them set up GoFundMe pages. We also raised money ourselves. We were determined that none of our people would be excluded from the convention because of the considerable cost. It was an enormous lift organizationally with our skeleton crew.

We also began organizing our convention "whip" operation to ensure that in the event of floor fights we would be able to effectively communicate with our delegates so that they could vote as a block. We were not necessarily anticipating floor fights at this point, but the platform and rules committees had not met, so we prepared just in case.

Even though we had come to agreement with the Clinton campaign on the college plans and the health care improvements, there were many other issues that Bernie was still dedicated to pushing in the platform and rules committees. Robby Mook and I tried to work out a solution to the superdelegate issue. We wanted no superdelegates. The Clinton campaign wanted vague nonbinding language, and so we were not able to resolve it prior to the rules committee meeting. All of us understood that there were issues that still had to be worked out. There was not really a lot of risk on the Clinton campaign's part—they knew they ultimately controlled the votes on both committees. That was a concern from our end.

The membership of the platform and rules committees was determined proportionately by the state-by-state results in the primary and caucuses. Because Hillary Clinton won more delegates, she would pick more platform and rules (and credentials) members than Bernie would. In addition, the chair of the party handpicked twenty-five members of each of the three committees.

Earlier in the year, chairwoman Wasserman Schultz had asked us to submit some names for her to consider in making her seventy-five committee picks. We submitted forty names. Exactly three were given slots. Combined with the chair's picks, the Clinton campaign could heavily outvote us. This was just another way in which the deck was stacked against not only Bernie but the progressive agenda he was advancing. This was on top of our concerns about the choice of chairs for the rules and platform committees, which Bernie had expressed personally to Hillary Clinton at their meeting.

The platform committee was to meet on July 8 and 9 in Orlando. Before it did, the fifteen-member Democratic Party Platform Drafting Committee was constituted in late May to create, as its name suggests, a draft of the platform to be considered and amended in Orlando. Technically, the DNC chair had the authority to appoint all fifteen members. But given that Debbie Wasserman Schultz had chosen only three of the forty names our campaign had submitted to fill her seventy-five slots on the three committees, we didn't have a lot of confidence (okay, we had no confidence) that her appointments would reflect the outcome of the Democratic primaries and caucuses.

Bernie called Wasserman Schultz in early May about the drafting committee. She told him that she would consider allowing each campaign to submit ten names; she would choose four from each list and then appoint the remaining seven herself. That sounded like we were being rolled. In truth, even by this point I had more confidence in the Clinton staff than I did in the chairwoman's office. The primaries were ending, and however they turned out, the Clinton people (who expected to win) did have an interest by this time in not completely blowing up the party. Debbie Wasserman Schultz had shown repeatedly that the health of the party was clearly secondary to her personal agenda and vendettas.

Bernie sent a letter to Wasserman Schultz on May 6 suggesting that the campaigns each pick seven representatives and jointly agree on the fifteenth member, who would serve as chair. This arrangement completely cut out Wasserman Schultz herself. Finally, a compromise was reached whereby the campaigns could submit names for a designated number of slots. Bernie was allowed to submit names for five of the slots on the drafting committee. The Clinton campaign got six slots and the DNC four. Even so, the chair had the final sign-off on which, if any, of the submitted names would be appointed.

When we sent over our list, the DNC immediately had problems. The first was that we had included the executive director of National Nurses United, RoseAnn DeMoro. It's no secret in Washington that the DNC establishment types do not like the straight-talking head of the nurses union. The DNC then came up with the rule that they did not want representatives of organized labor on the drafting committee. Wait a second, we said. Hillary Clinton's choice for the committee, Paul Booth, was from the American Federation of State, County and Municipal Employees (AFSCME). We had no objection to Paul Booth, but we wanted to be able to appoint a labor person as well. Then the rule was clarified to one where it was okay to have members from organized labor, just not the heads of unions.

The DNC had one other objection to our list of picks. They said that the seating of our list would put too many black people on the committee. I was flabbergasted when I heard it. We pushed back because it was so outrageous. But they would not budge.

The drafting committee met through June. During the deliberations, as reported by *Salon*'s Ben Norton, the committee defeated amendments by the Sanders delegates—led by Rep. Keith Ellison—to include a fully indexed $15 minimum wage, a requirement that federal contractors pay at least $15 an hour, opposing cuts to workers' pensions, and expressly stating opposition to the Trans-Pacific Partnership. In each case but one, all the Clinton and DNC appointees voted, as my old friend John Franco would describe it, with Leninist party discipline in opposition to the Sanders delegates' amendments. (The exception was that Rep. Barbara Lee voted with the Bernie delegates in favor of the $15 minimum wage; the chair, Rep. Elijah Cummings, didn't vote, as he only voted in case of a tie.)

The politics around the amendment relating to the TPP were complicated. Hillary Clinton had announced her opposition to the TPP during the campaign after calling it the gold standard while secretary of state. Her move was viewed by many as a means of boxing out Bernie and Vice President Biden and shoring up her standing with organized labor. There was a lot of doubt about how strongly she would oppose what was expected to be consideration of the TPP during the lame-duck session of Congress, that is the meeting of Congress after the election but before newly elected congresspeople are sworn into January, following the presidential election. (It never was considered because Trump, who campaigned actively against the TPP, ended up winning.)

The Obama administration was pushing hard for the TPP to be passed in the lame-duck session. As a result, the administration opposed including explicit language critical of the TPP in the Democratic platform. The Clinton campaign used President Obama's position—which was the opposite of her public position during the campaign—as the reason they would not support any TPP-specific language in the platform. The fight would play itself out again at the full platform committee in Orlando and on the Democratic convention floor.

The draft adopted by the fifteen-member platform drafting committee was now on its way to the full platform committee meeting in Orlando on July 8. In my conversations with Robby Mook in the lead-up to that meeting, the Clinton campaign agreed to support the stronger

$15 minimum wage language in Orlando. However, they remained adamant that the TPP not be included. (They also remained opposed to single-payer health care, a ban on fracking, a carbon tax, and other policies.)

We were determined to create as progressive a platform as possible. By the time of Orlando, the two campaigns had already agreed that Bernie would endorse Hillary Clinton on July 12 in New Hampshire. But that didn't mean that our campaign would stop pushing for a platform that represented the values of the Democratic rank and file. Our polling consistently showed that even among Hillary Clinton's supporters there was broad support for a far more progressive agenda than that put forward by the Clinton campaign. The platform was also, from Bernie's standpoint, an important tool for communicating to voters a set of policies that would set the Democratic Party—and Hillary Clinton—up for success in the fall.

Our campaign didn't have any interest in gratuitously highlighting the administration's difference with the overwhelming majority of Democratic voters—and the top two candidates for the nomination—on the issue of TPP. Despite Hillary Clinton's talking points, Bernie has always recognized—he spoke of it often on the trail—the disastrous situation that President Obama found himself in when he was first elected and a barrage of false Republican attacks was lodged against him day in and day out.

Of course, Bernie had tried to push the Obama administration in a more progressive direction. That was his job as a U.S. senator. But he had stood with the president on all his signature achievements—the Affordable Care Act, the auto rescue package, the stimulus package, the effort to commute the sentences of oversentenced people, the Iran nuclear deal, and more.

So I called David Simas, Obama's political director. We had talked many times, especially near the end of the primary season. I am sorry now that I never got to take him up on his repeated offer to swing by the White House.

"Is it the administration's intention to push hard for the passage of the TPP in the lame-duck session?" I asked him.

"Yes, it is," he replied.

Okay, question answered. Defeating what we viewed as yet another job-destroying trade agreement had to come first.

Our team arrived in Orlando on the seventh. We met with a group of Clinton and DNC folks. The meeting was late and seemed unnecessarily tense from the get-go. The purpose was to talk about the ground rules for the platform committee meeting. To be perfectly honest, I can't even remember what started us down an increasingly negative exchange. We were not only not making progress, but things were going in the wrong direction. At one point I zipped up my briefcase, stood up, and just stood there. The other members of the team looked at me and, without saying a word, packed their stuff. We all walked out. Tomorrow would be better, we hoped.

The next day started fine. We held a meeting with all our platform committee delegates. There were 187 total delegates. Clinton had 90, Bernie had 72, and Debbie Wasserman Schultz picked 25. Bernie had less than 39 percent of the delegates to the platform committee, even though he had received over 43 percent of the Democratic primary vote and convention delegates. Given that reality, we had to stick together. Even if we did, we would need 22 Clinton or DNC delegates to vote with us to overcome a Clinton objection. That was a tall order; the Clinton and DNC platform drafting committee members had been highly disciplined. To make progress on almost anything required that we negotiate with the Clinton campaign. They effectively controlled over 60 percent of the votes in the room.

Many of our delegates had submitted proposed amendments, in some cases a large number. Our position was that we would support the amendments of our delegates unless they were counter to a position Bernie had taken. We worked to figure out which ones were duplicates. There was no need to have multiple votes on the same amendment. We wanted to make progress, not waste time. Even so, there were going to be a lot of amendments offered.

We also met with the Clinton staff to see which of our delegates' amendments might be acceptable to them in their current form or with minor tweaks. There were many that we resolved that way. It was in everyone's interest to not take up a lot of time with things that were unobjectionable to both sides.

During our meetings with our delegates, we explained the system we would use for signaling what the campaign's recommended vote was on a particular amendment. Staff at each side of the room would hold up a green piece of paper for a yes vote and a red piece for a no vote. If the campaign had no position, then we would not hold up either. The Clinton campaign used a similar system, with people giving a thumbs-up or thumbs-down to their people, and in addition they used electronic communications.

The first major bump in the road happened when a completely baseless rumor spread through the Clinton camp that Bernie was on a flight to Orlando to personally lobby platform committee delegates on the TPP. By that time, Marc Elias, the Clinton campaign's lawyer, had arrived and was helping to coordinate their team.

Marc and his firm represented the Clinton campaign, the DNC, the Democratic Senatorial Campaign Committee, the Democratic Congressional Campaign Committee, Hillary Clinton's super PAC Priorities USA, and a host of other Democratic Party organs, related super PACs, and elected officials. He also is responsible for much of the up-to-the-line legal structures that were used by the Clinton campaign, including David Brock's super PAC that controversially coordinated with the Clinton campaign.

I have known Marc Elias for years. He represented Bernie's 2006 Senate campaign. And Marc was a student in Bernie's class when Bernie spent a semester teaching at Hamilton College between his 1988 and 1990 congressional runs. Marc owns a summer house in Vermont. (I promised if he behaved I wouldn't put out his address and affiliation to his Vermont neighbors.) So there was no personal animosity between us. But let's just say that he was and is a zealous advocate for his client, and he could be counted on to play hardball. All that being said, the fact that he and I knew each other helped smooth the process in Orlando—especially because he had a direct line to Robby Mook, who was not there in person.

It was Marc Elias who brought to me the somewhat panicked news that the Clinton campaign had heard that Bernie was on a plane headed to Orlando. It was a ridiculous rumor. I told him so. Assured, he walked away.

He came back to me not long after to tell me he was still hearing rumors that Bernie was coming to Orlando.

"If he was coming to Orlando, first of all I'd know about it, and second of all I'd just tell you he was coming to Orlando," I said. "He's not coming to Orlando."

"Can you check?" Elias asked a bit sheepishly. I got the sense that he was not asking for himself but wanted to calm the nerves of some anxious worrier.

"Can I check? Sure."

So I pulled out my cell phone with Elias standing there and pushed the speed dial for Bernie.

"Hello," Bernie said.

"Hey, Bernie, it's Jeff. Where are you right now?"

"I'm in my office, why?" he asked.

"You aren't coming to Orlando, are you?" I asked him.

"Orlando? Why would I come to Orlando?"

I then explained to him the rumor that was circulating.

"That's crazy. Well, you can tell anyone who wants to know that I'm not coming Orlando."

I hung up the phone. Elias was finally satisfied, and the rumor that Bernie was winging his way to central Florida was finally laid to rest.

The Clinton folks weren't the only ones suffering from a lack of trust. Pretty soon it was my turn. It happened when we and the Clinton campaign were reviewing the proposed amendments to see which might be acceptable. When we got to the amendment that called for a $15 federal minimum wage, the Clinton policy person indicated that they had a problem with it. That came as a complete surprise to me, because Robby Mook and I had specifically discussed it, and he had assured me that they were fine with it. No doubt we were being double-crossed.

I called Robby to explain the situation. He acknowledged that we had come to an agreement on the issue. "Well, you are going to have to talk to your people here, because that's not their understanding," I told him.

Conversations between Brooklyn and the Clinton team in Orlando ensued. Meanwhile, the proceedings of the platform committee were being held up while this was going on. The policy person was apparently unhappy that the agreement on the $15 minimum wage had not been communicated, with the result being that this person had made representations to others that the Clinton campaign position was opposed. This wasn't really my problem—until the policy person just disappeared, and the proceedings were in recess for hours.

I called Robby back somewhat annoyed. "What the hell, Robby?" I asked. "Where is your person? Did they go on strike because they didn't get the memo on the minimum wage?"

He was also clearly exasperated by whatever was going on. "Something like that," he replied. "I'm working on it." To me, the fact that the information had not been conveyed to the staffer in Orlando was completely understandable. Brooklyn was trying to win an election. What was incomprehensible is how one person thought it acceptable to keep almost 200 people waiting.

In the end, the agreement held. State senator Nina Turner offered the $15 minimum wage amendment and with a minor tweak it was approved, as was the language protecting workers' pensions that had been defeated at the platform drafting committee stage.

Not surprisingly, the amendment in support of a single-payer, Medicare for All program failed. One of the Clinton delegates was walking by as the vote was being tallied. She stopped for just a second. "That's what Obama should have done in the first place," she said.

"So you voted for the amendment?" I asked.

"No, I voted against it." And she turned and walked back to her seat. Leninist party discipline.

We did come together on a number of issues, including criminal justice reform. On environmental issues, we could not convince the Clinton people to endorse a carbon tax. But they did consent to language stating that "greenhouse gases should be priced to reflect their negative externalities, and to accelerate the transition to a clean energy economy and help meet our climate goals." Environmental activist and film director Josh Fox and 350.org head Bill McKibben, both of whom were in Orlando, confirmed that the language represented a major step forward.

On the issue of the TPP, the other side would not budge. We gave them two opportunities to do so. AFSCME head Lee Saunders offered an amendment to the platform laying out the criteria any trade agreement had to meet to be acceptable. Ben Jealous offered an amendment to that language stating that the TPP did not meet that standard. Jealous's amendment received the votes of the Sanders delegates, but the Clinton and DNC delegates, including those representing organized labor, voted against it. (By the way, for all those in the gallery who enjoyed the pizza the campaign provided during the long proceedings, you can thank Ben Jealous. He came up and asked if the campaign would buy it, and I immediately signed off on it.)

The second opportunity came when former Texas agriculture commissioner Jim Hightower offered an amendment that called for the TPP to not be passed during the lame-duck session of Congress. The vote was essentially the same. Our team was extremely disappointed by the results. Not only because the TPP was bad policy, but also because the Clinton campaign and the DNC were having major labor leaders vote against the unified position of organized labor, which was adamantly anti-TPP. The best hope of passing the TPP was in the lame-duck session of Congress coming up in the fall. All the unions were against it. Yet in Orlando their leaders were voting against amendments to stop it.

In our view, the other side's position was severely damaging Hillary Clinton's chance in the fall. If the campaign was just carrying water for the president, he was asking a very, very high price of her. Eric Bradner, writing for CNN, captured the dilemma:

> By keeping specific opposition to the Trans-Pacific Partnership out of the platform, Democrats avoided embarrassing President Barack Obama, whose administration has spent most of his two terms negotiating the massive 12-nation trade deal.

However, the decision also opens up Clinton and other Democrats to questions about whether their opposition to the Pacific Rim pact is sincere.

It's a politically precarious position as presumptive Republican nominee Donald Trump turns decades of Republican pro-trade orthodoxy on its head, regularly railing against the Trans-Pacific Partnership and other free trade deals on the campaign trail.

After the November election, one Clinton aide said to me, "Well, I guess we'll never know if Hillary Clinton was really against that TPP or not." That same confusion was shared by working Americans across the country and reinforced by the mixed signals the Clinton campaign was sending by, for example, torpedoing anti-TPP amendments in Orlando.

David Weigel quoted one of our delegates to the platform committee whose view summed up what many of us believed at the time: "'We're trying to save Secretary Clinton from herself,' said Brent Welder, a labor lawyer and Sanders delegate from Missouri." But in early July in Orlando, the Clinton campaign either didn't want to be saved or didn't feel they needed to be. The election results in the industrial heartland in November proved them wrong.

There was one surprising win at the platform meeting in Atlanta. An amendment to create a pathway for legalization of marijuana by the states won by one vote. During the debate, the Clinton campaign had signaled (perhaps mis-signaled) to its platform committee delegates that it had no position on the amendment, which allowed them to vote however they saw fit. There was an attempt to have a revote, but it would have completely blown up the meeting, so the Clinton folks quickly put a stop to it.

One can only imagine how many other amendments might have been passed if the delegates had been left to vote their conscience. That's not a criticism. The Clinton campaign was managing its delegation to get its desired result, as were we on our side. The only point here is that much of the Democratic Party is far more progressive than it has been allowed to show.

At the end of the day, Bernie's efforts to push the Democratic platform in a more progressive direction were an overwhelming success. NBC's

Alex Seitz-Wald noted that "Sanders' decision to stay in the race has baffled many and alarmed others, who worry he might help Trump by fracturing the Democratic Party. But this weekend's meeting of the Democratic Platform Committee showed that in defying norms, Sanders notched real victories and advanced his so-called 'political revolution.' "

Obviously, our side did not get everything it wanted. On the other hand, the Clinton campaign made concessions and worked with us to create a document that we all could embrace. They understandably felt that they were making concessions that no putative nominee had had to make in terms of the platform since 1988. It wasn't always a pretty process or even a friendly one. But it was an example of how talking, debating, and at times fighting could in fact bring the party together. The limits of what is possible can only be discovered by pushing up against the edge of what is impossible.

23

THE BIG ENDORSEMENT

ON JULY 12 BERNIE MADE his much-anticipated endorsement of
Hillary Clinton's candidacy. We had been working on the details of the
event for some time, as reported by ABC's MaryAlice Parks on July 6.
Various states had been considered before the campaigns mutually decided upon New Hampshire. While no longer a truly purple state, it
can be purplish.

Bernie's campaign had really taken off after his big victory in New
Hampshire, so holding the event there could have local benefits for the
Clinton campaign, in addition to the expected national impact. From our
perspective, it allowed us to say thank you to the Granite State.

I did not attend but was in close contact with Robby Mook. Bernie
gave a thirty-minute endorsement speech in a Portsmouth high school
gymnasium: "Secretary Clinton has won the Democratic nominating
process, and I congratulate her for that. She will be the Democratic nominee for president and I intend to do everything I can to make certain she
will be the next president of the United States."

He made the case for why people who supported his campaign should
join him in helping to elect Hillary Clinton: "I have come here to make
it as clear as possible as to why I am endorsing Hillary Clinton and why
she must become our next president."

He reminded his supporters what they had been fighting for during the nominating process, highlighting the areas where the campaigns had come together and going down a list of his central planks: higher minimum wage, affordable college, access to health care, the environment, criminal justice reform, immigration reform. And he made the case that electing Hillary Clinton would bring forward movement on these issues and that electing Donald Trump would move us backward.

He also assured everyone that he was not just endorsing Hillary Clinton at that event but that he would be campaigning for her across the country: "Our job now is to see that platform implemented by a Democratic Senate, a Democratic House and a Hillary Clinton president—and I am going to be in every corner of this country to make sure that happens." It was a promise that he followed up on through the fall.

In closing, he said, "Hillary Clinton will make an outstanding president and I am proud to stand with her here today."

I talked with Robby Mook after the speech. "Well, what did you think?" I asked.

He was very pleased. "It was great. It was perfect," he said.

Some in the media missed the entire point of the speech. Perhaps taking swipes at Bernie had just become a reflex. Chris Cillizza, in perhaps the most insight-free column on the endorsement, wrote: "It's hard to imagine that she or her campaign team were thrilled with Sanders." Actually, it wasn't hard to imagine at all, because they told us that they were. Hillary Clinton herself, caught on a hot mic as they embraced on stage, said to Bernie, according to the *New York Times*, "You were great, so great," and "Thank you so much."

Cillizza criticized Bernie for focusing on the issues that were central to his campaign and for talking about how the campaigns had found common ground on many after the primaries were over. But that's exactly what Hillary Clinton did in her remarks. If it wasn't obvious, and reading the Cillizza column it apparently wasn't to some, both Bernie and Hillary Clinton were speaking to the millions who had supported Bernie in the primaries. The millions who supported Hillary Clinton in the primaries didn't need convincing. They were already on board.

There was one more item of business before we arrived in Philadelphia for the Democratic National Convention, and that was the meeting of the party's rules committee. In addition to the policy changes Bernie worked to advance, his pre-convention agenda also included many changes to the Democratic Party's rules to make both the nominating process and the party itself more democratic, more transparent, and more open.

Chief among the concerns was the issue of superdelegates. That some 700 elected officials and party insiders had 50 percent more say over who would be the Democratic nominee than the over 39 million people in California was, well, undemocratic. The existence of superdelegates is justified by the antidemocratic impulse that the establishment needs a check on rank-and-file Democrats to prevent the nomination of an unacceptable candidate. The Republicans don't have superdelegates. The fallacy that party insiders are better able to pick a winning nominee than tens of millions of primary voters is borne out by the last general election. Donald Trump, who had little establishment Republican support, prevailed in November against Hillary Clinton, whom the Democratic establishment—in many cases before a single vote was even cast in the primaries and caucuses—was absolutely convinced was the strongest possible choice.

Back in November 2015 NPR had reported that Clinton had a 45-to-1 advantage over Bernie in superdelegates (359 to 8). By some counts, by mid-February 2016 Clinton had 415 superdelegates to Bernie's 14, meaning she had almost 17.5 percent of the delegates she needed. The reason for Clinton's broad support among superdelegates was obvious. Many of the superdelegates, although not all by any stretch, were more comfortable with Hillary Clinton's more moderate, establishment politics. She was also viewed as the likely winner of the nomination and by the overwhelming majority as the most electable against the Republicans—consistent public polling to the contrary notwithstanding. Why back a long-shot campaign and risk the wrath of the Clintons?

The way each candidate's delegate count was reported was that the number of superdelegates was generally combined with the number of pledged delegates. That meant Bernie was always shown as being way behind even as he was racking up wins with voters. In many ways this was most damaging early on, when relatively few pledged delegates had been chosen, because it created a sense of futility for those seeking an alternative to Clinton.

In that sense the existence of the superdelegates taints the entire Democratic nominating process. It has been said that superdelegates have never overturned the will of the voters. The candidate with the plurality of pledged delegates has always won the nomination. But that ignores the effect that superdelegates have on creating the momentum for a candidate to win the greatest number of pledged delegates. During the campaign, Bernie found an unlikely ally in critiquing the way superdelegates were being reported as part of a candidate's total: Debbie Wasserman Schultz.

People attain superdelegate status in different ways. Some are elected Democratic officials: U.S. House members, senators, governors, the president and vice president. Most are party officials: state party chairs and vice chairs and member of the Democratic National Committee (both those elected at the state level and those appointed by the chair).

Opposition to superdelegates is not limited to Bernie Sanders. Elizabeth Warren has publicly spoken against superdelegates, as has former congressman Barney Frank, who backed Clinton.

In our discussions with the Clinton campaign about electoral reforms, we could not come to a consensus on eliminating superdelegates altogether. Nor was it possible to come up with a mutually agreed-upon list of other electoral reforms and specific party reforms in the short period of time we had after the primaries. While we might have been able to come up with a short list of needed reforms, it would necessarily have been incomplete. As talks progressed, it was clear that what we would develop was a meaningful process to carry out electoral and party reform. Our main concern was that the process not be just window-dressing, and that the justified concerns about the electoral process and the operation of the party get addressed.

The strongest opposition to eliminating superdelegates came from the Congressional Black Caucus. As reported by *Politico* in June 2016, the caucus sent a letter to party leaders opposing the elimination of superdelegates and the creation of universal open primaries. The expressed concern about superdelegates was that the caucus members did not want to be put in a position of running against their constituents to gain delegate slots at the Democratic convention. Their expressed concern about open primaries was that they diluted minority voting influence. As we saw earlier, closed primaries may be disproportionately locking out young voters of color.

An issue the Black Caucus did not address is that the automatic inclusion of every member of Congress as a superdelegate undermines minority influence in the presidential nominating process at the Democratic National Convention. That's because the makeup of the combined Democratic caucuses of the U.S. House and Senate is less diverse than the pool of Democratic National Convention delegates as a whole. In fact, for the 2016 convention, the congressional superdelegation had 20 percent less African American representation than the delegates overall; Latinos, almost 36 percent less; Asian Americans, almost 25 percent less; LGBTQ, almost 78 percent less. For Native Americans the number is incalculable because the number in the congressional superdelegation is zero. That means automatic inclusion of every Democratic member of Congress creates a pool of votes for the nominee of the party at the convention that is marginally whiter, straighter, and more male than it would otherwise be.

We went back and forth with the Clinton campaign for weeks trying to come up with an acceptable way forward on rules changes. The issue of electoral reform was a critical one for our supporters. Many believed (rightly, in my view) that, despite what voters wanted, the nominating process—while not designed specifically to disadvantage Bernie Sanders—created tremendous additional hurdles for any candidate not fully embraced by the Democratic establishment.

The actual meeting of the rules committee was right before the convention. The ratios of representation on the rules committee was the same as on the platform committee. We were again in an environment where our delegates could be heavily outvoted by the combined numbers of the Clinton- and DNC-appointed delegates.

We continued negotiating as the rules committee proceedings continued. The main sticking points were issue of superdelegates and developing a serious process for considering and resolving the other issues after the election. The Clinton staffers preferred a looser, less binding process. We wanted more safeguards.

If we could not come to a resolution on the reform agenda with the Clinton campaign, we would have to quickly organize for a floor fight at the convention. If we could not come to terms, Bernie fully intended to take the issue of superdelegates in future nominating contests to the convention floor. It likely would have been messy, so it was something the Clinton campaign desperately wanted to avoid.

As the deliberations in the committee wound on, we finally struck what both sides believed was a workable compromise. We would establish a Democratic Unity Reform Commission with an open-ended mandate to take up these issues after the election. From our perspective, the commission contained two critically important elements. One, a series of procedural safeguards. These included representation ratios of ten Clinton appointees, eight Sanders appointees, and only three DNC appointees. In addition, the Democratic Party's Rules and Bylaws Committee is required to take up the commission's recommendations, and if it does not adopt the commission's recommendations, then those recommendations are taken directly to the full DNC membership. This was important to ensure that recommendations for reform did not get buried in the DNC bureaucracy.

Two, superdelegate reform. This tied the hands of the commission. The compromise didn't eliminate superdelegates or even reduce their overall number. But it required that the votes of all the superdelegates whose status was not based on being an elected official had to be cast at the convention in proportion to the will of the voters.

That addressed the primary concern raised by the Congressional Black Caucus that no current superdelegate would have to run against a constituent to be a delegate to a future convention. But it decreased the number of superdelegates who would be unpledged by over 60 percent. Even if a candidate could lock up every unpledged superdelegate—which even Hillary Clinton did not do—that total would equal only around 12 percent of the total delegates needed to secure the nomination—not 30 percent. The reduction puts more power in the hands of the Democratic rank and file.

Even though the campaigns had agreed to the compromise, we were determined not to proceed with it unless our delegates to the rules committee were on board. We hastily called a meeting with our delegates in a small conference room. It was a packed, standing-room-only gathering. We went over the details of the compromise. There were some questions from the assembled group, but they quickly saw the major breakthrough that had been achieved, particularly on the issue of superdelegates. We left our Bernie-delegate caucus meeting. The rules committee reconvened and the compromise was approved. And it was on to the convention.

24

THE REALLY BIG SHOW

WHEN BERNIE ENDORSED HILLARY CLINTON, he explicitly said that she would be the Democratic nominee for president of the United States. But he did not formally suspend his campaign or drop out. That was in part to maintain leverage in the successful negotiations over the platform and the rules. He was also committed to making sure his delegates had the opportunity to cast their votes for our campaign at the convention. This was important to our supporters. They wanted the roll call vote to happen. I suspect large numbers of them would have decided not to show up if that was not going to happen.

The Democratic National Convention was an opportunity to bring both sides together for the fight against the Trump candidacy. From our earliest discussions about the convention, the Clinton campaign was principally concerned about the political optics—that it not turn into a sectarian spectacle that the media and the Republicans would use to highlight Democratic divisions. Bernie shared their concern. He had run a long campaign, and there were still serious policy differences between him and Hillary Clinton. But they paled in comparison to his differences with Trump. For working people and poor people, especially, a Trump presidency would be a disaster (which it has been), and Bernie was committed to preventing Trump's election in every way possible. That included peace at the convention, as long as our delegates were respected.

In the run-up to the convention, the campaigns had negotiated most of the issues, including when Bernie would speak. Both sides understood that there would be a roll call, but we were working on the exact mechanics until well into the event itself.

One particular issue of concern was the role of Debbie Wasserman Schultz. Under the rules, she was to, at a minimum, gavel in and gavel out the convention. I told Robby Mook early in the process, "If Debbie Wasserman Schultz walks out on that stage in Philadelphia, half of the convention is going to be loudly booing, and there's not a thing I or anyone else can do about it. It's not like we are going to incite something. We can ask everyone to behave, but it is not going to make a bit of difference. It's going to be bad."

The Clinton folks said that they understood, but they didn't seem to be doing anything to take care of the problem. At the end of the day, it was their problem; they controlled the convention. They had been warned. If the first visual they wanted was discord, so be it. However, none of us could have anticipated the WikiLeaks grenade that was lobbed into the process on July 22, just three days before the convention opened. The release of the hacked DNC emails set our supporters ablaze. For anyone who had doubted that the DNC and Debbie Wasserman Schultz were actively trying to torpedo Bernie's campaign, the emails said it all.

The email dump showed repeated antagonism toward the campaign. I was personally honored and amused to be the subject of Debbie Wasserman Schultz's scorn. "Damn liar," "Particularly scummy," and "Ass." I must have been doing something right. To the "Ass" comment, I responded to *Politico*, "Isn't the ass the mascot of the dem party?"

What was troubling was the extent to which the national party was plotting against our campaign. The most incendiary email chain was from DNC CFO Brad Marshall to DNC CEO Amy Dacey and press team members Luis Miranda and Mark Paustenbach suggesting an attack on Bernie's religion ahead of the Kentucky and West Virginia primaries. "It might make no difference, but for KY and WVA can we get someone to ask his belief. Does he believe in a God. He had skated on saying he has a Jewish heritage. I think I read he is an atheist. This could make several points difference with my peeps. My Southern Baptist peeps would draw a big difference between a Jew and an atheist."

Marshall followed up a few minutes later: "It's these Jesus thing."

DNC CEO Amy Dacey replied, "AMEN."

While this was the most patently offensive exchange in the first nearly 20,000 emails, there were many others that demonstrated the close co-ordination of the Clinton campaign and the DNC. Later releases would reveal even more. DNC staffers had discussed planting stories that our campaign was in disarray around the time of the VANghazi data issue in December. "Wondering if there's a good Bernie narrative for a story, which is that Bernie never ever had his act together, that his campaign was a mess," wrote DNC deputy communications director Mark Pausten-bach. Another had the DNC consulting with Clinton campaign lawyer Marc Elias about responding to our campaign's charges about the abuse of the joint fund-raising agreements that looted funds raised for state par-ties. Although, as we have seen, Elias's firm also represented the DNC, we had been assured that there was a wall between lawyers representing the different parties. Elias's email does not contain legal advice but rather political messaging pointers:

> My suggestion is that the DNC put out a statement saying that the accusations the Sanders campaign [is making] are not true. The fact that CNN notes that you aren't getting between the two cam-paigns is the problem. Here, Sanders is attacking the DNC and its current practice, its past practice with the POTUS and with Sec Kerry. Just as the RNC pushes back directly on Trump over "rigged system," the DNC should push back DIRECTLY at Sanders and say that what he is saying is false and harmful [to] the Democratic party.

What we know now is that the points we had made were absolutely true, and that what was really hurting state Democratic parties was their impoverishment by the Clinton campaign. Other emails show Clinton and DNC press staffers frantically coordinating responses to the issue.

And there was so much more. The contents of the emails were in every news outlet. Although it didn't directly affect us, the emails were full of insults at major donors and even a swipe at President Obama. In many circles, the fallout from donors was creating more waves than the news that the DNC had worked against Bernie Sanders. Bernie-world was rightly incensed. Inside our campaign, we were not surprised by the revelations. They were just confirmation of what we already knew and had been complaining about—in some cases to a skeptical media. Be that as it may, the convention became a lot more complicated.

The Clinton campaign finally realized that it was time for Debbie Wasserman Schultz to go, but they didn't want it to be messy. They met with her privately to get her to resign for the good of the party. "I'm exhausted. It took five hours to get her to resign. She was just digging in her heels for most of it," Robby Mook told me shortly after the meeting. She finally agreed to resign after insisting on speaking personally to President Obama. The Clinton campaign gave her a title for some nonexistent role in the campaign. Even then, Wasserman Schultz insisted that she wasn't going to resign until after the convention. And she still intended to gavel it in and out!

"As Party Chair, this week I will open and close the Convention and I will address our delegates about the stakes involved in this election not only for Democrats, but for all Americans," she wrote in her resignation statement.

"Does she not get it?" I asked Mook.

"You don't know how hard it was just to get her to resign," he replied.

"It's going to be bad when she walks on that stage," I warned.

My concerns became very real to everyone when Wasserman Schultz's speech at the Florida delegation breakfast broke down as delegates angrily and loudly reacted to her appearance. It finally sank in.

"Okay, she's out. She won't be on the stage," Mook told me after the Florida breakfast debacle.

I was walking with Mark Longabaugh through the crowded corridors of the arena where the convention was being held when I heard someone call out my name. It was Senator Harry Reid. He rushed over to me with a big smile. He placed his hands on my upper arms and gave me a light shake.

"We did it. We did it. We finally got rid of her," he said with an ear-to-ear grin.

"Yes, we did, Senator," I replied, beaming back at him.

Interim chair Donna Brazile called me before the announcement. "I won't do it unless you and the senator are okay with it," she said. "When I get over there I'm going to clean house." She did just that. She issued a public apology to Bernie and his supporters for the DNC's conduct and "accepted the resignation" of the DNC's top staff in early August. We were pleased with the selection of Donna Brazile. (We did not yet know about the issue of the leaked debate questions at the Michigan debate and the Ohio town hall.) I called Bernie. He signed off on Brazile's selection.

Just because Debbie Wasserman Schultz was done did not mean that our supporters and our delegates were ready to forgive all the transgressions against Bernie and the campaign that had been exposed for all to see. Bernie wanted to address his delegates at the convention to thank them and to ask them to join him in working to defeat Trump. The Clinton campaign was nervous about the prospect—they thought that it could lead to a lot of anti-Clinton venting. We had gone back and forth about it quite a bit in discussions before the convention. But Bernie was insistent that the event occur, and it did. It was supposed to be a private, closed-press event.

It turned out the press was in the packed room. The Bernie delegates were in no mood to hear about the need to elect Hillary Clinton in the wake of the email disclosures. Every time Bernie mentioned her name, they broke into boos. The Clinton folks were apoplectic as the cable news networks streamed coverage of the raucous meeting.

Mook called me. "What the f*ck? This is a disaster. This was supposed to be closed to the press."

"Yes, it was. Not sure what happened," I replied. "It will all work out," I assured him. There wasn't much else to say. He continued his expletive-filled venting for a while longer. Had the roles been reversed, I might have used even more than he did.

Bernie put out a text message to our delegates asking them not to protest on the floor as a "personal courtesy" to him. Even so, the Bernie delegates on that first day were vocally unhappy from the floor of the convention.

I spent much of the day doing media appearances, including one with Bloomberg's Halperin and Heilemann. The interview was held in an area overlooking the convention floor. There was a considerable amount of audible commotion as they opened the interview by characterizing events as a "hot mess of a convention rollout." We went back and forth about whether the Bernie delegates would continue in the same vein over the course of the week. I assured them that as the week went on people would get more in the "spirit of unity." Halperin gave me a disbelieving eye roll. Heilemann said that based on the events of the day he expected Bernie delegates to boo Hillary Clinton's name during his speech that night. And Halperin bet me a copy of *Superman* #1 that it would happen.

I saw Heilemann later that night on the floor after Bernie's speech. He had to concede that his prediction had been wrong. Bernie's speech was enthusiastically received. I still have not received my copy of *Superman* #1 from Mark Halperin (let me be clear that I want the *Superman* #1 from 1939, not the inexpensive later relaunches).

In hindsight, it probably helped a lot that first lady Michelle Obama and Senator Elizabeth Warren spoke earlier in the evening. Elizabeth Warren had disappointed many Bernie supporters by not endorsing him during the primaries, but she still had their respect for her long-term and continuing fight against the financial oligarchs. And Michelle Obama was and is so deeply respected by people across the Democratic Party.

As Bernie was about to speak, the Clinton staff, in an act of sincere generosity, vacated their seats on the elevated stage and gave them to me and other Sanders staff. For me it was a very emotional moment. Seeing Bernie standing in front of the cheering delegates at the Democratic National Convention made me think back to the early days of Bernie and me driving the backroads of Vermont. It struck me what an incredibly unlikely path he had charted, taking his fight for a fairer America from our small state to, literally, the national stage.

He came to the podium to thunderous and sustained applause and cheers. He thanked his supporters and family and then laid out the case, in a detailed, policy-oriented speech, for the election of Hillary Clinton and the defeat of Donald Trump. In that environment, he appropriately focused on what the two candidates had in common, but he did not shy away from important issues such as the Trans-Pacific Partnership. He closed with a full-throated endorsement of Hillary Clinton, and the crowd cheered its approval. While there was still unhappiness on the floor in the coming days, Bernie's speech and the voting the next night really calmed the public displays of displeasure.

The next day, Tuesday, brought new challenges. That was the day that Bernie and Hillary Clinton were to be nominated and the votes of the delegates would be cast. Both Bernie and Clinton would have three people give nomination speeches. One of the people that Bernie wanted to nominate him was state senator Nina Turner. She had endorsed Bernie in the fall and had tirelessly and effectively campaigned for him from one end of the country to the other. She had never formally endorsed Hillary Clinton before endorsing Bernie, but from the time she announced her support, she experienced deep enmity from establishment circles. State senator Vincent Fort of Georgia, another African American supporter of Bernie's, also faced substantial blowback for his endorsement. It was another manifestation of the race-shaming our rank-and-file supporters faced online.

Bernie's view was that he should be able to choose the speakers who would nominate him. The Clinton campaign disagreed. The discussions about whether Nina Turner would be allowed to speak got very heated in both directions. Robby Mook contacted me by email on Tuesday afternoon with a rumor that folks were printing pictures of Monica Lewinsky to show on the floor. Included on his email were director of state campaign and political engagement Marlon Marshall and, on our team, Mark Longabaugh and Rania Batrice. Obviously, that was something we did not support. They wanted our help in dealing with it. I wanted theirs in letting Bernie pick his nominating speakers. They refused. So I replied to the email chain and added our top floor managers, Robert Becker, Rich Pelletier, and Pete D'Alessandro: "Becker, pete, rich Please stand down all sanders whip and floor operations."

Within minutes, Pete D'Alessandro replied, "Standing down until otherwise notified."

And all our staff walked off the floor of the convention and went to the holding room we were using in the Clinton staff area. They could deal with the Monica Lewinsky issue themselves.

I called Bernie. "This is outrageous," he said. "What's their problem? Go back and work on it." Which is exactly what we continued to do. But they would not budge.

The Clinton campaign kept suggesting that they couldn't have Nina Turner on stage because it would upset some group of supporters. One senior Clinton aide at one point said he wasn't going to burn his personal relationships with people to let her speak. I didn't give a damn about any staffer's "personal" relationships, mine included. At that moment, after the experience at the platform committee meeting, I was a little tired of all the personal feelings that a few Clinton staff felt they had every right to inject into the process.

Mark Longabaugh and I were left in the meeting room alone after the exchange. "What the hell, Mark. Don't you want your former opponents standing on stage endorsing you? What's wrong with these people, don't they get it?" I was convinced at that moment that I, Bernie Sanders' campaign manager, was more interested in getting Hillary Clinton elected than some of her own people. (I'm sure they'd disagree.)

The time ticked by and they stood firm. We had no choice as the hour drew near but to choose an alternate speaker. After all, that person would have to have a speech prepared. We suggested Paul Feeney, the labor organizer who had been our Massachusetts and Connecticut state director. The Clinton people agreed. Paul Feeney hit it out of the park with his speech. But we were bitterly disappointed that Nina Turner had been kept off the stage.

However petty it was for Nina Turner to be denied a speaking role, we were not going to let the floor situation fall apart. I sent an email to the previous email chain: "Turn the floor operation back on. Let's get people calmed. Rumors of Monica Lewinsky posters. Pls suppress."

In many ways the roll call vote on Tuesday night held as much significance as Bernie's speech the night before, if not more. With the casting of the votes at the convention, the process would be concluded. We had arranged that the full roll would be called and that Vermont would pass its turn to be in the final position. Then, when the Vermonters had voted, Bernie would rise and move the nomination of Hillary Clinton. Importantly for our delegates, the actual voters of each delegation as cast would be preserved in the record. It was a point that we had negotiated hard to protect.

As the roll was called, the various states would cast the aggregate vote of both pledged delegates and superdelegates. In many cases, this made it seem as if Hillary Clinton had won states that Bernie had won by wide margins. In retrospect, having each state report the votes individually was something we should have tried to negotiate.

The most emotional moment of the night came when Larry Sanders, Bernie's brother, cast the final vote for Democrats abroad. He spoke about his parents, their hard lives, their young deaths, and their love for Bernie. And he spoke of their love of FDR's New Deal and the pride they would have felt knowing that Bernie was renewing that tradition. Sitting with family, staff, and supporters in his box, Bernie visibly fought back tears. So did many of the rest of us in the hall. With all the pomp and parade going on, and all the vetted speeches, it was a truly genuine moment in one of the most scripted events you can find—a presidential nominating convention. In all my years with Bernie, I had never seen him so moved in public.

When Vermont was about to cast its votes, Bernie moved to where the Vermont delegation was sitting. After their votes were cast, he rose to the microphone: "I move that the convention suspend the procedural rules. I move that all votes, all votes cast by delegates, be reflected in the official record, and I move that Hillary Clinton be selected as the nominee of the Democratic Party for president of the United States."

Congresswoman Marcia Fudge, who was presiding, then put the motion to the convention. It was loudly seconded by the assembled delegates. By a thunderous voice vote, the convention approved Bernie's motion. And in that one split second, like a light going out, the campaign that for me had begun back in the Thunder Grill over a year before—and in many ways back in 1986—was over.

PART FIVE

WHERE WE GO FROM HERE

25

HOW TO WIN THE FUTURE

FOLLOWING THE CONVENTION, there were many heartfelt good-byes to comrades in arms who had trudged through Iowa snows and scorching hot southwest deserts. But the work continued to elect Hillary Clinton and defeat Donald Trump.

Bernie kept his promise and campaigned throughout the country for Secretary Clinton. Neither of us was convinced that her election was inevitable. And that made him work all the harder, day after day, in state after state, at rally after rally.

I appeared with some frequency on TV in support of Hillary Clinton's campaign and traveled to St. Louis to be a press surrogate for her after the presidential debate. At one point Donna Brazile asked if I would be interested in taking her DNC VP seat. And the Clinton campaign asked me to go on the DNC payroll to be a television surrogate for them. I was honored to receive both offers, but I had to turn them down.

Bernie and Jane had asked me to take the helm at Our Revolution, the fledgling nonprofit that was inspired by his race for president. It had been my intention to use the lessons we had learned in the presidential campaign to more directly help candidates in the 2016 cycle, but I had to put that aside. There were some serious start-up issues at Our Rev. The alternative to my coming on board, Bernie and Jane said, was that it would be shut down. I could not allow that to happen so soon after its inception.

Not everyone was happy with Bernie's decision, and there was some blowback. Having spent over a year in a hotly contested primary campaign, I was used to taking arrows. But not from behind. I am pleased to report that despite a few bumps, Our Revolution is thriving—organizing at the grassroots level around the country and helping down-ballot progressives get elected. And I was able, in the summer of 2017, to finally hand off the reins and focus more squarely on electoral politics.

As everyone knows, Hillary Clinton went on to lose the general election. Given the closeness of the general election, I am sure that there are many dedicated people from the Clinton campaign who would go back and do some things differently if they could. I know there are certainly many on our campaign who would love a do-over.

Hindsight is, after all, 2020.

But we now have to look ahead to 2020.

Bernie's hard-fought 2016 campaign for the presidency energized millions of voters and brought into the national mainstream the progressive vision he has articulated his entire political life. In the end, we did not secure the Democratic nomination. But, like his 1986 governor's race that I worked on, the 2016 race has laid the groundwork for future successes. I feel the same disappointment now that I felt back then. But I know what can come out of an "unsuccessful" campaign.

The genie is out of the bottle. The overwhelming support that Bernie received from young people of all ages (he received more votes from young people in the primary process than did Clinton and Trump combined) tells us that the future can indeed witness a transformation to a more just and equitable American politics and economics. In that sense he truly did win in 2016. But people cannot give up or check out. As Bernie pointed out so often on the campaign trail, real change only comes when people stand up and demand it.

But what does that mean in our representative federalist democracy?

THE IMPETUS FOR CHANGE COMES FROM THE BOTTOM, BUT IT IS ENACTED BY PEOPLE WHO ACTUALLY HOLD ELECTED AND APPOINTED OFFICE

Profound change throughout our country's history has originated with the "people." This is true of women's rights, civil rights, labor rights, and all other great movements that have worked to overturn unjust conditions and institutions. In every case, however, change was enacted by people in office. Women who marched in the streets for the right to vote ultimately got that vote because they built the political pressure that forced Congress and state legislatures, almost exclusively controlled by men, to pass the Nineteenth Amendment to the United States Constitution. Saying that does not diminish in any way the tremendous sacrifice, courage, and effectiveness of the activists for women's suffrage.

So many paid the ultimate price—their very lives—to fight for equal rights for African Americans. The names of many of the martyrs of that era are well known, and there are far, far more who labored for justice whose names we will never know. The outrageous injustice of the situation and the brave sacrifice of the African American community and allied civil rights activists sparked action in Congress to pass the Civil Rights Act.

In the most extreme example, it was President Abraham Lincoln—backed by the Union army of over 2 million men—that finally cut loose the shackles of America's most shameful institution, slavery. That fact does not and should not detract from the tireless and thankless work done by abolitionists of all races and by those who risked everything to help enslaved African Americans find freedom before emancipation.

The lesson here is twofold. One, through organizing and sacrifice, people can change the debate and transform the popular consciousness to the point that elected leaders are forced to act. Two, at the end of the day, change is put in place by the political leaders.

In 1981, Bernie won the Burlington mayor's office by a mere ten votes. Under his leadership, Burlington developed a perpetually affordable homeownership program, ensured that the waterfront was developed in a way that created large public spaces, supported programs for youth and the arts, and more—all while keeping property taxes down. If Bernie had not been elected, he certainly would have continued his lifelong work in support of everyday Vermonters. But all the accomplishments of his administration would never have been. His demonstrated vision and, frankly, competence at running Vermont's largest city would ultimately be the foundation of his successful runs for federal office.

That is why we need not only a movement that pushes elected officials to do the right thing but also to elect political leaders who will do the right thing even when a million people are not in the streets—political leaders whose first impulse is to make life better for the American people in every community rather than perpetuating an inequitable status quo. We are all living through an era where reaching that goal is imperative, where we are witnessing in the starkest of terms what it means to have a government that is antagonistic to the most basic needs of the clear majority of Americans in terms of economics, social justice, or environmental sanity.

This is the challenge that this generation faces. How do we create, as Bernie would call it, "a government that works for all of us"?

WE HAVE A LOT OF WORK TO DO, FOLKS

For those of you who have not tilled the fields of American electoral politics recently, the situation in not good. Having Donald Trump in the White House and a Republican-controlled Congress is bad enough. But it is worse than that. Since 2010, Democrats have lost almost a thousand state legislative seats. Prior to the 2017 elections, Republicans controlled the legislature in thirty-two states. To all of you who vote in presidential years and not in those "inconsequential" off-year state legislative elections, and to those national party leaders and donors who have ceded this arena to the Republicans and their big donors, let me lay out as plainly as possible why we are at the tipping point.

As we approach 2020, there has been increasing discussion of state leg-islative races in the context of congressional gerrymandering. Republi-cans now control thirty-three governors' mansions. Republican legislatures and governors, through their dominance of state government—run re-apportionment, have stacked the deck against Democratic congressio-nal candidates for a decade. That's a critically important point. But here's one that's even more troubling.

Republicans almost control enough state legislatures to call a conven-tion to amend the United States Constitution. Let's look at how close we are to that dystopian nightmare.

Article V of the United States Constitution allows the legislatures of two-thirds of the states to call a constitutional convention. That's thirty-four states. That puts the Republicans only two away. According to Stephen Wolf's analysis for *Daily Kos* after the 2016 election, in addition to thirty-two state legislatures being Republican-controlled, the legislatures in five states are split, with each party controlling one house. Flipping just two legislative houses nationwide gives the Republicans the power to call a constitutional convention. And only thirty-eight states are required to pass any proposed amendments that would come out of the convention. In November 2017, Wisconsin became the twenty-eighth state to call for a constitutional convention.

One can only imagine the litany of horrors that could come out of such a convention. How many millions could be impoverished, with wealth and income inequality made exponentially worse, by the repeal of the Sixteenth Amendment, which granted Congress the power to levy the income tax? How many rights would come under attack? How many liberties could be curtailed? How many Supreme Court–articulated protections—*Roe v. Wade, Brown v. Board of Education, Obergefell v. Hodges*—could not only be reversed but permanently barred by the Con-stitution from ever being considered again?

Is this danger imminent? Maybe not. But should we roll those dice when the stakes are this high? To turn this around, we must have the cour-age to ask how we got here and how we reverse it.

HOW COME THEY'RE WINNING, AND HOW DO WE START WINNING?

The empirical reality is that the Democratic Party and its candidates are failing to connect with voters in huge swaths of the country and in many communities. The "why" could fill many books all by itself. There is no one answer, but there are many contributing factors. For any readers who might be confused about the point of this section, it's not to bash the Democratic Party. It's about how we build a national party than can win at the local, state, and federal level.

THE REPUBLICANS ARE WINNING WITH THE DEMOCRATS' OLD PLAYBOOK

The role of big money on the Republican side and, since *Citizens United*, the enhanced role of corporate money, is a major factor. The Koch brothers can deploy nearly a billion dollars in an election cycle. And, as *Politico*'s Kenneth Vogel has reported, the Koch brothers alone operate a network of organizations that has "an infrastructure that rival[s] that of the Republican National Committee."

To be clear, it's not just the money but how you spend it that's important. According to NPR's Peter Overby, the Koch brothers network "is emulating what political parties and labor unions used to do." They are doing this through "a seamless system of grass-roots groups, designed to advance the network's conservative and libertarian goals year in and year out, *while also* helping like-minded politicians." (Emphasis added.)

The Koch brothers understand what the Democratic Party used to understand. They get that you have to be on the ground year in and year out to be successful electorally. The NPR story, which was broadcast on October 12, 2015, quotes the head of one of their front groups: "What makes this network different . . . is that we've been in these communities now for three, four years and we're going to be in them in 2017, 2018, 2019."

Those progressives who say we need more grassroots organizing and those who say we need more emphasis on elections are both right. The success of community organizing feeds electoral success, and vice versa. If Democrats and progressives hope to stem the tide of Republican advances over the long term, the national Democratic Party can no longer just be a fund-raising vehicle for presidential aspirants. It must invest in building permanent grassroots infrastructure in communities from coast to coast. This infrastructure is not a substitute for massive investments in actual elections, it is an indispensable part of it. This infrastructure is not just to build strength among red-state constituencies. It is a very common and justified complaint in many minority communities that the Democratic Party shows up at election time looking for votes and then disappears. This infrastructure needs to be everywhere.

THE DEMOCRATIC PARTY IS FAILING AS A NATIONAL PARTY, BUT IT'S NOT TOO LATE

There has been a lot of focus on our unexpected loss in November 2016. According to top Clinton staff I spoke with as late as the day before the election, Florida was supposed to be a lock, and the now-decimated blue wall in the industrial heartland was holding firm. Needless to say, that was not the real state of play.

In the wake of that disaster, there has been a lot of finger-pointing at data analytics, strategic decision making by the Clinton campaign, and even at Bernie Sanders (I'm not going to dignify that last one with a response). While it's clear that there were mistakes made by the Clinton campaign (as there were in ours), Monday morning quarterbacking and blaming technical staff misses the much broader and more important point. The Democratic Party has lost the trust of tens of millions of voters in large swaths of the country.

In that sense, the fate of Hillary Clinton's campaign was the result of the chasm that has developed between the establishment that runs the party and many voters of all races, including young voters, working-class voters, rural voters, and the progressive community both within and outside the Democratic Party. Is it true that a historically consequential political figure of incredible dignity and decency like Barack Obama can overcome that chasm in an election? Of course, Hillary Clinton herself won the popular vote in 2016. But the failure to address the Democratic Party's disconnect with voters will not win back Congress, or state houses, or even the presidency.

And this is not entirely a case of benign neglect. I cringe when I hear a member of the Democratic establishment elite or progressive activists who have convinced themselves that they don't even need to reach out to voters who have become disenchanted with the Democratic Party brand. They have all kinds of political theories to justify why they will win without the multiracial middle- and working-class coalition that has always been the foundation of past Democratic successes. There are coastal strategies, theories about the rising electorate, and even those who believe that the future of the party is affluent suburban Republicans. For many of those who control the party apparatus, these theories are comfortable. They do not require them to fundamentally challenge the reality that their adherence to a neoliberal agenda is killing the Democratic Party.

But let's admit that these theories have some application. Still, they will ultimately fail as a foundation for the Democratic Party because of our federal American political system. One can piece together an Electoral College victory some of the time with some of these approaches. But what about the United States Senate? What about state governments? You cannot create "a government that works for all of us" unless you want to win over much more of "all of us" than the Democratic Party has been able to do, or in some circles wants to do.

Regardless of one's political views, no one can maintain that the Democratic Party's current approach to politics has been effective. Look at the White House, Congress, thirty-three governor's mansions, sixty-eight state legislative houses. If the Democratic Party were a meritocracy, how many of the architects of its current political fortunes would still be gainfully employed in the field of politics?

Will the Democratic Party win back some congressional seats in 2018?

The party of the sitting president almost always loses seats, so one would expect so. Even if we win a dozen seats, it will not demonstrate that the party's problems are behind it.

Given Trump's betrayal of middle- and working-class voters at every turn and his bigoted attacks against so many communities, a failure to win a significant number of House seats in the 2018 off-year will be further evidence that the Democratic Party needs an abrupt change in course to avoid the fate of the Federalists and the Whigs.

Frankly, it's time to turn away from the aberrational rightward shift that has been tearing the party apart since the 1990s—time to return the modern Democratic Party to its historical trajectory of greater equality and inclusiveness. In an interview with NBC's Chuck Todd, I once said that Bernie was trying to reconstitute the FDR coalition. Chuck's response was that he was not sure that that coalition even existed anymore. He had a point. And that's exactly the problem.

THE DEMOCRATIC PARTY NEEDS AN AGENDA BASED ON SHARED ASPIRATIONS WHILE RECOGNIZING THE UNIQUE CHALLENGES THAT DIFFERENT COMMUNITIES FACE IN ACHIEVING THOSE ASPIRATIONS

The question then becomes: If the Democratic Party were to reconnect with its roots and were to commit to building a permanent grassroots infrastructure nationwide, what would it advocate? The answer is really the same. Return to your roots.

Anyone who's seen a lot of polling and focus groups is struck by the great commonality of aspirations shared by the vast majority of Americans regardless of their zip code. This commonality of the American aspiration is borne out in a February 2017 Harvard-Harris poll: "Voters across generation, gender, race, and political parties agree that job creation should be [the] top priority" for the Trump administration.

Most of what Americans want is found in that 1944 FDR State of the

Union from chapter 11. Put succinctly, they want economic security, they want their children to have a brighter future than they had, they want to be as free as possible from the vagaries of illness and unemployment, they want a retirement without poverty, and they want to live a life of dignity and social inclusion. That's the agenda that the Democratic Party must authentically champion. It is an agenda that lifts all communities. That is the message of common aspirations that fueled Bernie's campaign.

An agenda of common aspirations—an articulation of the type of life we want for every American—should not be read as a call to ignore the varied challenges that people in different communities face in reaching that goal. Quite the opposite. When we strive to achieve common aspirations—what Bernie calls "an economy and a government that works for all of us"—we necessarily address what Hillary Clinton in her campaign called "every barrier." But "every barrier" means "every barrier." That includes barriers rooted in prejudice and bigotry as well as those rooted in economic inequality and political oligarchy.

For too many Americans, systemic racism and other forms of discrimination are a bar to achieving common aspirations. For others, they are not. Many communities have underfunded schools that hinder the advancement of young people. Others do not. Some communities are suffering the effects of economic dislocation due to deindustrialization. Others are not. And so on. It's not a question of which barrier takes precedence or is most egregious. We must commit to addressing them all if we want to create a broad-based Democratic Party capable of winning in every state.

The person who has had one foot amputated is unlikely to draw a lot of consolation from the fact that the person in the next hospital bed has lost both. The pain of both has to be addressed, and voters understand that. When voters believe that you are standing with their family, they have no objection to your standing with others' families as well. Americans want a more just and equitable society not just for themselves but for the nation. If I did not believe that, I'd be out of politics in five minutes.

There is a reason that Bernie's call for an end to police shooting of African Americans and the need for criminal justice reform received the loudest applause at his rallies across the country even, and in many cases especially, when the audience was largely white. Outside of the context of an agenda of common aspirations, too often the justified efforts to address the needs of one community are painted as coming either at the expense of another or as a preference for one over the other. We have let the Republicans cynically define us that way for too long. We cannot fall into their trap, which allows us to be divided.

An example of one policy proposal that reflects the approach I am advocating is Rep. Jim Clyburn's 10-20-30 federal funding proposal. As described on his website, it would guarantee that 10 percent of funds for federal programs be invested in counties where at least 20 percent of the population has been in poverty for the last thirty years: "These counties mired in persistent poverty are as diverse as our great nation; Appalachian communities in Kentucky and North Carolina, Native American communities in South Dakota and Alaska, Latino communities in Arizona and New Mexico and African American communities in Mississippi and South Carolina. They lack access to quality schools, affordable quality health care and adequate job opportunities."

Poverty is an enduring blight on our nation in a way that it is not in other industrialized western democracies. As Representative Clyburn notes, it affects people of every race and from all parts of the nation. Would Clyburn's proposal, if adopted, disproportionately benefit people of certain races? Of course it would. And it should, because people of color disproportionately live in the counties he describes. But it offers help to all similarly situated people and represents a unifying frame in much the same way as raising the minimum wage does. Is this one proposal enough to base a party around? No, of course not. But its logic is.

That is why efforts like the Fight for $15 has been so successful even in red states, and why half the hands went up at one postelection meeting with Trump supporters when they were asked who supported a single-payer health care system. And that is why even with his radically pro-corporate, anti-working-family agenda, President Trump has yet to even suggest laying a finger on such universal, and therefore universally popular, programs as Social Security and Medicare.

THE PARTY'S COMMITMENT
MUST BE AUTHENTIC

Voters don't always get the nuance of every policy proposal. Nor should they. They actually have real lives, unlike us political types. They want to elect people they believe will do right by them (or at least better than the other candidate). That being said, voters are keenly sensitive to what is known in professional political circles as bullshit. In a world increasingly dominated by the virtual, voters more and more are looking for political leadership that is authentic.

Bernie's appeal to voters across the country in 2016 had a lot to do with people's accurate assessment that he was an authentic messenger of the vision he articulated. We saw that in our focus groups. Even when people didn't agree with a position he held or felt it was not achievable, they believed, correctly, that his support for that position was genuine.

As research by the super PAC Priorities USA (which backed Hillary Clinton) and others has shown, many of the voters who supported President Obama and then voted for Trump hold the view that the Democratic Party's economic policies favor the wealthy. Many party regulars can and do respond indignantly that that's not true. But that's not going to win any hearts and minds, let alone elections.

We Democrats need to ask serious questions about why people have that impression. When big banks were being propped up, corporate bonuses were being paid, and no one was held accountable, what message did it send to voters who, because of the Great Recession, lost their jobs, their homes, and their life savings? How about a recent legacy of job-destroying free-trade deals, including NAFTA and the TPP? Washington insiders may not see the lost jobs as any to aspire to, but that type of economic snobbery is symptomatic of the problem. How about all the coddling of wealthy donors that was revealed in the DNC's leaked emails? The DNC certainly has not spent hours on seating charts to figure out which unemployed coal miner from West Virginia or struggling parent in Baltimore was going to get to sit next to the president.

The typical response to this critique is that, well, the Republicans do it, and they win. But that fundamentally misses the cynical message that Republicans are peddling. The Republicans are the ones trying to convince Americans that government is incompetent, corrupt, and stacked against the average person. Their behavior merely reinforces the entire theme of their messaging.

On the other hand, Democrats, by and large, favor greater government intervention in the economy, a social safety net, and social equality. Democrats, by virtue of who we are, face the greater challenge. We actually want to accomplish something, and we need people to trust that we are doing it in a way that is meant for their benefit.

Lose that trust and we will lose elections. Imagine the choice that voters face in that situation. One party you view as corrupt promises to do nothing, to leave you alone and spend less of your money. The other party you view as corrupt wants to have a more active role in a number of economic and social spheres and may even ask you or someone else for more money. I can tell you already who Americans are going to choose. It's not even close. Democrats have got to pick a side—the 99 percent or the 1 percent—and then, as Priorities USA recommends, we have "to name names."

REASSEMBLING THE SHATTERED GRAND DEMOCRATIC COALITION IS THE ONLY ALTERNATIVE

The shattered components of the grand Democratic coalition need to be reassembled if we are again to become a broad-based national party capable of winning in every zip code in America. I'm not going to sugarcoat the problems of the old coalition, in which some segments were not full participants or had their interests sacrificed at times. But we can re-create a grand Democratic coalition around an agenda of common aspirations without re-creating those inequities. In truth, we can only succeed if we pull all the constituent parts of the coalition toward shared prosperity and dignity. We have no alternative if we are to win. There are no other options.

The failed New Democratic experiment of the 1990s showed that neoliberalism, which is antithetical to the economic interests of working people, only succeeded politically when it relied on triangulation policies that resulted in millions being imprisoned, impoverished, or socially ostracized. That course is unacceptable. The other alternative—continued loss to the Republicans—is also unacceptable.

It's time to really open up the Democratic Party to as many people as we can and let them interact with the party in the way they feel comfortable—even if they want to be part of our nominating process without getting a laminated membership card. It's time to start supporting down-ballot candidates who don't necessarily fit Washington's neoliberal cookie-cutter formula for success. In most parts of the country, no one likes the taste of those cookies anymore, and they haven't for a long time. It's time to get back to our modern roots, with a real agenda of broad-based prosperity and a commitment to include every American. It's time . . . but time is running out.

26

ONWARD TO 2020

TALKING ABOUT BERNIE'S HISTORIC 2016 race and the impact that he and his millions of supporters are having on politics would not be complete without some discussion of the 2020 presidential race.

The 2020 race will look very different from those in 2008 and 2016. The most visible difference will be the much larger field of candidates. Many of them will not be well known at the beginning and will have to work to establish themselves as viable choices. That is exactly the position in which Bernie found himself at the beginning of the 2016 campaign. It is critical that if the forces of progress are to win in 2020, each of these candidates must have a fair chance to introduce herself or himself to the Democratic rank and file in a process that is as fair as possible. We cannot lose sight of the fact that job number one is defeating Donald Trump.

On issue after issue his administration has betrayed the people he asked for support. He promised to drain the swamp but has filled his administration with Wall Street insiders. He promised better health care and then tried to add millions to the roles of the uninsured. He promised to favor the middle class over the elites but pushed a tax agenda that would benefit the super-rich and endanger funding for schools, health care, and transportation. As of this writing he couldn't even keep his promise to release the government's JFK assassination files, a decision derided by the Republican

Senate judiciary chair and a federal judge. People all across this country rightly wanted change in 2016 and still do. However, this is not the change that working people thought they were getting when Trump sold them a false bill of goods in 2016.

In addition, the Trump administration has demonstrated its incompetence at the most basic level of governing. For many of us this has come as a mixed blessing. President Trump's lack of competence has meant that agenda items like the repeal of the Affordable Care Act have failed. But no one can argue that it is good for our country to have an administration that at times looks more like the Keystone Cops than the leadership of the free world.

There are some auspicious signs that we can in fact replace the most divisive, pro-corporate-elites, anti-working-family president in modern American history in 2020. But it is not a given. President Trump still enjoys support in the Republican Party as a whole and in many regions of the country. He will have access to mountains of billionaire-class dollars. And he will have the very powerful weapon of the bully pulpit of the presidency. There can be little doubt that the media will not have learned anything from 2016 and will once again give him billions of dollars more in free airtime than his opponents will get. The business imperative that drove the coverage of the empty podium has not gone away. Despite what the media believes, the moral indignation repeatedly expressed by commentators and TV hosts over Trump's behavior and untruths does not compensate for the wall-to-wall coverage he gets. Trump knows that better than anyone else and will use it to his advantage.

What are we to do in this historically important moment? What we cannot do is to continue what we have been doing. That failed in 2016, and it has failed for nearly a decade now with consistent losses at the local, state, and federal levels. Being "not Trump" is not going to cut it. Now is the time for Democrats to demonstrate what they are for, not just what they are against. That has been difficult for a number of reasons.

All of the serious contenders for the Democratic nomination in 2020 are rightly focused now on resisting the Trump agenda rather than putting themselves out as the alternative. The American people don't want to live in a world of perpetual political campaigns. That said, the run for the 2020 nomination has already begun. Everyone testing the waters will not ultimately be a candidate. But like a chess game, the pieces are moving, and in the early part of the game the pawns get positioned first.

Some are still relitigating the 2016 election. Some are doing so out of bitterness at the outcome either because they thought they were going to win, they thought the election was stolen from them, or understandably to protect the legacy of Hillary Clinton. Her career in politics is itself historic in many ways, and her accomplishments are many. Her loss to Trump in their eyes mars that lifetime of hard-fought achievements. I don't agree but I understand it. Campaigns are fought in a historical moment that candidates have no control over. 2016 was a change election (as 2020 will be). Hillary Clinton was not viewed as the candidate who was going to make enough change—by working-class people of all races, by young people, and by independent voters—to be elected easily to the presidency in 2016. At another historical moment that might not have been true. That is not unique to her. In my view, Bill Clinton would not be able to secure the Democratic nomination today. The grass roots of the Democratic Party has rejected neoliberalism.

But except for the Clinton-world insiders and some of her most strident supporters, the relitigation of 2016 increasingly has nothing to do with 2016 and everything to do with 2020. There are already highly organized online operations—reminiscent of the Brock trolling program discussed in chapter 7—whose mission it is to attack Bernie and his supporters. In truth, it never really stopped after the primaries. Too many at the top of our own party are scared to death of the regular people in every corner of the country that Bernie Sanders gave voice to in 2016 and continues to give voice to.

Consistent polling shows Bernie Sanders as the most popular active political figure in America, which has those people in a panic. But what is below those top-line numbers is even more panic-inducing. Bernie Sanders is most popular with voters of color. That flies in the face of what can only be called a lie of Trumpian proportions: that progressive change only appeals to rabid white, male, hipster Berniebros. It's not true now and never was.

This reality is a threat to politicians whose views are out of sync with the rank and file of the Democratic Party but who want to be elected anyway, and to the political and economic elites in the Democratic Party who want to cling to power. They are willing to do most anything to turn back the clock, even if it means in practical terms that we are in a weaker position to defeat Donald Trump in 2020. To hold onto power, they must tear apart the grand coalition that we need to build if we are to beat the Republicans and create a more equitable and inclusive society. They have to drive a wedge between progressive voters of color and progressive white voters, a wedge between progressive women and progressive men. They have to erase the very existence of the 77 percent of black voters who have a positive view of Bernie Sanders. In other words, they have to engage in the same divisive tactics that Trump relies on—and frankly that the neoliberals in the Clinton administration played with welfare reform, the crime bill, and DOMA. Divide and conquer.

Let me give an example of how this disgusting politics played out this past fall. I was attending a Democratic Party Unity Reform Commission meeting in Las Vegas in October 2017. It was scheduled to precede the Democratic Party's semiannual meeting. DNC chair Tom Perez had just made new at-large appointments to the DNC and its various committees.

There was a perception that Perez had purged those who had supported his opponent for chair or who were viewed as too close to the progressive wing of the party. (Calling it a *wing* really understates it. Among the rank and file it's getting to be almost the entire bird.) The purge included some DNC members with decades of service to the party, including New Hampshire party chair Ray Buckley (who had run for DNC chair and then endorsed Keith Ellison's bid) and DNC member Jim Zogby (who supported Bernie's bid for president and has been a vocal proponent of increased transparency and accountability at the DNC). While both remained on the DNC, they were demoted on important committees. There was some unhappiness about it.

So the two of them decided to run for open positions within the DNC that would put them on the executive committee. Zogby, in particular, was objectionable to the establishment because he has not backed down in his opposition to what I call the imperial DNC chair. Rules and bylaws of the party constrain the chair's powers and require consultation with the executive committee and other committees. Those rules are routinely ignored now as they were by the previous chair, and I suspect chairs before that. But that doesn't make it right. Zogby's goal is to make the Democratic Party more democratic.

I decided to leave Las Vegas after the Unity Reform Commission meetings were concluded and not stay for the larger DNC meeting. I was sitting in the airport terminal grabbing a quick bite before my flight when a call came through from Symone Sanders. Symone had been the national press secretary on Bernie 2016 and had worked on the Clinton campaign during the general election. She had also just been appointed as an at-large member of the DNC.

"Well, hello, Ms. DNC committee member," I said playfully as I picked up the phone.

"Well, maybe not for long," she replied.

"What's up?" I said, my tone turning more serious.

Symone explained that there was a rumor circulating around the DNC that Jim Zogby was trying to have Symone, Leah Daughtry, and Minyon Moore—all black women—removed as at-large members of the DNC and replaced with Bernie supporters. It didn't make any sense.

First of all, Symone had been a Bernie supporter. Second, the deadline for nominations for at-large delegates had passed. Finally, I had just spent the past couple of days with Jim Zogby, who is also on the Unity Reform Commission, and the rest of the Bernie appointees to that commission. There was never a single word expressed about such a thing. Nor could I imagine there would be. Jim has been leading the call for the party to be more inclusive of various communities, not less. I told Symone I would check into it and get back with her. Something stunk badly. I sent a text to Larry Cohen, the vice-chair of the Unity Reform Commission and a Bernie appointee. He responded quickly that there was no truth to it.

I had to get on my plane, but during my layover I hit the phone to track down this false rumor. By the time I landed in Detroit on the way back to DC, the rumor had changed. Those peddling it must have realized the internal inconsistency of Jim Zogby trying to get rid of Symone Sanders, a former Bernie staffer. So now the rumor was that Zogby was trying to get rid of Leah Daughtry, Minyon Moore, and Donna Brazile. That may have improved the consistency of the slander against Zogby and Bernie supporters in general, but didn't make it any more true.

This amateurish attempt at dark political arts took another hit when it came out that Zogby had decades-long friendships with Leah, Minyon and Donna that went back to their work on Jesse Jackson's 1984 presidential campaign. Whoops! Leah Daughtry for her part publicly embraced Jim Zogby and endorsed his run for the executive committee. Minyon Moore put out a statement saying she did not believe that Zogby would do such a thing. And in my conversation with Donna Brazile, she could not have been more clear that she did not believe it either. The lie was unravelling.

So the rumor changed again in one last gasp to keep it alive. Instead of Zogby, other Bernie supporters were said to be the source of it. The fact that we know the whole thing was made up didn't mean it wasn't effective in the short term. In an environment such as a DNC annual meeting, where everyone is meeting in small groups and receptions, rumors like this spread like wildfire and are easier to spread than to undo. Jim Zogby narrowly lost his bid to get on the executive committee.

I was not content to let this scandalous tactic go without further investigation. In my more than a dozen conversations with members of the media and DNC members from all factions, it appears that this shocking smear originated with top DNC staffers who claimed to have personally overhead discussion of this nonexistent plan to depose Leah, Minyon, and Donna (or was it Symone?). To me this was 2016 revisited, when DNC staffers were scheming to attack Bernie's religion.

This episode foreshadows the type of self-destructive politics that we can expect to see from establishment elements of the party in 2020. They understand the fault lines in the party. They understand that many African Americans rightly perceive that their consistent support for the Democratic Party is taken for granted. They also understand that starting a lie about black women being targeted would find some resonance. Black women and many other constituencies are used to being sidelined both within the party and without and are therefore vigilant. Using lies to play on that justifiable anxiety for political advantage is, to borrow a term from Hillary Clinton, deplorable, and Donald Trump thanks you for it. Only by dividing by race (or gender, sexual orientation or identity, religion, country of origin, and so forth) people who want and need transformative change the most can these insiders hang on to their petty trappings of power while the country continues to elect the far right.

This episode also highlights one of the reasons why, despite all his betrayals and incompetence, Donald Trump may be reelected in 2020. The *Titanic* may be going down, but as long as the establishment have the first-class cabin everything's okay.

Whoever is the standard bearer in 2020 must be committed to uniting the country around an agenda of common aspirations while recognizing the unique challenges every community experiences in realizing that ideal. Our standard bearer's message of change cannot just be change from Trump and the Republicans, but also of change from the same old same old that has too many people falling behind. Any honest appraisal of the 2016 general election shows where we failed. Working-class voters in the so-called blue wall left us, and younger voters of color chose to stay home.

Many of those voters were unhappy with their choices for president, but many were also turned off by what they justifiably perceived as an unfair process. To that end, the DNC's role in the next presidential nominating process should be completely hands off. Let the candidates speak to the rank and file and may the best candidate win. Insiders claim there needs to be an active role for establishment players. After all, the Republicans did not have sufficient insider checks and balances, they argue, and Trump was able to win the nomination.

But in terms of picking the most electable general election candidate, it turns out that a process left solely to the rank and file like that of the Republicans produced a candidate, however distasteful, that empirically was more electable than the anointed choice of the Democratic establishment. It is after all the people who elect the president in November. Doesn't it make sense that they, including independents, are the best judge of who will appeal to them and their neighbors?

The Democratic Unity Reform Commission is currently working to reform the superdelegate system, a highly undemocratic element of the Democratic nominating system. By the time you read this that reform will hopefully be adopted and the number of unpledged superdelegates will be greatly reduced. If it is not, it will be a strong signal that there is no serious appetite for letting the people control the party.

In addition, the DNC should have no part in setting up or sanctioning debates. They add needless bureaucracy to the process and, as we have seen, open up the process to mischief by partisans. The candidates and the sponsors of debates can negotiate directly just as effectively.

The DNC should not enter into any joint fund-raising agreements with any candidates until the primary season is over. In 2016, those agreements were used to skirt federal election laws to the benefit of one candidate. If candidates want to help raise money for the party, that's fine. But the candidate herself or himself should not be part of the agreement. As an aside, the DNC should pledge to no longer loot state parties as it did in 2016. This was another circumvention of federal election law and has the long-term effect of destroying the viability of state parties in much of the country.

As evidenced by the Las Vegas meeting, senior DNC staff seem unable to refrain from taking sides. Some of the most disgusting attacks seem to originate there—whether attacks on a candidate's religion or lies meant to paint loyal party members as racist. In addition, it was DNC staff who actively conspired with the Clinton campaign to rig the debate schedule. Until the primaries are over, no DNC staff should have contact with representatives of any campaign without representatives of every other campaign present. No exceptions. If the chair needs to speak with the various campaigns, he or she can arrange it through the candidates themselves. Too many Democratic operatives seem to put their own professional, personal, or petty interests ahead of the party and the country when they are supposed to be neutral actors.

Finally, no strategic contractor or vendor who represents the DNC should be allowed to work for one of the campaigns. In the 2016 campaign we saw a top lawyer at the firm representing both the DNC and the Clinton campaign giving advice to DNC staffers about how to respond to our campaign's criticism of the questionable joint fund-raising agreements. This happened despite a firewall that supposedly existed at the law firm to prevent such a conflict.

There is a role for the DNC during the primaries. The DNC should ensure that every possible voter in the Democratic coalition can participate in the nominating process. As we saw, the participation of young African Americans lags way behind other racial groups. That is bad for the party and bad for the country. Contributing to that problem are the closed primaries that lock out independent, Democratically aligned black youth in New York, Pennsylvania, Maryland, Florida, and elsewhere. The same is true of young Latino and white voters.

Testimony before the Unity Reform Commission revealed that the Democratic Party has the power to force Democratic nominating contests open to nonaligned voters even when state legislatures refuse to act. If state parties refuse to remedy the disenfranchisement of the next generation of voters of color, the DNC should step in. It should publicly lobby Democratic governors and legislatures to make changes. It should also go to court to force those primaries open and to aggressively fight every other kind of voter suppression and disenfranchisement.

Just a word about the candidates. If the DNC removes itself as a partisan in the nominating process, it will be important that the candidates carry on their campaigns in a way that allows the candidate with the most support among rank-and-file Democrats to win and for the party to come together to win in November 2020. One way to accomplish that is for each campaign to pledge to a list of principles.

The first is that every candidate should pledge to not participate in a debate if every bona fide candidate for the nomination is not included, as Bernie did in 2016 when one network wanted to exclude Governor O'Malley. A minimum threshold could be established, such as polling at 1 percent in some number of respected public polls.

Each candidate should also pledge to wage their campaign with only hard money. We don't need super PACs funded by a few rich donors interfering in our nominating contest or propping up candidates who have no base of support other than a rich patron. It makes the process much more base when candidate-affiliated super PACs are used to launch dirty attacks on their opponents. In the current campaign finance environment, the eventual nominee may have to rely on a super PAC against the Republicans because they will use them. But that does not mean that we as Democrats have to taint our own nominating contest.

The third principle is that each campaign should refrain from the kind of negative campaigning that turns off so many voters. Understandably there will be a lot of sharp elbows in the nominating process. The line between policy and personal is sometimes blurry. I find nothing wrong with hard-nosed comparisons of candidates' positions and records. It should not be acceptable, however, for candidates to adopt the disqualify-defeat-and-worry-about-unifying-the-party-later mantra that the Clinton campaign adopted in New York. This approach does long-term harm to our party and the political process in general. Candidates should focus more time on why voters should support them and their policies rather than why voters should not support their opponents.

Finally, let me be up-front about what I am sure is painfully obvious. The polling in 2016 was right. Bernie Sanders was the stronger candidate against Trump. Bernie would have won. Period. It's not a view I am shy about.

I also believe he is the strongest candidate to reclaim the White House in 2020 in this moment in history. His authentic message of positive change and his appeal to a broad range of voters gives Democrats the best opportunity to put together the coalition that can reclaim elected offices at all levels. That being said, he has not decided to run again. I am sure that is the case with all the potential 2020 contenders. But he has not decided not to run either. Run, Bernie, Run!

INDEX